The You
Making Th

The Young Are Making Their World

Essays on the Power of Youth Culture

Edited by YUYA KIUCHI *and*
FRANCISCO A. VILLARRUEL

McFarland & Company, Inc., Publishers
Jefferson, North Carolina

LIBRARY OF CONGRESS CATALOGUING-IN-PUBLICATION DATA

Names: Kiuchi, Yuya, editor. | Villarruel, Francisco, editor.
Title: The young are making their world : essays on the power of youth
    culture / edited by Yuya Kiuchi and Francisco A. Villarruel.
Description: Jefferson, North Carolina : McFarland & Company, Inc.,
    Publishers, 2016 | Includes bibliographical references and index.
Identifiers: LCCN 2016019355 | ISBN 9780786498840 (softcover : acid
    free paper) ∞
Subjects: LCSH: Youth—Social conditions. | Youth—Political activity.
Classification: LCC HQ796 .Y58175 2016 | DDC 305.235—dc23
LC record available at https://lccn.loc.gov/2016019355

BRITISH LIBRARY CATALOGUING DATA ARE AVAILABLE

ISBN (print) 978-0-7864-9884-0
ISBN (ebook) 978-1-4766-2512-6

Front cover image, youths and technology © 2016 Rawpixel Ltd/iStock

Printed in the United States of America

McFarland & Company, Inc., Publishers
   Box 611, Jefferson, North Carolina 28640
      www.mcfarlandpub.com

Table of Contents

Introduction

The transitions from childhood to adolescence and from adolescence to early adulthood are important times when lifelong habits are established, self-assurance and identity are solidified, futures are defined, and mobility is increased. These transitional periods are also times of mixed messages. Adults and policies both create and restrict opportunities. For example, there are restrictions on driving, alcohol and tobacco purchases, curfews, working at jobs, and even on education that youth everywhere must conform with.

Yet in the last forty years, researchers (e.g., Lerner; Villarruel, Perkins, Borden, & Keith 2002) have reminded us that there have been changes in the services offered to young people and the roles they themselves play in their futures. Gone are the days when youth needed proscriptive programs or institutions to successfully transition to adulthood. As our world has expanded, so too have the opportunities for youth to flourish. Some of these opportunities are created by youth themselves as they have become active participants in defining what is important to them and how they view their roles in the world. Look at how they have incorporated technology in multiple aspects of their lives.

The notion of youth culture is not altogether new, but perhaps youth popular culture is new for some. The notion of youth popular cultures provides society with a different means of viewing youth: it is not as much about systematic planning and development as it is about expression. In other words, youth culture is no longer defined by what youth do or do not do, but rather in how they support and are supported by their communities, the opportunities they have, and a context for identity development. Using hip hop, poetry slams, theater, street art, and dance, for example, youth have taken an active role in the social construction of their communities; they are building a social movement that defines their roles and places in society.

Examining the intersection of youth culture and popular culture, therefore, provides a way to better understand how youth view their own lives and how they actively pave their own paths for the future while recognizing their

1

pasts and heritage. The idea of youth popular culture is particularly important as our society experiences what Don Tapscott (2008) called a generation lap. It is not only when a parent has to ask his or her child to set up a new wireless router at home or when a grandparent has to ask his or her grandchild to set up an email account that we can see the evidence of youth driving our society forward. Media may seize on young people's obsession with their smartphones, but just as often their parents are using their phones to answer their work emails at their children's athletic event while teenagers are using their phones as a social device to find each other at a game or to take pictures together for their favorite social media.

This volume offers insight into what these young people are doing through the lens of positive youth development, a model that helps us look at their popular culture as an asset rather than a deficit. Yuya Kiuchi leads off with an examination of youth-led and technology-mediated activism after the death of Michael Brown in Ferguson, Missouri. Despite the common labeling of cyber-activism as slacktivism, Kiuchi reveals that Facebook, Twitter, and other social media enabled young people both inside and outside of Ferguson to create a virtual public space where geographical barriers were overcome. While thousands protested in the streets of Ferguson, many more protested in the virtual public space, #Ferguson. #Ferguson was where powerful hashtag activism took place, including #iftheygunnedmedown and #handsupdontshoot. Youth challenged images of African American youth circulated by mainstream media while feeding the reality to the rest of the society through their own means.

Vicki Burns and Asia A. Eaton focus on one of the most iconic behaviors of youth in the U.S. today: the use of social media for countless endeavors in their everyday lives, from entertainment to education. One important way youth are now using social media is as an instrument for activism, empowerment, and resistance against sexism. Social network sites and online communities have the ability to connect girls from diverse backgrounds to share ideas and create communities that can demand accountability and change from individuals, groups, and organizations that promote gender bias. While a significant number of online communities are working to improve perceptions of and opportunities for women and girls, both online and off, few are directed and run by girls themselves. Often, adult women end up advocating on behalf of girls in these communities, missing the voices of their key stakeholders. Through a review of online communities and an in-depth case study of a successful girl-fueled online grassroots movement, it becomes apparent that girls need to continue to be at the forefront of the conversation to end sexism and sexist discrimination. Methods to increase girls' participation in online movements to combat sexism are discussed.

Nicole Polen-Petit examines the documented use of online spaces by

LGBTQ youth and explores the connection between sexual literacy and the two main ways youth, and specifically LGBTQ youth, engage with the online world: the pursuit of information and knowledge and the desire for self-expression, identity and community. This is particularly important since we live in a world where most individuals approaching adulthood in developed nations have never known a time or a place when and where the online environment or the use of tools connected to the online environment was not an intimate part of their lives and everyday activities. Issues concerning the importance of congruence between online and offline identities as well as social capital are discussed. Polen-Petit offers directions and recommendations for further research and inquiry.

John A. Oliver and Willie S. Anderson explore music and media as vehicles for youth to express and articulate their voices. Historically, particularly over the past 40 years, youth have commonly used music to "speak truth to power." Oliver and Anderson include examples of ways youth and adults form educational partnerships, engage in activism, and participate in key social change initiatives. They observe youth as consumers, citizen journalists, and social activists. Oliver and Anderson also contend that youthful adult partnerships are key to social change and that collaboration promotes positive dialogue and action within educational institutions, corporations, and communities. Oliver and Anderson challenge readers, especially educators, to reframe or re-mix historical perspectives and embrace paradigm shifts that bridge multiple gaps of race, culture, class, faith, sexual orientation, and disability.

Bryan Currie focuses on religion and youth popular culture. He argues that as almost 70 percent of youth have been involved in religious youth groups, and at least half of the youth in community programs say faith is important to them, youth development professionals should understand how religious youth interact with popular culture. These "faithFull" youth are likely influenced by one of the world's major faiths, many of which believe popular culture is a potential contaminant to be either avoided or handled carefully. While their friends establish identities and form peer groups based on pop culture preferences, faith-involved youth may stand at a crossroads. Will they sacrifice social standing and peer relationships to reap the benefits of being faithFull? Or will they risk putting themselves at odds with family, faith leaders, and faithFull peers to explore the forbidden fruit of popular culture? Given that both popular culture and faith culture provide valuable developmental resources, is disengaging from either a good option? With these guiding questions, Currie explores the relationship among youth, popular culture, religion, and faith.

Jenifer K. McGuire and Alison Chrisler argue that body art, which once was seen as a marker of social outcasts, is now widely accepted among various social groups, including young people. Today's youth have developed norms surrounding body art. Queer identified youth have developed their own set of practices that both mark their cultural group membership and serve as a way to communicate their personal identity. McGuire and Chrisler focus on the body art narratives of transgender young people in a sample drawn from the American, Canadian, and Irish community groups. When analyzing the body art descriptions of transgender youth, they used a queer cultural lens and resiliency framework and considered both the image and the process of obtaining the body art and how it revealed a queer identity or concept. Young people described their body art as a way to document their changing relationships with their physical and psychological selves. Though much of the body art literature focuses on the risks associated with and the impulsivity of obtaining body art, this study found that the act of obtaining body art was both a planful and thoughtful process that enabled youth to mark and solidify social relationships, reclaim their bodies, and use their bodies to create a narrative of their gender experience.

Elizabeth Sharp, Darla J. Johnson and Nicole Wesley explore possibilities of dance as a medium for positive youth development by studying a dance-theater project among high school youth (the JUSTICE Project). Sharp, Johnson and Wesley focus on how the JUSTICE Project informed teens' artistic vision, working strategies, dance making interests and choreographic processes, and how it helped them more deeply engage with themselves, each other, and larger issues of justice in their high school and communities. Using the AP cornerstone principles of (a) authentic decision-making, (b) natural mentors, (c) reciprocal activity, and (d) community connectedness, the essay showcases how the JUSTICE Project offers a unique way to promote positive youth development.

Jesse Silva, Stella Silva and Joshua Quinn examine the use of Hip Hop, Hip Hop culture, and code switching as a methodology in addressing inequities, disparities, and issues for youth in Austin and San Marcos, Texas. The target population included predominantly Hispanic/Latino and African American/black youth enrolled in TRiO programs sponsored by the Office of Student Diversity & Inclusion at Texas State University. The conditions in which Hip Hop was created as well as the culture it created provide a framework for understanding how code switching is used to connect, educate, and empower youth. Ethnography self-reflection, content analysis of language used in workshop titles and descriptions, and findings from a master's applied research project were used as examples. Code switching proved to be a viable tool and strategy for enabling youth to understand and engage their social realities and educational opportunities.

Scott Westfall and Daniel Gould look at the intersection of sports and youth culture. They examine the various athletic experiences that today's youth encounter, including different levels of physical activity (or inactivity), rising obesity rates, and pressures/threats from social media. They also study both the benefits and detriments of sports. Some of the benefits include sports' ability to serve as a platform for teaching life lessons to youth. Yet current detriments can include sport specialization—which often leads to overuse injuries and mental burnout. Additionally, sports are no longer entirely controlled by educators or governing bodies with pure intentions; many of today's youth sports leagues focus on developing only the most talented athletes and therefore ignore the educational athletics component. The overarching message is to maintain positive elements of contemporary youth sports while at the same time adapting youth sports to meet the needs of a very new and ever-changing generation of young people.

Martha Montero-Sieburth describes how a targeted group of 12 students from the United States who attended the University of Amsterdam's International School for a semester used "Ethnic Diversity and Popular Culture," an undergraduate course during 2008–2012, to deconstruct stereotypes experienced prior to their leaving the U.S. and during their research of popular culture. Writing from her perspective as the instructor of the course, and drawing from the experiences of students as reflected in their final papers, Montero-Sieburth explores the mapping of the realities of coffeehouse practices and the depiction of sex workers. Montero-Sieburth's students reflected on their own prejudices after conducting interviews and gaining insights from managers to customers about the coffeehouse scene and red light district clients, sex workers, and Dutch policies as they operate in and make up aspects of Dutch culture. The students tested their attitudes and values as well as their own stereotypes by assessing their unfounded fears about sexuality, work, education, and being adults. These changes became evident initially from comments from their European peers, and later through their own reflections which showed their limited sense of "cosmopolitanism" and cross-cultural ignorance. They sought ways to overcome stereotypes as they gained greater agency and developed a sense of community-building unknown to them in this new terrain.

Mariko Izumi and Naomi Kagawa focus on the "no-gal" subculture in Japan. It provides a case study that challenges the general anxiety about the role of fashion in the development of youth. These Japanese "gals," whose subculture identity revolves around anime-inspired make-up, bleached hair and flamboyant outfits, connect their obsession with fashion and trend with agriculture, the "uncool" industry that has been struggling to attract the young generation. Izumi and Kagawa examine the no-gal subculture to explore the processes of identity development among Japanese youth. In particular, they pay attention to Shiho Fujita, the icon and the initiator of the "no-gal project," by reading her blog posts and publications. By applying the theory of positive youth development, Izumi and Kagawa illustrate how Fujita's no-gal project engages in the positive youth development and creates an empowering social environment that offers a space for the youth to imagine their impact on the society.

Lori Hoisington and Noah S.L. Crimmins discuss how brain development contributes to popular culture among adolescents. Of particular focus are the differences in adolescent and adult brain development and function with explanation for how these differences contribute to adolescent behavior. Two popular myths about adolescents are debunked: *Adolescence is just a phase that individuals must get through* and *Adolescents are immature and irrational.* Findings from research studies are presented to explain why characteristic adolescent behavior is normal for this developmental stage and necessary to achieve full maturity as an adult.

Fairy Cham-Villaroman, Charles W. Bates and Francisco A. Villarruel study the intersection of immigrant youth and public policy. They argue that regardless of their status as immigrants, these youth are influenced and influencing popular culture that emerges from the intended and unintended consequences of public policy development and implementation. In many cases, their participation in popular culture takes forms of civic engagement and advocacy that help them acquire 5 Cs of positive youth development and succeed in their lives.

This volume, a collection of thirteen essays written by academics, professionals, and community organizers, shows how popular culture and youth culture function can lead to positive youth development. Because of the richness and diversity of youth popular culture, the book cannot be and does not try to be comprehensive. Rather, its goal is to highlight some real-life examples of youth engaged in various social activities. Being young comes with a set of disadvantages: not being able to vote, not having much money, not having decades of experience and knowledge, and so on. But youth is a powerful phase in life. Especially with the rise of communication technologies that are both mobile and affordable, many young people are socially aware and are active for the cause of social justice. The essays that follow demonstrate the power of youth and their popular culture in the early 21st century.

Youth in Virtual Public Space
Social Justice and Youth Mobilization in #Ferguson

Yuya Kiuchi

On August 9, 2014, Michael Brown, an unarmed African American male, age 18, was fatally shot by a 28-year-old white police officer, Darren Wilson, in Ferguson, Missouri, a suburb of St. Louis. Before the incident, Brown, accompanied by his friend Dorian Johnson, stole a box of Swisher cigars, leading Wilson to respond to a police dispatch call about the robbery. Although varying witness accounts and information exist about what happened between Brown and Wilson, reports suggest that the two had an altercation at Wilson's police car, that Wilson fired his gun twice and hit Brown's hand, that Brown ran away from the car with his back turned to Wilson, and that Wilson shot Brown multiple times with two of the bullets fatally hitting his head and chest (Freivogel, 2014). The U.S. Department of Justice (2015), however, also revealed that the evidence was inconclusive if Brown had actually had his back turned to Wilson when he was shot. Witness accounts also vary in terms of what Brown exactly did when he was shot, especially with his hands and arms. It is still unknown if Brown had his hands up in surrender.

No matter what actually happened between Michael Brown and Darren Wilson, the shooting did not happen in a "vacuum" (Beer, 2014, par. 3). It happened in the context of America's persisting racism despite American society being frequently labeled as colorblind or post-racial (Kiuchi, in press). In this so-called post-racial society with persisting evidence of racism, criminalization of African Americans, especially males and youth, and mainstream media's continuing bias against African Americans are all too common. To combat such social injustice, grassroots movements led by youth and assisted

7

by technology, namely social media, have become a major source for justice. Furthermore, by the summer of 2014, many youth across the nation had become aware of the power of grassroots bottom-up activism thanks to various campaigns on immigration reform, LGBTQ and same-sex marriage issues, educational and residential segregation and inequalities, and other forms of systemic discrimination.

Immediately after the shooting, unrest ensued in Ferguson. Protesters were convinced that Brown was shot despite his hands being up in the air in surrender. Yan (2014) quoted Dorian Johnson, commenting, "At no point in time did they [Brown and Wilson] struggle over the weapon because the weapon was already drawn on us" (par. 7). The protest continued for several days. While the protests started peacefully, Ferguson eventually witnessed instances of violence and looting ("Looting erupts," 2014). Demonstrators were met with about 50 police officers in riot gear ("Protests near St. Louis," 2014). Claire McCaskill, senator from Missouri, commented that the militarization of the police escalated the unrest ("McCaskill," 2014).

Soon after the shooting, the incident became another avenue to examine the latest American racial dynamics. Criminal justice scholars discussed the relationship between African American communities and the police (Scholosser, Cha-Jua, Valgoi, & Neville, 2015; Chapter One, 2015). The case received multidisciplinary attention: through the lens of social class and racism (Lanhan, 2014), medicine (Reid, 2015), and African American history and studies (Kelley, 2104; McTighe, 2014; Lindsey, 2015). Others looked at the ways in which race in the U.S. could be discussed in classrooms and communities (Cuenca & Nichols, 2014; Falcon, 2015; Green & Green, 2015). Dyson (2014; 2015) examined the Ferguson case within a larger context of America's racial dynamics.

Social Media Activism and Youth Around Ferguson

Today, 64 percent of Americans in the U.S. own a smartphone. On average, 75 percent of those are between the ages of 18 and 29, 46 percent are between 30 and 49, and 31 percent of Americans over 50 have used their phone to capture a video at least once during a seven-day period (Smith, 2015). Therefore, it is no surprise that the deaths of Eric Garner, John Crawford III, and other unarmed African American men in recent years have become widely debated events on social media. Although the smartphone ownership gap between African Americans and whites is no longer significant (Smith, 2014), the new technology once again gave voice to the population whose voice has traditionally been silenced or ignored.

The Michael Brown shooting was also significant in that social media and other digital communication technologies impacted the way people heard, read, and talked about it. Within five days after the death of Brown, over six million tweets were sent about the incident (Fung, 2014). Within ten days, the number was up to about eight million. While the protest was at its height, on August 13, close to 4,500 tweets were sent mentioning #Ferguson every minute (Zak, 2014). These numbers are the proof that #Ferguson went viral. But a critical question is what these numbers really meant. Other key facts about Ferguson and its digital experience—the popularity of #iftheygunnedmedown, two GoFundMe campaigns that jointly raised over $500,000 for Darren Wilson, the NAACP's constant updates on the events unfolding in Ferguson, just to name a few—also suggest that digital experiences around Ferguson were a critical part of how people lived and will remember the highly controversial and saddening event in August 2014.

The Ferguson case was, however, far from being the only or the first event in which media technologies made a significant impact on a major social issue. The images of Emmett Till in his coffin, of Bull Connor's attack on protesters, and of many others also galvanized many Americans. Fifty years before Ferguson, during the height of the civil rights movement, Martin Luther King, Jr., was fully aware of the power of the images disseminated through network television to politicize Americans and to advance his civil rights agenda (Kiuchi, 2012; Torres, 2003). More recently, it was thanks to a VHS tape of Rodney King's case in 1991 that long-felt resentments against the LAPD surfaced. The history of technology is filled with instances of the marginalized population using new technology of the time for their own cause. What makes smartphones and social media stand out is that now images and stories are instantaneously shared. As Axelrod (2014) discussed, the images of Bull Connor's police dogs were not seen until the day after the incident when the newspaper was printed and delivered while events that unfolded in Ferguson were shared almost simultaneously.

The case in Ferguson showcased the power of social media activism driven by African American youth. When it comes to broadband access at home, there is a significant difference between whites and blacks—74 percent of whites and 60 percent of blacks have broadband access at home. But the difference is statistically insignificant when focused on whites and blacks between the ages of 18 and 29. Furthermore, for these young Americans, racial differences are again insignificant in terms of access to a smartphone. In addition, African American youth between the ages of 18 and 29 are 6 percent more likely to be on social media than their white counterparts. The gap is 12 percent for Twitter. African Americans with high school education or less are 9 percent more likely to use Twitter than their white counterparts. Blacks from a household making less than $30,000 a year are also 9 percent more likely to use the social media service than whites from a similar household (Axelrod, 2014; Smith, 2014). All these numbers underscore the importance of social media for many African American youth.

Despite the common assumption that youth today are apathetic and are only interested in themselves, they are actually socially engaged and motivated (Tapscott, 2009; Harris, Wyn, & Younes, 2010). From the youth-led effort to elect Barack Obama president in the mid–2000s and the Occupy Movement later in the decade to other social issues both inside and outside the U.S., youth have demonstrated their commitment for social justice and taken advantage of their skills in utilizing the latest communication technology to mobilize their peers (Costanza-Chock, 2012; Damodar, 2012; Porfilio, Roychoudhury, & Gardner, 2013; Kimball, 2014; Velasquez & LaaRose, 2015). Of course, this is not to suggest that social media caused uprisings, revolutions, and activism. Social media did not cause protests in Ferguson, either. Instead, these examples show that social media were significant part of various mobilizing efforts (Gerbaudo, 2012; Kellner, 2012; Howard & Hussain, 2013).

In Ferguson, as was the case with other recent examples of youth-led social activism, youth successfully created a space for social engagement. Such social engagement is different from simply acquiring information about the latest news events or uploading pictures and videos as a form of citizen journalism. Smith (2015) reported that about a third of smartphone users frequently used their phone to follow breaking news and that 35 percent shared images and videos about events in their community with others. About 70 percent of smartphone users do so occasionally. However, with the younger population more in tune with the latest technology, and Twitter being a significantly more important form of social media for African Americans (Axelrod, 2014; Smith, 2014), youth in and around Ferguson were able to create a virtual public space for social justice, rather than just for information sharing. Out of this interaction between the virtual and the real, #Ferguson as a virtual public space was born.

#Ferguson, as a virtual public space, was different from Ferguson. On the one hand, Ferguson, Missouri, was, of course, where Michael Brown was killed and where protesters were seen on the street. Therefore, Ferguson as a physical space emerged as a locus of protest for social justice out of a specific event and fueled by frustrations on the street level. On the other hand, #Ferguson was a virtually constructed space. This is not to say that Ferguson and #Ferguson were separate. The split between the virtual and the real is almost non-existent, if it exists at all. Many live in both spheres simultaneously. But #Ferguson offered opportunities for African Americans' and young people's voices to be heard and for them to be engaged in multiple ways.

Youth Engagement in #Ferguson

An increasing number of students are organizing themselves in the U.S. for various causes (Walton, 2015). Therefore, it is no surprise that along with adult protestors and demonstrators, many youth also participated in social justice activism in Ferguson. At different points, youth made sure they remained relevant. For example, during a protest event with notable participants including Cornel West and other local faith and community leaders, young people began to realize that their voice had been overshadowed by that of more high-visibility speakers. When the chants of "Let the youth speak!" The Rev. Traci Blackmon, chair of the event, spoke with youth in attendance and decided to give them opportunities to speak (Haas, 2014). Blackmon "spoke with youth and organizers to come up with a new plan. She apologized to those who were asked to forgo their time at the podium, including [the Rev. Jim Wallis]. She said it was the right thing to do, however, because these youth had been leading the movement in Ferguson from the beginning" (Haas, 2014, par. 5). This is not unique to Ferguson or Missouri.

These young people were active both in Ferguson and #Ferguson. Demby (2014) noted that at a march event held by Al Sharpton's National Action Network in Washington, D.C., youth activists from St. Louis County expressed their frustration that those who spoke were not the ones marching in Ferguson. Some activists said, "It should be nothing but young people up here!" (par. 9). Ned Alexander, a 25-year-old member of the Young Voices, stated, "I never imagined myself doing anything like this. But I felt now that I'm at the age I felt like I can make a change, so I might as well make a change while I can" (Corley, 2014, par. 7).

While those in Ferguson protested against the system of racism and police brutality that took away Brown's life, those in #Ferguson also fought against the traditional media and challenged them to re-examine America's racial dynamics. As will be discussed later, citizen journalism led by social media did not always bring positive outcomes. Questions about the benefits and downfalls of reports from the streets were raised, including how social media actually worked as an instigator rather than a source of solutions, and how they affected the grand jury's decision in March 2015 (Byers, 2014; Diem, 2014; Ingram, 2014; Stelter, 2014). Nonetheless, Stelter (2014) notes, "it's one thing to hear a news anchor say that police fired nonlethal rounds to disperse protesters on Monday night; it's another to see photos of the pepper balls and wooden pellets and the bloody injuries they caused" (par. 8). Social media became a new method of information distribution and acquisition for many. But the benefit of social media was not limited to the diversified means of information distribution and acquisition. Simultaneously, social media had proven themselves to be an effective "early warning service" for mainstream news outlets (Carr, 2014, par. 6).

For many youth, social media also offered a means for engagement and involvement for their cause. Berkatsky (2015) wrote, "We were able to document [the movement against police brutality] and share it quickly with people in a way that we never could have without social media" (par. 4). Demby (2014) explained that for young people of color, nothing worked better as a megaphone than Twitter. It was on such media that young people's frustrations were expressed. Lee commented on NPR's *On the Media* that "some young people say they've been waiting for a moment like this, where they can express themselves, whether they do it peacefully or violently—the death of this young man in this community by a police department that they say has been harassing them for years, they finally now are saying, 'Enough is enough'" (View from, par. 10). Furthermore, it was not just those young people in Ferguson that took advantage of social media to partake of what Lee termed a "rebellion" that went "viral" (View from, par. 10). #Ferguson became a place where young people who could not join the protest on site were nonetheless able to participate in the movement in the way they could.

Stories of Youth Heard in #Ferguson

Social justice and storytelling cannot be separated. Being able to tell one's own story without relying on others is particularly important for marginalized populations. David Karpf mentioned, "Because of social media, the police don't have control of this story.... It's opened everything up, changed how the media decides what's worthy of coverage—and who to trust" (Deutsch & Lee, 2014, par. 3–4). Many of the stories in #Ferguson were told by those who were there during the immediate aftermath of Brown's death and by those who felt close to the experience of Ferguson residents even though they might have been hundreds or thousands of miles away from Missouri.

African American youth participating in #Ferguson effectively used hashtags to voice their feelings, thoughts, experiences, and criticisms about the realities of racial dynamics in the U.S. both within and beyond Ferguson. Sarah Jackson, a professor at Northeastern University, was quoted saying, "What we saw was the first people who hashtagged Mike Brown's name were young people who lived in Ferguson and who saw his body laying in the street.... The people driving the Michael Brown story and Ferguson—and this is also true of the Trayvon Martin case—were young and had some connection to the victim. It was young folks from those communities who don't necessarily Tweet about political things or even have many followers" (Demby, 2014, par. 25). Even though they were not professional journalists or renowned social media gurus, participants found their voices were powerful and viral. For example, #iftheygunnedmedown encouraged African American youth to ask, "If the police killed me, what picture of me would the media use to show who I was?" The hashtag, a form of protest to the mainstream media that showed Brown wearing a red Nike tank top with his right hand making a peace sign according to some or a gang sign according to others, challenged the ways in which media characterized African American youth. A high school graduation picture of Brown with a cap and gown would have portrayed him differently. The problem of negative black representation clearly is not a thing of the past. #iftheygunnedmedown highlighted a reality of American racial politics.

Rod Winzer, an 18-year-old African American male, for example, posted two pictures of himself on Twitter as a part of the #iftheygunnedmedown campaign. One picture showed him in a dark blue graduation gown while the other was of him in a t-shirt with a gold chain around his neck, dangling to his chest. Similarly, Tyler Atkins, another African American young male in his senior year in high school, juxtaposed two pictures of himself. In one he wore a tuxedo with a saxophone around his neck. The picture was from a jazz concert at his high school. The other was of him in a black t-shirt with a blue bandana on his head and with his finger pointed to the camera. Atkins explains that the picture was from a rap music video he made with his friend for a math project in his class. He commented, "Had the media gained ahold of this picture, I feel it would be used to portray that I was in a gang, which is not true at all" (Vega, 2014, par. 4). Twitter can easily be criticized for its conciseness with 140 characters, but the conciseness enabled a very powerful discourse about one of the most challenging realities about contemporary American society to take place.

Hashtag campaigns were not limited to #iftheygunnedmedown. #handsupdontshoot was another example that many African American youth were involved in. Of course, the aim of this hashtag was to shed light on the fact that Brown, according to some, had his hands up in surrender when he was shot. One of the most prominent pictures of the campaign came from the students of Howard University, a historically black university. The picture of its students holding their hands up was posted by the university officially. The picture contained no smiles. The image is filled with young African American men and women quietly keeping their hands up. The university's caption reads, "We are proud of our students who have united peacefully to show they will not stand for the senseless violence anymore. Thank you to the Howard University Student Association for leading and organizing this display of solidarity. #HandsUpDontShoot" (Howard University, 2014).

In many ways, these hashtag campaigns are similar to historical examples of slogans. "We shall overcome" and "Black is beautiful" during the civil rights era had comparable goals of using memorable phrases to bring people together for social justice. These slogans undoubtedly connected activists and citizens across geographic boundaries. What made the hashtag campaigns unique from these historical cases is the creation of the aforementioned dynamic virtual public space. Young African Americans were able to participate in #Ferguson in many different ways from many different places. They remained connected and relevant. Their voice was heard by both those on the street in Ferguson and those who worked for the traditional mainstream media outlets.

Decentralized Participation Led by Youth

In #Ferguson social media enabled young people both inside and outside Ferguson as well as students on college campuses including Howard University to actively participate in the same movement simultaneously, youth took the leadership in the movement. On one level, the protest in Ferguson was part of the ongoing struggle for African American civil rights. Berlatsky (2015) therefore asks, "The civil-rights movement of the '60s obviously didn't have Twitter of social media or the Internet, but it was able to get its message out to the media in other ways. Why wouldn't traditional media be adequate now?" (par. 7). DeRay McKesson, one of the leading organizers of activism against police brutality, responds by stating, "What is different about Ferguson, or what is important about Ferguson, is that the movement began with regular people. There was no Martin, there was no Malcolm, there was no NAACP, it wasn't the Urban League. People came together who didn't necessarily know each other, but knew what they were experiencing was wrong" (Berlatsky, 2015, par. 8).

Demby (2014) calls this decentralized model of social protests the "Fannie Lou Hamer-Ella Baker model" or "an approach that embraces a grass roots and in which agency is widely diffused" (par. 5). This diffused model somewhat reminds us of Mark Granovetter's (1983) concept of weak ties and their strength. The relationship among hashtag activists in #Ferguson might be much weaker than that among activists marching down the street in Ferguson. But as a 19-year-old student at Spelman College in Atlanta, Georgia, stated, "Hashtag activism is activism.... We might be tweeting from a couch, but we're also getting up and doing the work that needs to be done" (Vega, 2014, par. 23). Thanks to these activists activism in Ferguson gainrd additional momentum and attention both inside and outside the U.S. This is to say that hashtag activism that followed the decentralized model showed the power that weak ties possessed to achieve what strong ties could not.

There are, of course, critics of such cyberactivism. Often termed as slacktivists, cyber activists are often characterized as those who sit on a comfortable couch in their living room watching TV or interacting with others solely on social media and websites. Philip Howard also explained that few cases of hashtag activism had actually led to policy changes or initiatives, or changed public opinions (Brewster, 2014). Diem (2014) speculates that social media might "have hurt the legal proceedings in Ferguson more than it helped" (par. 16). It is also possible that some violence observed in Ferguson was instigated by those who were on social media (Diem, 2014). Many young people were committed to their social cause, nonetheless. August Schaller, a junior at Buncombe County Early College, was quoted saying, "This is an opportunity for young people to change things" (Walton, 2015, par. 25).

But #Ferguson was exceptionally successful, with its associated hashtag and other forms of digital activism. The Ferguson National Response Network had more than 100 sites for protests and demonstrations in preparation for the grand jury's decision later in the year. (Richardson, 2014). From #iftheygunnedmedown to #handsupdontshoot and similar examples of activism such as #icantbreathe, social media kept feeding news stories to various media outlets. Despite his critical views on the impact of activism from #Ferguson, Howard (2014) also commented that hashtag activism enabled "massive public demonstrations and sustained news coverage…. It kept #Ferguson events in public consciousness and the national headlines" (par. 13).

Conclusion

Using hashtags in the ways described above is clearly different from hashtags as an indexing tool. Rather, social media users marked each individual's stories with hashtags. In other words, hashtags enabled Twitter users to generate or engage in a particular discourse around a topic. For example, Carl L Miller (2014) tweeted, "His [Michael Brown's] 'crime'? Not allowing an officer to search his car without a warrant" and added #NYpolice and #Ferguson. Similarly, Deray McKesson (2014) wrote, "White privilege, illustrated. #Ferguson." In both cases, the authors of the tweets joined the existing conversation about Ferguson through the use of a hashtag. Furthermore, since Twitter users are free to add any hashtag, #Ferguson can be, and turned out to be, chaotic and rhizomic. #Ferguson does not necessarily predicate that a particular tweet is for social justice. It could as well be in support of Darren Wilson. In reality, about 10 percent of the tweets were in favor of Wilson (Diem, 2014). The lack of #Ferguson in a tweet similarly does not preclude tweets from being about the death of Brown. However, what social media did as a whole in August 2014 was once again generate a new space for social engagement.

Ashley Yates, one of the founders of the Millennial Activists United and who is in her twenties, said, "Younger people … were utilizing the tools that we were utilizing so effectively to get the word out and really become our own media" (Corley, 2014, par. 13). The outcome of this youth-led and technology-mediated activism was the formation of a virtual public place. #Ferguson challenged what Lipsitz (2011) termed "a white spatial imaginary." He underscored the "importance of acknowledging the degree to which our society is structured by a white spatial imaginary and for confronting the serious moral, political, and social challenges mounted against it by a black spatial imaginary" (p. 13). Youth utilized social media to mobilize themselves and others for social justice to challenge the established mass culture.

REFERENCES

Axelrod, J. (2014, August 14). How social media galvanized the community in Ferguson. *CBS News*. Retrieved from http://www.cbsnews.com/news/how-social-media-galvanized-the-community-in-ferguson/.

Beer, T. (2014, August 18). Racism and the police: The shooting of Michael Brown in Ferguson. *Sociology Tool Box*. Retrieved from http://sociologytoolbox.com/racism-police-ferguson/.

Berlatsky, N. (2015, January 7). Hashtag activism isn't a cop-out. *The Atlantic*. Retrieved from http://www.theatlantic.com/politics/archive/2015/01/not-just-hashtag-activism-why-social-media-matters-to-protestors/384215/.

Brewster, S. (2014, December 12). After Ferguson: Is "hashtag activism" spurring policy changes? *NBC News*. Retrieved from http://www.nbcnews.com/politics/first-read/after-ferguson-hashtag-activism-spurring-policy-changes-n267436.

Byers, A. (2014, August 20). #Ferguson: Social media more spark than solution. *Politico*. Retrieved from http://www.politico.com/story/2014/08/ferguson-social-media-more-spark-than-solution-110202.html.

Carr, D. (2014, August 17). View of #Ferguson thrust Michael Brown shooting to national attention. *New York Times*. Retrieved from http://www.nytimes.com/2014/08/18/business/media/view-of-ferguson-thrust-michael-brown-shooting-to-national-attention.html?_r=0.

Chapter one: Policing and profit. *Harvard Law Review, 128*(6), 1723.

Corley, C. (2014, October 24). With Ferguson protests, 20-somethings become first-time activists. *NPR*. Retrieved from http://www.npr.org/2014/10/24/358054785/with-ferguson-protests-20-somethings-become-first-time-activists.

Costanza-Chock, S. (2012). Youth and social movements: Key lessons for allies. Retrieved from http://cyber.law.harvard.edu/sites/cyber.law.harvard.edu/files/KBWYouthandSocialMovements2012_0.pdf.

Cuenca, A., & Nichols, J.R. (2014). Ferguson is about us too: A call to explore our communities. *Social Education, 78*(5), 248–253.

Damodar, A. (2012). The rise of "great potential": Youth activism against gender-based violence. *Harvard International Review, 34*(2), 48–52.

Demby, G. (2014, December 31). The birth of a new civil rights movement. *Politico*. Retrieved from http://www.politico.com/magazine/story/2014/12/ferguson-new-civil-rights-movement-113906.html#.Vdy_dn01YZw.

Department of Justice. (2015). Memorandum: Department of justice report regarding the criminal investigation into the shooting death of Michael Brown by Ferguson, Missouri police officer Darren Wilson. Retrieved from http://www.justice.gov/sites/default/files/opa/press-releases/attachments/2015/03/04/doj_report_on_shooting_of_michael_brown_1.pdf.

Deutsch, L., & Lee, J. (2014, August 19). No filter: Social media show raw view of #Ferguson. *USA Today*. Retrieved from http://www.usatoday.com/story/news/nation-now/2014/08/14/social-media-ferguson-effect/14052495/.

Diem, N. (2014, December 4). Ferguson and the effect of social media activism. *Law Street: Law & Policy for Our Generation*. Retrieved from http://lawstreetmedia.com/issues/entertainment-and-culture/ferguson-and-the-effect-of-social-media-activism/.

Dyson, M.E. (2014, November 29). Where do we go after Ferguson? *New York Times*. Retrieved from http://www.nytimes.com/2014/11/30/opinion/sunday/where-do-we-go-after-ferguson.html.

Dyson, M.E. (2015, April 17). Racial terror, fast and slow. *New York Times*. Retrieved from http://www.nytimes.com/2015/04/17/opinion/racial-terror-fast-and-slow.html?_r=0.

Falcon, S.M. (2015). The globalization of Ferguson: Pedagogical matters about racial violence. *Feminist Studies, 41*(1), 218–221.

Freivogel, W. (2014, October 30). What we know—and don't know—about Michael Brown's Shooting. *St. Louis Public Radio*. Retrieved from http://www.news.stlpublicradio.org/post/what-we-know-and-dont-know-about-michael-browns-shooting.

Fung, B. (2014, August 14). Watch Twitter explode along with Ferguson. *Washington Post*. Retrieved from https://www.washingtonpost.com/blogs/the-switch/wp/2014/08/14/watch-twitter-explode-along-with-ferguson.

Gerbaudo, P. (2012). *Tweets and the streets: Social media and contemporary activism*. New York: Pluto Press.

Granovetter, M. (1983). The strength of weak ties: A network theory revisited. *Sociological Theory, 1*, 201–233.

Green, S., & Green, B. (2015). If you want a revolution, the only solution, evolve: The use of culturally responsive teaching in today's classrooms. *Black History Bulletin, 78*(1), 12–16.

Haas, R. (2014, November 22). Young activists take the state in Ferguson. *National Catholic Reporter*. Retrieved from http://ncronline.org/news/peace-justice/young-activists-take-stage-ferguson.

Harris, A., Wyn, J., & Younes, S. (2010). Beyond apathetic or activist youth: "Ordinary" young people and contemporary forms of participation. *Young, 18*(1), 9–32.

Howard University. (2014, August 14). We are proud of our students who have united peacefully to show they will not stand for the senseless violence anymore. Thank you to the Howard University Student Association for leading and organizing this display of solidarity. #HandsUpDontShoot. Retrieved from https://www.facebook.com/howarduniversity/photos/a.247650612184.116180.38238012184/10151995916112185/.

Howard, P., & Hussain, M. (2013). *Democracy's fourth wave? Digital media and the Arab Spring*. New York: Oxford University Press.

Ingram, M. (2014, November 25). Did social media make the situation in Ferguson better or worse? Gigaom. Retrieved from https://gigaom.com/2014/11/25/did-social-media-make-the-situation-in-ferguson-better-or-worse/.

Kelley, R.D.G. (2014). Another freedom summer. *Journal of Palestine Studies, 44*(1), 29–41.

Kellner, D. (2012). *Media spectacle and insurrection, 2011: From the Arab uprisings to occupy everywhere*. New York: Bloomsbury Academic.

Kimball, G. (2014, August 4). Why recent global uprisings are led by youth. *Heathwood*

Institute and Press: Critical Theory for Radical Democratic Alternatives. Retrieved from http://www.heathwoodpress.com/why-recent-global-uprisings-are-led-by-youth-gayle-kimball/.

Kiuchi, Y. (2012). *Struggles for equal voice: The history of African American media democracy*. Albany: SUNY Press.

Kiuchi, Y. (in press). *Race still matters: Reality of African American lives and the myth of post-racial society*. Albany: SUNY Press.

Lanhan, L. (2014). Ferguson before #Ferguson. *Columbia Journalism Review, 53*(4), 35–38.

Laura, C. (2015). Teaching Ferguson: Meaningful classroom dialogue about the Michael Brown case. *Black History Bulletin, 78*(1), 6.

Lindsey, T.B. (2015) Post-Ferguson: A "herstorical" approach to black violability. *Feminist Studies, 41*(1), 232–237.

Lipsitz, G. (2011). *How racism takes place*. Philadelphia: Temple University Press.

Looting erupts after vigil for slain Missouri teen Michael Brown. (2014, August 11). *NBC News*. Retrieved from http://www.nbcnews.com/storyline/michael-brown-shooting/looting-erupts-after-vigil-slain-missouri-teen-michael-brown-n177426.

"McCaskill: Police 'militarization' escalated unrest in Ferguson." (2014, August 14). *NBC News*. Retrieved from http://www.nbcnews.com/video/nbc-news/55867114 #55866941.

McKesson, D. [deray]. (2014, November 9). White privilege, illustrated (cont.) #Ferguson https://twitter.com/deray/status/531470912391217153.

McTighe, L. (2014). Moment or movement: Here's another story. *Fellowship, 78*(10–12), 19–21.

Miller, C.L. [Vote4CarlMiller]. (2014, November 9). His "crime"? Not allowing an officer to search his car without a warrant. #NYpolice #Ferguson http://fb.me/3ve7O9GRz. Retrieved from https://twitter.com/Vote4CarlMiller/status/53167180 5350924288.

Porfilio, B.J., Roychoudhury, D., & Gardner, L. (2013). Ending the "war against youth": Social media and hip-hop culture as sites of resistance, transformation and (re)conceptualization. *Journal for Critical Education Policy Studies, 11*(4), 85–105.

"Protests near St. Louis continue for slain teen after riot, arrests." (2014, August 11). *Chicago Tribune*. Retrieved from http://www.chicagotribune.com/news/nation world/chi-missouri-police-shooting-20140811-story.html.

Reid, R. (2015). Reflections on Ferguson. *The American Journal of Psychiatry, 172*(5), 423–434.

Richardson, V. (2014, November 24). In Ferguson, young activists emerge as movement leaders. *Washington Times*. Retrieved from http://www.washingtontimes. com/news/2014/nov/24/in-ferguson-young-activists-emerge-as-movement-lea/?page=all.

Schlosser, M.D., Cha-Jua, S., Valgoi, M., Neville, H.A. (2015). Improving policing in a multiracial society in the United States: A new approach. *International Journal of Criminal Justice Sciences, 10*(1), 115–121.

Smith, A. (2014, January 6). African Americans and technology use. *Pew Research Center*. Retrieved from http://www.pewinternet.org/2014/01/06/detailed-demo graphic-tables/.

Smith, A. (2015, April 1). U.S. smartphone use in 2015. *Pew Research Center*. Retrieved from http://www.pewinternet.org/2015/04/01/us-smartphone-use-in-2015/.

Stelter, B. (2014, August 13). Missouri shooting furor shows how social media users help and harm. *CNN*. Retrieved from http://www.cnn.com/2014/08/12/us/missouri-teen-shooting-social-media/.

Tapscott, D. (2009). *Grown up digital*. New York: McGraw-Hill.

Torres, S. (2003). *Black, white, and in color: Television and black civil rights*. Princeton: Princeton University Press.

Vega, T. (2014, August 12). Shooting spurs hashtag effort on stereotypes. *New York Times*. Retrieved from http://www.nytimes.com/2014/08/13/us/if-they-gunned-me-down-protest-on-twitter.html?_r=0.

Velasquez, A. & LaRose, R. (2015). Youth collective activism through social media: The role of collective efficacy. *New Media and Society, 17*(6), 899–918.

View from "Fergustan." (2014, August 15). *On the Media*. Retrieved from http://www.onthemedia.org/story/view-fergustan/transcript/.

Walton, B. (2015, February 22). A new wave of activism: Young people fight for justice. *Citizen Times*. Retrieved from http://www.citizen-times.com/story/news/local/2015/02/21/new-wave-activism-young-people-fight-justice/23810189/.

Yan, H. (2014, November 13). Get up to speed on the Ferguson shooting investigation. *CNN*. Retrieved from http://www.cnn.com/2014/11/13/justice/ferguson-up-to-speed/.

Zak, Elena. (2014, August 19). How #Ferguson has unfolded on twitter. *Wall Street Journal*. Retrieved from http://blogs.wsj.com/dispatch/2014/08/18/how-ferguson-has-unfolded-on-twitter/.

#GirlsFightBack

*How Girls Are Using Social Network
Sites and Online Communities
to Combat Sexism*

Vicki Burns *and* Asia A. Eaton

Online social network sites are an integral part of adolescents' lives today (e.g., Lenhart & Madden, 2007; Rideout, Foehr, & Roberts, 2010). As of 2012, 95 percent of all U.S. youth aged 12–17 reported going online (Madden, Lenhart, Duggan, Cortesi, & Gasser, 2013) and 81 percent of these reported using social network sites, up about 25 percent from 2006 (Lenhart, Purcell, Smith, & Zickuhr, 2010). Teen social media users typically visit social network sites daily (Madden, Lenhart, Duggan et al., 2013), and most access the Internet on mobile devices- meaning that youth are connected to online social networks every day and everywhere.

Over the last 10 years, from 2005–2015, social network sites like Facebook, MySpace, Twitter, Instagram, Pinterest, Tumblr, and Vine have become the most dominant forms of social media communication (Boorstin, 2014; boyd, 2008; Marquart, 2010; Sloan, 2011). Youth today rely heavily on Facebook for social networking, with 94 percent of teen social media users having a Facebook profile (Madden, Lenhart, Cortesi et al., 2013). Twitter is less popular, with 24 percent of online teens using Twitter in 2012, but its usage is growing rapidly, having doubled since 2011 (Madden, Lenhart, Cortesi et al., 2013). High school age girls and African American teens are particularly likely to use Twitter compared to other groups (Lenhart et al., 2010; Madden, Lenhart, Cortesi et al., 2013).

The rapidly increasing accessibility and popularity of social network sites, which are cited as one type of social media classification (Kaplan & Haenlein, 2010), has had myriad effects on youth development outcomes.

20

Many scholars have pointed to the seemingly negative effects of social media on youth behavior and culture. For example, it has been argued that social media enable youth violence, including bullying, stalking, and gang violence (for a review, see Patton, Hong, Ranney, Patel, Kelley et al., 2014). Others have demonstrated a negative relationship between social well-being and social media use among girls (Pea, Nass, Meheula, Rance, Kumar et al., 2012), especially compared to face-to-face communication. Some argue that social media use can exacerbate youth consumption of alcohol and tobacco (Cavazos-Rehg, Krauss, Spitzmagel, Grucza, & Bierut, 2014; McCreanor, Lyons, Griffin, Goodwin, Barnes et al., 2013). The American Academy of Pediatrics has even released a clinical report on potential problems youth may face due to social media activity, urging parents to watch for signs of depression and exposure to inappropriate content (O'Keeffe & Clarke-Pearson, 2011).

However, the overall relationship between social media use and youth well-being is inconsistent (Best, Manktelow, & Taylor, 2014), because some forms of social media engagement can promote positive youth development. In this essay, we will examine one way social media are being used by girls as a means for self-expression, empowerment, and to level engagement in political and social movements. In this essay, the term "girls" is specifically referring to youth between the ages of 12–17. Furthermore, the current essay will examine how girls are using social media to undertake meaningful and impactful social change efforts to combat sexism. First, we review how girls use social network sites such as Facebook and Twitter, and online communities such as SPARK and Powered By Girl (PBG), as activist tools in the fight against sexism. We also examine some of the positive outcomes of these efforts for girls and communities. Finally, we discuss areas for future research on online activism and ways to continue to support girls' activism moving forward.

Definition of Online Activism

Activism, or efforts to enact or direct social, political, economic, or environmental change, can occur on a local or individual level as well as in larger social movements (Martin, Hanson, & Fontaine, 2007). An example of individual feminist activism might be a person's decision to challenge a friend who makes a sexist comment. Other examples of individual activism may involve addressing injustices occurring within a local school, neighborhood, or government agency. While these efforts are crucial to enacting change, they co-exist with larger activist efforts that draw from and unite a diverse group of people dedicated to a common cause. The primary emphasis in this type of activism is to create social change via a collective vision and the shared belief that a particular facet of society needs to be addressed and improved (Taft, 2011). The current essay will focus on such larger social movements.

For hundreds of years, social activism included media communication such as leaflets and newsletters (van de Donk, Loader, Nixon, & Rucht, 2004a). Young people also have a long record of being "key actors in nearly every major social movement in modern history" (Chock, 2012, p. 2). However, youth activism that originates and is hosted primarily through media communication is an entirely new phenomenon. Online social activism, also known as Internet activism, digital activism, digital campaigning, cyberactivism, e-activism, online participation, online organizing, e-movements, eParticipation, etc. (e.g., McCaughey & Ayers, 2003; Earl & Kimport, 2011a; Earl, Kimport, Prieto, Rush, & Reynoso, 2010; Seabo, 2008; van de Donk, Loader, Nixon, & Rucht, 2004b) can be defined as politically-motivated social movements that rely on the Internet (Vegh, 2003). Often cited as beginning in 1990 (Gurak & Logie, 2003), online activism ranges the gamut from passive information sharing to mobilizing online and offline action, including participation in petitions, protests, boycotts, fundraising, politically-motivated hacking (e.g., hacktivism), demonstrations, voting, and email and letter-writing campaigns (Earl & Kimport, 2011b; Vegh, 2003).

Despite its recency, online activism has spread rapidly and widely, helping mobilize youth in political and social actions. The low-cost, high-speed, and wide accessibility of the Internet and social media have enabled youth across the globe, from diverse socioeconomic, political, and racial/ethnic backgrounds, to become involved in activism (Earl & Schussman, 2008; Raynes-Goldie & Walker, 2008). The Internet is a vehicle youth can use to sidestep some of the limitations they face in dominant structures, both to voice their personal opinions and experiences and to participate in and organize cooperative efforts. Though youth typically lack conventional power and status (such as the right to vote, economic independence, or mobility), online activism provides them a platform for challenging the "true powers" of this world (Stasko, 2008). In fact, social network sites and online communities can empower youth as "information leaders" when they connect their families and peers with mobilizing information and opportunity (McDevitt & Butler, 2011). Furthermore, these virtual spaces allow youth to utilize activism for important social issues. For example, researchers have cited the Internet and social network sites as important places for youth to understand, respond, and challenge gender-based violence (Motter, 2011; Salter, 2013).

Research supports a strong, positive relationship between social media use and youth political engagement. In fact, social media use has been found to be a stronger predictor of activism in youth than various demographic variables, such as socioeconomic status. Social media appears to be an accessible space for diverse youth to engage in political and social activism as it is familiar, youth are already spending their time on the sites, and they can participate without having to step outside their comfort zones (Raynes-Goldie & Walker, 2008). This has been documented in advanced democracies, such as the U.S., Australia, and the U.K. (Xenos, Vromen, & Loader, 2014), as well as in Africa (Iwilade, 2013), Chile (Valenzuela, Arrigada, Scherman, 2012), Iran (Wojcieszak, & Smith, 2014), Lebanon (Maamari & Zein, 2014), and Singapore (Skoric & Poor, 2013), for example. Internet activism has even penetrated the U.S. White House, where the first lady, Michelle Obama, publicly participated in the #BringBackOurGirls hashtag tweeting campaign (aka "hashtag activism") to end the 2014 Chibok kidnappings (McVeigh, 2014). Furthermore, the White House has created the "It's On Us" campaign, which is aimed at addressing and reducing the sexual victimization and rape that is prevalent on college campuses (RAINN, 2014). The White House and other organizations supporting this campaign have utilized social media and hashtag activism by promoting the #ItsOnUs hashtag, which urges everyone to take a pledge to fight campus sexual assault.

The Use of Social Networks and Communities

The most popular forms of online activism have changed over the years. The "zines" of the 1980s and early 1990s transformed into personal websites and blogs for many, or morphed into online newspapers and magazines. The late 1990s and early 2000s saw the birth and popularity of "blogging" and "ezines" which have also become an important online contribution (McCaughey, 2013; Piepmeier, 2009). Much research and writing has already covered the content and outcomes of girl's online blogging and ezines (e.g., Keller, 2014), with some even identifying "zines" and blogs as the new feminist frontier (e.g., Hammer, 2005; Keller, 2012).

Online communities have been defined as sites that have one or more "maintainers" who serve in a supervising or administrative role to manage the site's activities, content, and users (Bers, 2012). "Online community" appears to be a general umbrella term that can describe different types of activity, with social network sites being one type of online community (boyd & Ellison, 2008). According to boyd and Ellison (2008), social network sites can be defined as a web-based service that permits users to "construct a public or semi-public profile within a bounded system, articulate a list of other users with whom they share a connection, and view their connections and those made by others in the system" (p. 211). In addition to connecting with other users, these sites are popular places to share text-based information and other forms of media such as pictures and videos (Kaplan & Haenlein, 2010). Although the terms "social network site" and "online community" are often used interchangeably in the literature, boyd and Ellison (2008) specify that recent social network sites are often revolved around people and not "topics" or "interests," with the "individual at the center of their own community" (p. 219), while previous online communities may have been revolved around a specific topic or interest. In this sense, it appears that "online communities" can describe social network sites such as Facebook, which can be deemed a community organized around "people," or they can describe online sites that are a community organized around a certain "interest" (e.g., combating sexism). Online "movements" have been described as both identifiable, episodic movements that have occurred online (e.g., #BringBackOurGirls) as well as ongoing online movements that have active members coming together to change an aspect of society based on a specific topic or interest (e.g., the SPARK Movement). For the purposes of this essay, the latter conceptualization of an online "movement" can be used interchangeably with the term online "community" when the movement is geared towards an ongoing topic or social change and the movement is made up of members who can contribute and also manage the website for that movement. Both social network sites and online communities can be a place where online social action groups are formed and enforced, online petitions and their topics are conceived and circulated, and other grassroots social movements can be found.

Although blogging and ezines are still popular, they can be written in relative isolation and do not necessarily involve communities of girls or social activist outreach. Here, we are particularly interested in online activism that is created by girls to reach and inspire other girls. We will briefly mention a few adult-led or adult-majority communities that provide resources or space to girls, but these are not the focus of this essay. Instead, we will focus on the use of public social networks (e.g., Facebook) and online communities that are girl-powered (e.g., the SPARK Movement) that connect girls and help them become agents of their own lives. This focus was chosen because one of the most exciting, novel, and empowering features of activism for girls is that it holds the potential for them to create representative communities in which they control information and lead initiatives. The ability to autonomously create content and direct action is what sets girls' online activism apart from all previous forms of social and political action they might have participated in.

Girls as Creators and Change Agents in Online Activism

Online social network sites allow a level of active participation that did not exist before the Internet. For example, social network users can view and comment on information posted by those in their network, including on comments posted by an out-of-network person on an in-network person's feed. Users can also share other's posts in their own profile feed, for all of their in-network members to see, comment on, and share. Finally, users can create and post their own content in their profiles, including everything from text to links to photos and videos. In all these ways, girls can become contributors to culture instead of simply passive consumers through social network sites (De Ridder & Van Bauwel, 2013; Stasko, 2008; Harris, 2008).

Sites such as Facebook and MySpace also have groups and activist opportunities that enable people to band together on topics that are important to them (Kann et al., 2007). For example, Facebook has a "Causes" application where people are able to "share ideas, find supporters, and make an impact." Users are able to create and/or support a social cause campaign. Furthermore, Facebook has open and closed groups such as "Feminism on Facebook" with 8,706 members, which highlights current events and issues relevant to grassroots feminist movements. Users are also able to "like" topics that are categorized as "interests," to learn more about the topics and connect with other users who are interested in similar topics. For example, the topic of "gender equality" has 12,071 "likes," or 12,071 people who have publicly endorsed an interest in this topic.

Online petitions have also become a popular vehicle for girls' participation in online activism (Earl & Schussman, 2008). Earl and Schussman (2008) claim online petitions demonstrate that girls are making a shift from passive to active, and are demanding change from people in power. Change.org is one online petition website where girls can identify an issue related to sexism that needs awareness, attention, and change, and where they can find like-minded others to stand with them in solidarity. Social network sites such as Twitter and Facebook are places where these online petitions are often circulated for public awareness and response, and where young girls can "talk back" to various forms of pop culture. In this way, social network sites and online petitions sites such as Change.org have amplified girls' voices to the point where they can catch the attention of traditional producers of media and advertising (Earl & Schussman, 2008; Stasko, 2008).

For example, in 2014 a female high school student from Virginia started a Change.org petition urging Disney to include plus-sized princesses in their movies which reached 37,181 signatures. In 2012, an 8th grade girl from New Jersey started a Change.org petition on behalf of her four-year-old brother who wanted an Easy Bake Oven for Christmas but found no gender neutral oven sets for purchase. The 8th grader petitioned the company requesting that they make a less gender stereotypical version of the product along with non-gendered promotional materials. Her petition garnered 45,502 signatures and got the attention of the company, Hasbro. Hasbro invited her to their headquarters and ultimately agreed to make Easy Bake Ovens geared towards both boys and girls. Although Hasbro did not agree to the full extent of her requests, including making a non-gendered product, her advocacy resulted in real change from a multi-billion dollar company. These examples are evidence that girls are finding a voice in online social activist sites such as Change.org.

Culture Jamming and Media Activism

Certain types of websites and online communities provide girls with opportunities to create and deconstruct the popular culture that surrounds them. This is particularly important when it comes to the media's depiction of girls and women in music, movies, and television, where multidimensional female representation is lacking on and off the screen (Smith & Cook, 2008; Smith & Choueiti, 2010). Furthermore, producing their own content and media online helps girls to resist and challenge mass culture and to create and express their own realities (Harris, 2008; Hasinoff, 2012). For example, researchers have found that being able to actively produce and create media online assists girls with responding to and protesting the objectification of women and girls they see in mainstream media (Durham, 2008; Kearney, 2006). For example, the site "My Pop Studio" was developed by researchers and media scholars from the Media Education Lab. My Pop Studio provides girls experiences with different virtual options to increase media literacy skills by actively creating and recreating media. According to its site, My Pop Studio has a "Magazine Studio" where girls can create magazine layouts and have the opportunity to experience the impact of Photoshopping. The "TV Studio" allows girls to edit portions of television shows while the "Music Studio" affords girls an opportunity to create their own music stars and even compose a song. They are also able to experience the influential role of music when it comes to selling various consumer products.

This phenomenon of young girls creating and deconstructing pop culture reflects a concept that has developed in the culture in response to the overwhelming presence of media messages. "Culture jamming" is a form of media activism that has become popular over the Internet as more people, especially young people, disapprove of many of the underlying messages that are portrayed in mainstream popular media culture (Stasko, 2008). Although culture jamming has different forms and began offline by utilizing in-person protests, artwork, billboards, disseminating leaflets, and graffiti in public areas, the Internet has made the prospect of culture jamming quite accessible (Cammaerts, 2007). According to Mackey-Kallis (2012), "Culture jammers hoax corporate practices and products or spoof mass media messages in a way that unveils hidden agendas or counteracts meaning in order to negate their impact or success" (p. 51). Users culture jam, for example, by making parodies of existing media (e.g., advertisements) in order to "talk back" or "fight back" to marketers and expose the underlying harmful messages the media contains and is communicating to consumers (Harold, 2004). Even though anyone can be a cultural "jammer," Merskin (2006) specifically explores the evolution of what she calls a "Jammer Girl." Jammer Girls are groups of young girls that want to fight back against and change sexist depictions of girls, especially in the media. Merskin describes these girls as rejecting the "tenets of thinness, fashion, and passivity" (p. 51) and those wanting to actively redefine "beauty" in mainstream media and replace it with a more balanced and healthy representation of women and girls. The increase of culture jamming sites on the Internet has been noted as a significant advantage for girl-fueled online activism, particularly when it comes to unidimensional depictions of girls and women in the media and in the culture (Merskin, 2006).

There are many culture jamming sites, movements, and technologies that have been created specifically to "fight back" against modern media such as AdBusters, LAMPlatoon, and the LAMP's Media Breaker, to name a few. Many of these culture-jamming sites and technologies are not restricted to issues of sexism only, but most do address issues related to sexism to some degree. For example, AdBusters, which has been cited to be one of the most well-known culture jamming organizations (Mackey-Kallis, 2012) "spoofed" a Calvin Klein ad from the 1990s that featured one of their most popular models who was also extremely thin. AdBusters inserted the words "Feed me" into the ad, in an effort to highlight the true problematic nature of the marketing campaign for this popular consumer brand.

Some culture jamming movements and technologies are geared towards girls and sexism specifically. For example, the Representation Project is a movement that utilizes activism to critique film and media content that reinforces harmful gender stereotypes as well as objectification and violence against women and girls. The Representation Project utilizes social network sites and "hashtag activism," which is a way for people to support issues or causes such as sexism through social network sites and social media (Hill, 2014). The Representation Project started a hashtag called #NotBuyingIt, which allows the public to identify specific ads, episodes, and messages that are harmful, cite their reasoning for why they believe the message is harmful, and end it with #NotBuyingIt. The rationale is that companies will decrease sexist advertising if they believe it will cost them sales or public support. #NotBuyingIt has been successful in multiple campaigns, and they specifically target ads that are sexist to girls. From getting authors of children's books to remove sexist content, to pressuring Halloween costume businesses from marketing to girls in a sexualized way, this form of online activism is making changes (Indiegogo, n.d.). The Representation Project is, however, an adult-led organization that is speaking out on behalf of girls. Although many girls contribute to the creation of the different #NotBuyingIt hashtags, they still do not have ownership over this online movement. Although this type of online activism is geared towards girls and for girls, it is not necessarily a girl-initiated or managed online community.

About-Face.org "equips girls and women with tools to understand and resist harmful media messages that effect their self-esteem and body image." The site has a "Gallery of Offenders" and a "Gallery of Winners" that depicts media content that is both harmful and empowering towards girls and women, respectively. Girls and women can send in their own recommendation for both galleries. The site also has three online activist opportunities for young girls and women; petitions, "tweaking" a media ad, and an action section. The petition portion allows girls and women access to petitions for each ad/company in their Gallery of Offenders. They also provide a guide for how girls can create their own original petitions. In their tweak an ad section, they show examples of "tweaked" ads and an opportunity to send About Face their ads so they can be placed on the website. Lastly, their action section provides examples of social action projects and an opportunity to submit this so their own unique action projects can be highlighted on the site. Although girls and women can contribute in many different ways to About Face, the community appears to be led primarily by adult women who wish to assist girls and women in culture jamming and social activist processes.

Whether online movements and communities are geared towards culture jamming or are simply seeking a decrease in sexism geared towards girls, entirely girl-fueled online social movements against sexism are rare. While many anti-sexist online movements work towards improving girls' lives, many of these are run by adult women. There are some movements that invite girls to be the originators or the creators of activism (such as contributing to the Gallery of Offenders at About Face), rather than simply recipients of information. However, these movements showcase girls' work within a larger, adult-led change effort. In other words, girls' activism is a part of many online feminist communities, but girls rarely lead these communities. However, we found at least two established online activist communities and movements based in the United States in which girls are the major change agents. It is important to learn more how these unique communities operate, as they offer the most direct route towards understanding what girls want and need in today's feminist movement.

One online community called Powered By Girl (PBG) is "an online media activism movement and campaign for girls by girls." PBG is girl-fueled and was created by the Hardy Girls Healthy Women (HGHW) organization.

PBG's purported mission is to challenge, interrupt, and eventually decrease sexism in the media. PBG is known to focus on sexism and ways it uniquely interacts with racism, classism, and heterosexism. PBG is an international online movement and community, where its contents are created and uploaded by female guest contributors as well as social media interns. PBG welcomes the culture jamming of drawings, cartoons, poems, and remakes of ads and they encourage the use of humor and satire when "fighting back" against sexist media images. PBG provides a culture jamming app (the idea of this app came from young girls themselves) that allows girls to create their jam and can then post their work on the site. PBG bloggers are also all young girls who write commentary on sexist media aimed at girls. PBG reports having a presence across the Internet, but is specifically visible on Twitter, Facebook, and other social network sites.

A Case Study of the SPARK Movement

The SPARK Movement is a prime example of a successful online community where girls (ages 13–22) fight everyday sexism. SPARK is an intergenerational grassroots community and movement that is girl-fueled and girl-driven with the aim of ending all forms of sexualization. SPARK has had a number of influential campaigns that have led to tangible changes in society. For example, SPARK has focused on gender stereotypes and equality in the toys marketed to girls and boys, body image issues in advertisements in the media (e.g., magazines), and issues related to sexual assault and violence. SPARK utilizes various forms of online activism in their campaigns (e.g., online petitions, blogs), and they define themselves as a movement by girls, for girls. As online communities continue to be a place for girls to galvanize for social change against sexism, it is crucial to take an in-depth look at a successful online community that operates by having girls as an integral part of the problem-solving team and leadership. The following information was gathered through the SPARK website and also through an in-person interview with the first author and the SPARK executive director, Dr. Dana Edell. This interview was audio recorded and transcribed, and took place at the National Women's Studies Association National Conference in San Juan, Puerto Rico, on November 14, 2014.

SPARK is open to all girls ages 13–22 to participate and become a part of the SPARKteam, including girls from across the globe. The SPARKteam has been responsible for creating blogs, creating online petitions, fundraising, and heading national movements with large corporations who they have identified as being a part of the sexualization that hurts girls. SPARK is designed to be a movement fueled by girls for girls, yet has an intergenerational structure that allows adult women as part of the leadership team to help guide, support, and make girl activism possible.

Dr. Dana Edell, SPARK executive director, estimates that as of 2014 about 65 percent of SPARK girls are girls of color living in 14 U.S. states and eight different countries. Girls come from various socioeconomic classes and also range in terms of urban, suburban, and rural dwelling areas. Edell reports that one-third to one-half of the girls would also identify as lesbian, bisexual, and/or transgender in terms of their sexual orientation and gender identity. One of SPARK's strength areas is its diversity of participants, and given that it is a mainly online community, the Internet affords an international reach that enriches the experiences of the SPARK girls themselves as well as the impact they can have on other girls. In fact, Edell believes part of why SPARK is so important is that it allows girls who are in geographically-limited areas to share their voices and a place to find like-minded individuals. SPARK as an online community addresses the lack of access problem that leaves many young girls who want to fight back against sexism feeling alone. Edell says girls often come to her and say, "I'm the only feminist in my high school" or "I'm the only feminist in my community." Edell says SPARK's online presence is important because

> suddenly girls can foster all these relationships with girls who are incredibly different from them and incredibly connected to them. It's a space where girls are sharing feminist ideologies and activist passions. A girl living in a small town in Maine can connect with a girl living in New York City and a Trans girl in Connecticut can connect with a Trans girl in North Carolina. They might not have another space where they can actually communicate with each other.

In addition to connecting girls with other girls who think and feel like they do, SPARK allows flexibility as an online community that meets the demands and obstacles some young girls face. Given that they often lack independence in their schedules and mobility, it may not be realistic to expect girls who want to be involved in social change to attend weekly or biweekly in-person meetings. According to Edell, SPARK has online chats every two weeks with its members. These chats are automatically recorded and therefore girls who cannot attend the chat can catch up on the meeting when their schedules permit. The flexibility of having a social movement that is accessible 24 hours a day and seven days a week makes it manageable and possible for many young girls who would otherwise be unable to consistently participate.

One attribute of SPARK that distinguishes it from other online activist movements for girls is the way in which they structure the role and power of girls who join their movement. SPARKteam members attend one face-to-face annual retreat where they discuss the issues that are important to them and they begin to make plans for the SPARK Actions they will work on for the year. While the retreat is not mandatory, attendance is crucial. Edell reports that about 70–75 percent of girls attend in person, and Skype participation is setup for the girls who are unable to attend. Additionally, SPARK is able to provide full and/or partial financial support for girls in need so they are able to attend the retreat.

During the actual retreat, the girls brainstorm different issues that they believe are important to them and all members vote on which initiatives should be pursued for that year. Edell reports that at the most recent SPARK-team retreat, SPARKteam members came up with 27 possible actions/initiatives. Some example actions/initiatives that they suggested were related to women and immigration issues, girls in STEM fields, and issues related to feminist television analysis. Edell explains,

> Girls had to pitch why each of the proposed actions should be a Spark Action for the year. Then we narrowed that down into 6 or 7 of those 27 actions and we split the girls into groups. Girls within each of those groups had to strategize long term plans for that action. We have a whole action pitch form that is about 15 questions that the girls have to answer when they have an idea for an action and pitch it.

SPARK maintains flexibility by merging current events and issues with predetermined SPARKteam actions/initiatives. Edell reports that members of SPARK leadership and the SPARKteam will often expedite a SPARKteam action if something has occurred in society that is relevant to that action. Edell mentions that this flexibility is important because it can be "a moment where it [the action/initiative] could take off."

Even though there are a limited number of slots for girl leaders on the SPARKteam, Edell reports that SPARK has created additional online-only SPARK spaces for young people to participate in the movement.

> We currently have about 150 people in the SPARK Action Squad. It is a private Facebook group that is an online-only space where applicants fill out an application but most young people who express sincere interest in their application is accepted. The SPARK Action Squad is more diverse than the Spark Team. There are boys and a larger age range; we have people younger than 13 and young women or young adults in their 20s that are older than 22 but want to be engaged in this community. The SPARK Action Squad is moderated by three girls on the actual SPARKteam and SPARK recently hired a part time adult staff member to partner with the SPARKteam girls and co-facilitate. And every day there's a different focus. For example, there's Take Action Tuesday and every Tuesday there is a post about taking action this week. If they watch documentary films online together they are then able to talk about them together, and there is also a weekly book club. It is truly a hundred percent online space.

SPARK's Impact

SPARK has had a number of successful campaigns that take on sexism from a diverse lens. One of SPARK's campaigns that received high amounts of attention was geared towards *Seventeen* magazine and their use of Photoshop to alter the images of girls and women in their magazines. When Edell was asked which SPARK initiative she felt had the biggest impact on SPARK girls and other girls around the country thus far, the *Seventeen* magazine initiative was at the top of her list.

Members of the SPARKteam, who were supported and guided by a number of adult women from the SPARK leadership team, demanded that *Seventeen* magazine change how they represent girls in their magazines. One girl from the SPARKteam created a Change.org petition asking *Seventeen* to print at least one unaltered, un-Photoshopped image per month and to start committing to showing diverse images of girls in their magazines. Along with full participation from all the girls on the SPARKteam, SPARK counted on their dozens of partner organizations and friends in the media across the country to continue to put pressure on *Seventeen* and to collect petition signatures. With 86,436 signatures on their petition, *Seventeen* agreed to meet with Julia Bluhm, the SPARKteam member who wrote the petition along with Edell, and following the meeting made a pledge to promise to never alter the body size and face shape of the girls featured in their magazines and to feature more diverse girls in the magazine. They published this pledge in the Body Peace Treaty in their August 2012 issue. Edell reported that there was even a bigger success to the campaign than *Seventeen*'s Body Peace treaty—the overall level of public attention given to the issue of media representations of girls.

> If we had just had a private meeting with the editor of Seventeen and nobody ever knew about it, I would not have felt like it had a huge impact as it was never called out. But the fact that we got people talking about the impact of Photoshopped images, about the ways girls are represented, about who is missing from these teen magazines, which body sizes, which ethnicities- that felt great.

In addition, Edell believes the *Seventeen* magazine initiative fostered positive identity development in the teenage girls who were a part of SPARK, as well as impacting the teenage girls who were witnessing it. "We had a media firestorm around their office for weeks leading up to demanding a meeting questioning, 'Why won't you meet with a girl?' 'Why won't you sit down with a teenage girl?' It [the *Seventeen* magazine success] ended up building the confidence that their [teenage girls] voice matters. That they have something to say and that it's worthwhile. Look at what girls can do, they have the power to make change." Edell also mentioned that the *Seventeen* magazine initiative was successful because of the intentional targeting of a company that had something to lose. *Seventeen* magazine purports to be a magazine that wants girls to love themselves and love their bodies, and it relies on girls' interest and support to be profitable. The accusation that the magazine was harmful for girls and not in girls' best interest had dire implications for their bottom line.

Alternatively, Edell cited one additional SPARK victory that she believes was impactful for the SPARK girls and for the movement against sexism. In this case, the action involved the Google search engine homepage. The Google homepage honors successful and influential people with doodles of themselves that are showcased on the Google homepage. After extensive research by girls on the SPARKteam counting every published Google Doodle over four years, SPARK purported that the Doodle representation was sexist, in that 82.7 percent of the doodles were images of men. SPARK also pointed out that the doodles were not representative of racial/ethnic minorities. Edell reported that unlike other organizations, Google reached out to SPARK once they brought the issue into the public conversation and made it known to SPARK that they were committed to a more balanced representation of gender and race.

> Part of our contribution to the movement is igniting certain conversations and dialogue like this. But I also believe strongly that the girls who are on the SPARKteam have had transformative experiences working with us and that is also a huge success. I'm very proud of that, I think we work with girls in a unique way that the girls feel and they become aware that this space is pretty sacred for them, that they don't have other spaces like this. And that we've been working really hard to ensure that this exists, these intergenerational spaces of activism where girls can talk authentically and honestly about, feminism. [The message is] girls, we should give them a chance. We should listen to them.

According to Edell, an important theme when it comes to fighting media sexualization online is fighting "fire with fire." In other words, in order to effectively fight back against sexism that is often in public spaces like the media, one must also use media itself. It is important for online social change communities to utilize the tools that oppress them as a means to fight them.

> We have to use those tools and that language and that vocabulary in order to impact that space. And part of what we're doing is trying to create an alternative to sexualization and so we have to be using those same methods and tools in those online spaces. [We must use] strategies with positive messages so that we can interrupt and eventually draw out the negative.

Girl's Use of Social Network Sites and Online Communities and Their Relationship to Identity

After examining the purpose and impact of successful girl-fueled online activism, the theme of identity development emerges as a critical by-product for girls. Social network sites and online communities provide girls an unparalleled opportunity to shed, adopt, and explore identities both online and offline. Specifically, social network sites have been cited as important for the identity development of girls, as it gives them a place to create and explore "possible selves" (Manago, Graham, Greenfield, & Salimkhan, 2008) that can defy norms and stereotypes. Additionally, the negotiation of online identity and activity has been found to increase self-esteem and positively impact the way young people see themselves (Gonzales & Hancock, 2011). Some scholars believe the very act of having a social media online presence forces the adolescent to critically think about the way in which they want to be perceived by others (Fleur, 2014). In essence, making decisions about the different ways in which a teen will portray themselves and their activist efforts online triggers a negotiation of the identity development process which impacts them both on and offline. Guzzetti (2006) found that young teenage girls utilize online communities to "discuss, promote, and explore" aspects of their identities and that as a result, their online and offline identities often end up blending together. Sherman and colleagues (2000) assert that online actions and behaviors are actually extensions of what would be seen offline. Furthermore, Valentine and Holloway (2002) suggest a reciprocity effect in which young people's virtual world or persona actually become a part of their offline world or persona, and vice versa. For example, the exploration of an online self can become a type of identity "dress rehearsal" before the young girl decides to show newly found parts of herself to the offline world (Milford, 2013). Participating in online activism and online communities positively impacts girls' identity development on and offline, and it is important to consider this in future activism and research on girls.

Social network sites and online communities are critical venues for girls to explore their identities specifically as gendered and sexualized beings. Sexual objectification, which occurs externally and internally, serves to silence girls' internal experiences, such as their attitudes, needs, and feelings (Fredrickson & Roberts, 1997). An online community, as compared to a face-to-face community, may lessen the influence of the activists' gender or appearance (Valentine & Holloway, 2002), eliminating stereotyping and objectification on the basis of these social category memberships. For example, online communities appear to overrule strict gender norms and stereotypes that girls face in their everyday lives. The presence and relevance of their "femaleness" and their "femininity" can often result in the adherence of rigid gender roles that they place on themselves and that others place on them. However, online communities allow girls to take on less traditional and stereotypical norms, and allow exploration of more "masculine" attributes that they identify with but for one reason or another do not feel comfortable to express in their daily lives (Currie, Kelly, & Pomerantz, 2009). This flexibility in the expression of different parts of their gender and sexual identity is crucial for young girls going through the pivotal stages of identity development.

The anonymity the Internet can provide is also relevant for girls of varying races, ethnicities, classes, sexual orientations, religions, and abilities. In fact, research has noted that women who are a part of marginalized and disadvantaged groups seem to be the ones getting the most involved in online social action (Rapp, Button, Fleury-Steiner, & Fleury-Steiner, 2010; Roker, 2008). While the Internet does not eliminate the presence of gender, race, or other forms of discrimination, it does appear to afford girls a way to present themselves and be heard in unique ways. For example, some face-to-face social activism, such as sit-ins or protest marches, brings a risk to one's physical safety. Online networks and communities allow girls, particularly minority girls, to challenge injustices in society and to begin conversations surrounding change while remaining somewhat or completely anonymous (Motter, 2011). This affords freedom from physical harm and from the experience of "surveillance" that many minority women experience from dominant groups and even from themselves while in the presence of dominant groups (Harris, 2004). Additionally, girls and can be influential on issues that do not just impact them locally, but nationally. Allowing girls an opportunity to positively impact a situation that is occurring on the other side of the country gives them visibility, power, and a reach that previous generations of girls and women simply did not have.

As stated by Turkle (1999), the positive effects of exploring online can be likened to the exploration Erik Erikson outlined as a "psychosocial moratorium" where young people can interact with many different concepts and groups of people, which assists with the identity development stage. Online activism can be considered a prime example of this "psychosocial moratorium" as young girls are able to learn about social problems, find other girls who care about these same problems, and troubleshoot and brainstorm ways to ameliorate these issues. As was noted as a result of the SPARK Movement victories, engaging in online activism, particularly activism that leads to observable change, leads girls to feel differently about themselves. It appears that participating in an online activist community (such as SPARK) increases not only a sense of efficacy for girls, but a deeper sense of who they are as girls, future women, and valuable, capable citizens.

Future Directions and Suggestions for Girl-Led Online Activism

Although there has been some research and evaluation done on advocacy and activism efforts related to girls and girls' issues (Brinkman, Brinkman, & Toomey, 2011; Chen, Weiss, & Nicholson, 2010), studies are most often limited to face-to-face interventions with girls who are part of an after-school organization or as part of an outside study. Given the crucial role social media and online activism plays in the lives of young girls, it is noteworthy that there is little empirical research on these efforts. According to Kimball (2014), academic scholars largely ignore in-depth analyses of youth activism and youth social movements. Kimball studied the frequency of article titles that reflect youth activism in popular empirical youth journals. In her analysis of article titles in the 2011–2014 volumes of the *Journal of Youth Studies,* only 11.6 percent of titles reflected youth activism or political attitudes. Yet, according to the 2013 Youth Organizing Field Scan, there was a 15 percent increase in the amount of youth online and offline activism efforts surrounding gender and young women's issues from 2010 to 2013 (Braxton, Buford, & Marasigan, 2013). Braxton et al. (2013) surmise the increase can be a combination of young people responding to issues that are particularly relevant to their community, as well as experiencing an increase in solidarity around certain issues. Yet, research documenting girls' online activism in regards to these very issues is sparse.

A number of scholars who focus on ways to improve online activism cite the lack of structured methodology, empirical evidence, and evaluation as a pivotal area of weakness (Earl 2000, 2006; Grant, Finkelstein, & Lyons, 2003). Saebo (2008), who categorizes online activism as a type of "eParticipation," cites that since research on online activism spans across many different academic disciplines and is relatively new, there is not always a general consensus on the best research methods to utilize. Additionally, without structured research methods, researchers may have difficulty comparing studies and learning from each other's work (Saebo, 2008). Therefore, establishing appropriate research methods for the various forms and types of online activism may provide a useful blueprint for evaluating and comparing activist methodologies, designs, and outcomes (Earl, 2006; 2013; Saebo, 2008). While empirical research has been conducted on general youth online activism (Raynes-Goldie & Walker, 2008), online and offline activism against sexism by women (Ayers, 2003), offline activism against sexism by girls (Taft, 2011), girls who blog about sexism (Keller, 2012), and girls who write e-zines about sexism (Kearney, 2006), few studies have empirically investigated girl-fueled activist online communities that combat sexism. It is critical to explore this phenomenon not only because of the dearth of empirical research on girl-fueled activism but to evaluate the efficacy of these efforts and incorporate new strategies to increase their efficacy and expand their scope.

One reason for the lack of research on online community actions may be that it is difficult to define online activism. In the last few decades, news increasingly takes the form of a "media spectacle," which is when a story becomes "viral" through mass circulation on many different forms of social media (Kellner, 2011). Individuals have many opportunities to promote these stories in their networks, and they can use social network sites such as Facebook and Twitter to become a micro-contributor to the spectacle. It has therefore become challenging to differentiate between online activism and simply reposting, commenting on, or forwarding a news article or other form of media. In fact, this kind of viral effect can even lead to observable and significant social changes (Kellner, 2011), further blurring the line between activism and spectacle.

Additionally, scholars note that online activism is a "broad term" and can be seen many in different forms (e.g., culture jamming, online petitions). Careful attention is needed when defining and operationalizing online activism in order to avoid the obstacles academics face when attempting to study it (Vraga, Bode, Wells, Driscoll, & Thorson, 2014). Harris (2008) investigated online communities/cultures that are created by young women and girls to address "girl-centered feminism and racism." Harris contends that although these girl-fueled websites are often themselves a form of activism, analysts and researchers may not attend to these sites as they are not typically "outcome oriented." In this sense, part of the reason for the lack of research is not only the murky definition of what constitutes online activism but also whether online activism must or even can reliably result in observable, successful outcomes. For example, there are opposing views on the efficacy and impact of online petitions, which have been cited as both a popular online activist tactic and also a tactic that has earned the term "slacktivism." According to the *Stanford Daily*, online petitions are simply not effective and can in fact hurt social movements, "Many believe that online petitions have greatly risen in popularity because the strategy allows the signatories to feel good because they have done something, without necessarily having accomplished anything substantive" (Editorial Board, 2012, par. 4). However, Randy Paynter, founder of thepetitionsite.com, insists that online petitions provide an opportunity to "do something" for an otherwise overwhelming social problem. He sites that online petitions are a first step for many activists and likens online petitioning as a "gateway" to the online activist world. In fact, research has found that individuals who sign a petition are significantly more likely to donate money to a related charity (Lee & Hsieh, 2013). In this way, tracking the impact not only of the online petition but also the long-term activity and efforts of the people who sign a petition proved to be an important way to determine multidimensional longitudinal outcomes.

Therefore, implementing a system to track multidimensional outcomes can likely increase the occurrence of empirical research on girl-fueled online activism. One way to track outcomes may be to incorporate thorough evaluations of the experiences of girl online activists. For example, SPARK asks its members to fill out annual evaluations of their experiences in order to get a sense of the impact and ways they have grown and changed over the year. Additionally, online communities with heavy blog sections can document the perceived impact of various blog posts by noting the number and type of responses from the public (Keller, 2012). For example, researchers have utilized various techniques related to content analysis, a quantitative research method, and applied this to the study of online blogs (Herring, 2010). Furthermore, given the demonstrated relationship between online activism and identity for girls, it will be important to include empirical investigations that specifically target and measure identity development in online activists. In order to track and evaluate outcomes and to assist with the research and evaluation component, online communities may wish to partner with local universities, colleges, or professors. For example, multiple members of the SPARK leadership team are psychologists, professors, and/or researchers who are able to utilize their expertise in research methods and girls' activism to publish empirical journal articles that provide in-depth exposure to girls' experience with online activism. Additionally, research universities in particular have doctoral students that must complete theses or dissertations and may have a keen interest in exploring and evaluating girl-fueled online activist communities. Online communities that make efforts to evaluate outcomes will not only be more attractive for funding agencies, but will make future replication and improvements to activism more likely.

Another way to increase research and evaluation on online communities and online action is to expand our definition of what we consider to be "observable outcomes" in this area. While not every activist effort results in large and permanent social changes, changes on a smaller scale are telling and crucial. For example, changes in the composition or number of individuals in certain activist communities can signal important shifts in political and social climate. Also, public discussions within these groups can provide information to researchers and practitioners on girls' interests and concerns, enabling them to better support girls in starting their own online activism. Thus, researchers in areas related to social work, clinical and counseling psychology, sociology, public health, and other disciplines are encouraged to increase their attention towards girl-fueled activism and discussions that are already occurring online but are largely being ignored. Future directions should focus not only on tracking outcomes for research purposes, but also publicizing the outcomes of girl-fueled online activist efforts. It is critical to provide young girls with examples of other young people who have had positive outcomes who can serve as a model that the efforts of young people are valued and effective. In fact, there is a webpage dedicated solely to highlighting "23 Inspiring Feminist Digital Campaigns That Changed the World," however all of these feature adult women leading change and not a single one mentions girls. For example, a feminist group called UltraViolet waged a successful social media and online protest to pressure Reebok to drop a musical artist from brand ambassador status after he allegedly rapped about drugging and raping women. *Everyday Sexism,* another feminist online community, pressured iTunes to remove an app that allowed young girls to perform plastic surgery on virtual female characters. The Representation Project had a hand in pressuring GoDaddy to alter their advertising strategy and therefore decrease the sexist ads they produced. Once again, some of the examples given had a profound and positive impact on the lives of girls, but all appeared to be primarily adults advocating on behalf of those girls. While these are crucial examples that underscore the power online social activism has for combating sexism, it is imperative that journalists, scholars, and academicians make efforts to highlight online social change that is a direct result of girls. This is not to say that adult women should not be a part of these efforts. In fact, movements such as SPARK are as successful as they are due to the combined efforts of the adult leadership team in conjunction with the SPARKteam. However, the girls on the SPARKteam are afforded decision making power, and are asked to be a part of not only identifying the problems, but coming up with solutions to those problems.

Organizations and communities that are girl-centered but run by adults may increase the impact they have on girls by creating a youth advisory board or recruiting youth representatives who have power in organizational decision making. In addition, it is hoped that secondary and post-secondary institutions, in-person organizations, and after-school programs that serve girls may consider adding an online activist component to their programming. Students are often able to choose elective courses in school, yet options to take elective courses that utilize the Internet to promote activism or social justice on feminist topics are less commonplace. Implementing these types of opportunities can trigger a developmental process of empowerment that research has shown positively impacts youth development.

For example, Earl and Schussman (2008) argue that youth-driven online petitions with even a few hundred signatures have been able to create visible change. They also argue that this visible change leads young people to feel their voices count for something, which can lead to a sense of efficacy in relation to personal, social, and political power that may not have been possible before online petitions. Earl and Schussman (2008) write, "A personal sense of efficacy may be an important factor that prompts people to engage in collective action. That sense of efficacy may be something young people are gaining from their cultural contestation that they do not get from interactions with government" (p. 89). The creation of webpages, blogs, and articles that underscore the importance of digital petitioning by and for girls is a great example of how we can highlight the things girls are already doing while ensuring younger girls feel empowered to follow in their footsteps. The more young people look to the Internet as a place where they see their activist efforts work, the more online-only activist communities (Earl & Schussman, 2008) and girl-led online movements we will see.

Social network sites and online communities have afforded girls a new and critical opportunity to increase their voice and power in their everyday lives and in the larger society in which they live. These virtual spaces allow girls to communicate with other like-minded individuals from around the globe. In this way, virtual spaces provide the opportunity for girls from diverse backgrounds to develop solidarity and purpose in a way that has never before existed in our history. Through these connections, girls have found a way to capture the attention of major organizations and power holders and, in certain instances, convince them to change their approaches and practices. In addition to influencing organizations, girls, women, and even boys and men are being awakened to girls' needs and efforts through the use of online communities. Due to the accessibility of online activism, girls are able to nourish their leadership skills, critical thinking skills, and innovative thinking at even younger ages than before. These experiences increase girls' self-efficacy and support healthy identity development. Providing young girls spaces where their opinions and experiences have value and influence has the potential to create a new generation of women who will shatter old gender gaps. In fact, it is the belief of the authors that online communities are one key to decreasing and eliminating harmful gender stereotypes and inequities in income, violence, and power that girls and women experience. We hope that this essay has highlighted how important online activism is for girls when it comes to issues surrounding sexism, and that we can all assist girls in fighting back and (re)claiming their innate agency.

References

Ayers, M. D. (2003). Comparing collective identity in online and offline feminist activists. In M. McCaughey & M. D. Ayers (Eds.), *Cyberactivism: Online activism in theory and practice* (pp. 145–164). New York: Routledge.

Bers, M. U. (2010). *Designing digital experiences for positive youth development: From playpen to playground.* New York: Oxford University Press.

Best, P., Manktelow, R., & Taylor, B. (2014). Online communication, social media and adolescent wellbeing: A systematic narrative review. *Children and Youth Services Review, 41,* 27–36.

Boorstin, J. (2014). With 300M users, Instagram is now bigger than Twitter. Retrieved from http://www.cnbc.com/id/102256195#.

boyd, d. (2008). Why youth (heart) social network sites: The role of networked publics in teenage social life. In D. Buckingham (Ed.), *Youth, identity, and digital media* (pp. 119–142). McArthur Foundation Series on Digital Media and Learning. Cambridge: MIT Press.

boyd, d., Ellison, N. B. (2008). Social network sites: Definition, history, and scholarship. *Journal of Computer-Mediated Communication, 13,* 210–230.

Braxton, E., Buford, W., & Marasigan, L. (2013). 2013 National field scan: The state of the field of youth organizing. *Funders' Collaborative on Youth Organizing.* Retrieved from www.fcyo.org/media/docs/7343_FCYO-11-01.pdf.

Brinkman, B. G., Brinkman, K. G., & Toomey, S. (2011). What do to do about the boys? Advocating for system change when doing social justice work with girls. *Journal for Social Action in Counseling and Psychology, 3*(2), 53–70.

Cammaerts, B. (2007). Jamming the political: Beyond counter-hegemonic practices. *Continuum: Journal of Media and Cultural Studies, 21*(1), 71–90.

Cavazos-Rehg, P., Krauss, M. J., Spitznagel, E. L., Grucza, R. A., & Bierut, L. J. (2014). Hazards of new media: Youth's exposure to tobacco ads/promotions. *Nicotine & Tobacco Research, 16*(4), 437–444.

Chen, P., Weiss, F. L., & Nicholson, H. J. (2010). Girls study Girls Inc.: Engaging girls in evaluation through participatory action research. *American Journal of Community Psychology, 46,* 228–237.

Chock, S. (2012). Youth and social movements: Key lessons for allies. *The Role of Youth Movements for Social Change: Kinder & Braver World Project Research Series.* Retrieved from http://cyber.law.harvard.edu/node/8096.

Currie, D. H, Kelly, D. M., & Pomerantz, S. (2009). *Girl power: Girls reinventing girlhood.* New York: Peter Lang.

De Ridder, S., & Van Bauwel, S. (2013). Commenting on pictures: Teens negotiating gender and sexualities on social networking sites. *Sexualities, 16*(5–6), 565–586.

Durham, M. G. (2008). *The Lolita effect: The media sexualization of young girls and what we can do about it.* New York: Overlook Press.

Earl, J. (2000). Methods, movements, and outcomes. *Research in Social Movements, Conflicts and Change, 24,* 155–187.

Earl, J. (2006). Pursuing social change online: The use of four protest tactics on the internet. *Social Science Computer Review, 24,* 362–377.

Earl, J. (2013). Studying online activism: The effects of sampling design on findings. *Mobilization: An International Quarterly, 18*(4), 389–406.

Earl, J., & Kimport, K. (2011a). *Digitally enabled social change.* Cambridge: MIT Press.

Earl, J., & Kimport, K. (2011b). Introduction. In J. Earl & K. Kimport (Eds.), *Digitally enabled social change* (pp. 3–20). Cambridge: MIT Press.

Earl, J., Kimport, K., Prieto, G., Rush, C., & Reynoso, K. (2010). Changing the world one web-page at a time: Conceptualizing and explaining Internet activism. *Mobilization, 15,* 425–446.

Earl, J., & Schussman, A. (2008). Contesting cultural control: Youth culture and online petitioning. In W. L. Bennett, D. John, & T. Catherine (Eds.), Civic life online: Learning how digital media can engage youth (pp. 71–96). McArthur Foundation Series on Digital Media and Learning. Cambridge: MIT Press.

Editorial Board. (2012, March 4). Editorial: Activism is more than just clicking a button. *The Stanford Daily.* Retrieved from http://www.stanforddaily.com/2012/03/05/editorial-activism-is-more-than-just-clicking-a-button/.

Ferguson, C. J., Muñoz, M. E., Garza, A., & Galindo, M. (2014). Concurrent and prospective analyses of peer, television and social media influences on body dissatisfaction, eating disorder symptoms and life satisfaction in adolescent girls. *Journal of Youth and Adolescence, 43*(1), 1–14.

Fleur, G. (2014). Sexting, selfies, and self-harm: Young people, social media, and the performance of self-development. *Media International Australia, 151,* 104–112.

Fredrickson, B. L., & Roberts, T. (1997). Objectification theory: Toward understanding women's lived experiences and mental health risks. *Psychology of Women Quarterly, 21,* 173–206.

Gonzales, A. L., & Hancock, J. T. (2011). Mirror, mirror on my Facebook wall: Effects of exposure to Facebook on self-esteem. *Cyberpsychology, Behavior and Social Networking, 14,* 79–83.

Grant, K. E., Finkelstein, J. S., & Lyons, A. L. (2003). Integrating psychological research on girls with feminist activism: A model for building a liberation psychology in the United States. *American Journal of Community Psychology, 31*(1–2), 143–155.

Gurak, L. J., & Logie, J. (2003). Internet protests, from text to web. In M. McCaughey & M. D. Ayers (Eds.), *Cyberactivism: Online activism in theory and practice* (pp. 25–46). New York: Routledge.

Guzzetti, B. J. (2006). Cybergirls: Negotiating social identities on cybersites. *E-Learning, 3*(2), 158–169.

Hammer, R. (2005). Third wave feminism. *Contemporary Youth Culture: An International Encyclopedia.* Retrieved from http://ezproxy.fiu.edu/login?url=http://search.credoreference.com.ezproxy.fiu.edu/content/entry/gwyouth/third_wave_feminism/0.

Harold, C. (2004). Pranking rhetoric: "Culture jamming" as media activism. *Critical Studies in Media Communication, 21*(3), 189–211.

Harris, A. (2008). *Next wave cultures: Feminism, subcultures, activism.* New York: Routledge.

Hasinoff, A. (2012). Sexting as media production: Rethinking social media and sexuality. *New Media and Society, 15*(4), 449–465.

Herring, S. C. (2010). Web content analysis: Expanding the paradigm. In J. Hunsinger, L. Klastrup, & M. Allen (Eds.), *International handbook of Internet research* (pp. 233–249). Dordrecht: Springer.

Hill, A. (2014). Hasthtag activism: Is it #effective? *Law Street.* Retrieved from http://lawstreetmedia.com/issues/technology/hashtag-activism-effective/.

Indiegogo, (n.d.). The "not buying it" app: Challenging sexist media. Retrieved from https://www.indiegogo.com/projects/the-not-buying-it-app-challenging-sexist-media.

Iwilade, A. (2013). Crisis as opportunity: Youth, social media and the renegotiation of power in Africa. *Journal of Youth Studies, 16*(8), 1054–1068.

Kann, M. E., Berry, J., Grant, C., & Zager, P. (2007). The Internet and youth political participation. *First Monday*, 12(8). Retrieved from http://www.firstmonday.org/ojs/index.php/fm/article/view/1977/1852.

Kearney. M. C. (2006). *Girls make media.* New York: Routledge.

Kellner, D. (2012). *Media spectacle and insurrection 2011: From the Arab Uprisings to Occupy Everywhere.* New York: Bloomsbury.

Keller, J. (2014). Making activism accessible: Exploring girls' blogs as sites of contemporary feminist activism. In C. Mitchell & C. Rentschler (Eds.), *The politics of place: Contemporary paradigms for research in girlhood studies.* New York: Berghahn Books. Retrieved from http://www.academia.edu/5617191/Making_Activism_Acessible_Exploring_girls_blogs_as_sites_of_contemporary_feminist_activism_forthcoming_2014_.

Keller, J. (2012). Virtual feminisms: Girls' blogging communities, feminist activism, and participatory politics. *Information, Communication & Society, 15*(3), 429–447.

Kimball, G. (2014). Why recent global uprisings are led by youth. *Heathwood Press: Critical Theory for Radical Democratic Alternatives.* Retrieved from http://www.heathwoodpress.com/why-recent-global-uprisings-are-led-by-youth-gayle-kimball/.

Lee, Y., & Hsieh, G. (2013). Does slacktivism hurt activism? The effects of moral balancing and consistency in online activism. *CHI '13 Proceedings of the SIGCHI Conference on Human Factors in Computing Systems,* 811–820.

Lenhart, A., & Madden, M. (2007). Teens, privacy, & online social networks: How teens manage their online identities and personal information in the age of MySpace. *Pew Internet and American Life Project Report.* Retrieved from http://www.pewinternet.org/files/old-media//Files/Reports/2007/PIP_Teens_Privacy_SNS_Report_Final.pdf.pdf.

Lenhart, A., Purcell, K., Smith, A., & Zickuhr, K. (2010). Social media and mobile internet use among teens and young adults. A Pew Research Center report. Retrieved from http://www.pewinternet.org/files/old-media//Files/Reports/2010/PIP_Social_Media_and_Young_Adults_Report_Final_with_toplines.pdf.

Maamari, B. E., & Zein, H. E. (2014). The impact of social media on the political interests of the youth in Lebanon at the wake of the Arab spring. *Social Science Computer Review, 32*(4), 496–505.

Mackey-Kallis, S. (2012). Culture jamming. In M. Kosut (Ed.), *Encyclopedia of Gender in Media.* Thousand Oaks, CA: Sage.

Madden, M., Lenhart, A., Cortesi, S., Gasser, U., Duggan, M., Smith, A., & Beaton, M. (2013). Teens, social media, and privacy. *A Pew Research Center Report.* Retrieved from http://www.pewinternet.org/files/2013/05/PIP_TeensSocialMediaandPrivacy_PDF.pdf.

Madden, M., Lenhart, A., Duggan, M., Cortesi, S. & Gasser, U. (2013). Teens and technology 2013. *A Pew Research Center Report.* Retrieved from http://www.pewinternet.org/files/old-media//Files/Reports/2013/PIP_TeensandTechnology2013.pdf.

Manago, A. M., Graham, M.B., Greenfield, P.M., & Salimkhan, G. (2008). Self-presentation and gender on MySpace. *Journal of Applied Developmental Psychology, 29,* 446–458.

Marquart, E. (2010). Microblog sensation: The growing popularity of Tumblr. *3PM Journal of Digital Research and Publishing, 2,* 70.75.

Martin, D. G., Hanson, S., & Fontaine, D. (2007). What counts as activism? The role of individuals in creating change. *Women's Studies Quarterly, 35*(3&4), 78–94.

McCaughey, M. (2013). Technology is my BFF: What are new communications technologies doing to/for girls? *Media Report to Women, 41*(1), 6–11.

McCaughey, M., & Ayers, M. D. (2003). *Cyberactivism.* New York: Routledge.

McCreanor, T., Lyons, A., Griffin, C., Goodwin, I., Barnes, H. M., & Hutton, F. (2013). Youth drinking cultures, social networking and alcohol marketing: Implications for public health. *Critical Public Health, 23*(1), 110–120.

McDevitt, M., & Butler, M. (2011). Latino youth as information leaders: Implications for family interaction and civic engagement in immigrant communities. *Inter-Actions: UCLA Journal of Education and Information Studies, 7*(2), Article 2.

McVeigh, T. (2014). Michelle Obama raises pressure over kidnapped schoolgirls. *The Guardian.* Retrieved from http://www.theguardian.com/world/2014/may/10/michelle-obama-nigeria-presidential-address.

Merskin, D. (2006). Jammer girls and the World Wide Web: Making an about-face. *Global Media Journal, 5*(9). Retrieved from http://lass.calumet.purdue.edu/cca/gmj/fa06/gmj_fa06_TOC.htm

Motter, J. L. (2011). Feminist virtual world activism: 16 days of activism against gender violence campaign, guerrilla girls broadband, and subrosa. *Visual Culture & Gender, 6,* 109–118.

O'Keeffe, G. S., & Clarke-Pearson, K. (2011). The impact of social media on children, adolescents, and families. *Pediatrics, 127*(4), 800–804.

Patton, D. U., Hong, J. S., Ranney, M., Patel, S., Kelley, C., Eschmann, R., & Washington, T. (2014). Social media as a vector for youth violence: A review of the literature. *Computers in Human Behavior, 35,* 548–553.

Pea, R., Nass, C., Meheula, L., Rance, M., Kumar, A., Bamford, H., … Zhou, M. (2012). Media use, face-to-face communication, media multitasking, and social well-being among 8- to 12-year-old girls. *Developmental Psychology, 48*(2), 327–336.

Piepmeier, A. (2009). *Girl zines: Making media, doing feminism.* New York: NYU Press.

RAINN. (2014). White House launches "It's On Us." *Rape, Abuse, & Incest National Network.* Retrieved from https://rainn.org/news-room/White-House-Launches-Its-On-Us.

Rapp, L., Button, D. M., Fleury-Steiner, B., & Fleury-Steiner, R. (2010). The internet as a tool for Black feminist activism: Lessons from an online anti-rape protest. *Feminist Criminology, 5*, 244–262.

Raynes-Goldie, K., & Walker, L. (2008). Our space: Online civic engagement tools for youth. In W. L. Bennett (Ed.), *Civic life online: Learning how digital media can engage youth* (pp. 161–188). McArthur Foundation Series on Digital Media and Learning. Cambridge: MIT Press.

Rideout, V. J., Foehr, U. G., & Roberts, D. F. (2010). *Generation M2: Media in the lives of 8-to 18-year-olds.* Menlo Park, CA: The Henry J. Kaiser Family Foundation.

Roker, D. (2008). Young women and social action in the UK. In A. Harris (Ed.), *Next wave cultures: feminism, subcultures, activism* (pp. 243–260). New York: Routledge.

Saebo, O., Rose, J., & Flak, L. S. (2008). The shape of eparticipation: Characterizing an emerging research area. *Government Information Quarterly, 25*(3), 400–428.

Salter, M. (2013). Justice and revenge in online counter-publics: Emerging responses to sexual violence in the age of social media. *Crime, Media, Culture, 9*(3), 225–242.

Sherman, R. C., End, C., Kraan, E., Cole, A., Campbell, J., Birchmeier, Z., & Klausner, J. (2000). The internet gender gap among college students: Forgotten but not gone. *Cyberpsychology and Behavior, 3*, 885–894.

Skoric, M. M., & Poor, N. (2013). Youth engagement in Singapore: The interplay of social and traditional media. *Journal of Broadcasting & Electronic Media, 57*(2), 187–204.

Sloan, P. (2011). Pinterest: Crazy growth lands it as top 10 social site. Retrieved from http://www.cnet.com/news/pinterest-crazy-growth-lands-it-as-top-10-social-site/.

Smith, S. L., & Choueiti, M. (2010). Gender disparity on-screen and behind the camera in family films. Retrieved from http://seejane.org/wp-content/uploads/key-findings-gender- disparity-family-films-2013.pdf.

Smith, S. L., & Cook, C. A. (2008). *Gender stereotypes: an analysis of popular films and TV.* Retrieved from http://www.thegeenadavisinstitute.org/downloads/GDIGM Gender Stereotypes.pdf.

Stasko, C. (2008). (r)Evolutionary healing: Jamming with culture and shifting the power. In A. Harris (Ed.), *Next wave cultures: Feminism, subcultures, activism* (pp. 193–219). New York: Routledge.

Taft, J. (2011). *Rebel girls: Youth activism and social change across the Americas.* New York: New York University Press.

Turkle, S. (1999). Cyberspace and identity. *Contemporary Sociology, 28*(6), 643–648.

Valentine, G., & Holloway, S. (2002). Cyberkids? Exploring children's identities and social networks in on-line and off-line worlds. *Annals of the Association of American Geographers, 92*(2), 302 -309.

Valenzuela, S., Arriagada, A., & Scherman, A. (2012). The social media basis of youth protest behavior: The case of Chile. *Journal of Communication, 62*(2), 299–314.

van de Donk, W., Loader, B., Nixon, P. G., & Rucht, D. (2004a). Introduction: Social movements and ICTs. In W. van de Donk, B. D. Loader, P. G. Nixon, & D. Rucht (Eds.), *Cyberprotest: New media, citizens and social movements* (pp. 1–25). New York: Routledge.

van de Donk, W., Loader, B., Nixon, P. G., & Rucht, D. (2004b). *Cyberprotest: New media, citizens and social movements.* New York: Routledge.

Vegh, S. (2003). Classifying forms of online activism: The case of cyberprotests against the World Bank. In M. McCaughey & M. D. Ayers (Eds.), *Cyberactivism: Online activism in theory and practice* (pp. 71–95). New York: Routledge.

Vraga, E. K., Bode, L., Wells, C., Driscoll, K., & Thorson, K. (2014). The rules of engagement: Comparing two social protest movements on YouTube. *Cyberpsychology, Behavior, and Social Networking, 17*, 133–140.

Wojcieszak, M., & Smith, B. (2014). Will politics be tweeted? New media use by Iranian youth in 2011. *New Media & Society, 16*(1), 91–109.

Xenos, M., Vromen, A., & Loader, B. D. (2014). The great equalizer? patterns of social media use and youth political engagement in three advanced democracies. *Information, Communication & Society, 17*(2), 151–167.

Internet, Social Media and Sexual Literacy
Help or Hindrance for LGBTQ Youth?

NICOLE POLEN-PETIT

The Internet is, arguably, one of the greatest advances in media technology this world has ever seen because it enables individuals to learn, communicate, teach, connect, and express the self directly and emotionally with others on a global scale at any point in any given day. Electronic communications and interactions evolved from simple electronic mail into the new world of instant messages, status updates, tweets, and visual communication, whereby people are able to instantly and intimately connect to world events, politics, family, and friends (Herdt & Polen-Petit, 2014). This kind of instant and deep connection to the world is a completely new and different world for most adults. We are, however, also coming to an age in which most individuals approaching adulthood have never known a time or place when and where the online environment or the use of tools connected to the online environment was not an intimate part of their lives and everyday activities (Brooks-Gunn & Donahue, 2008).

Twenty-five years ago, the landscape of the adolescent world looked drastically different than it does today. At the time, if a young person needed advice or information on a particular issue, they were forced into a library or bookstore to, more than likely, consult a large set of alphabetized encyclopedias where they would find a cold and stale description of that which they sought more knowledge about. Today, encyclopedias often collect dust on library shelves, but interestingly sound a lot like Wikipedia, the popular online, user-created repository of information used by many as a point of reference for a myriad of subjects.

That same adolescent twenty years ago, in coming into an awareness of their own identity, would have only his or her surrounding peers and community in which to explore that identity. For a young person coming into an awareness of a LGBTQ identity, the experience may have had greater, specific challenges. If they were lucky, their identity would be supported and their own personal narrative would be a familiar thread within their surrounding communities. However, if they found that their identity seemed separate or unfamiliar, these youth often suffered in silence, doing all they could to try and understand themselves in a context that felt completely foreign and potentially harsh and disapproving. Today, the online environment and social media allow for explorations and expressions of identity that are historically unparalleled. For LGBTQ youth, this online environment has proved to be a critical component of their personal exploration and identification (DeHaan, Kuper, Magee, Bigelow, & Mustanski, 2013). While there has been much conjecture on the subject of the benefits and drawbacks of the dual interaction between youth and social media, the indisputable reality is the online world is inextricably tied to the process of identity formation and expression (Davis, 2011). Trying to understand how youth development is influenced by the virtual world of Internet sites and social media outlets is an undertaking that will be continuous and quickly changing, as does the Internet and social media change in an instant (Brooks-Gunn & Donahue, 2008). While we do have access to some research that investigates the larger youth population and the whys and hows of Internet access and use of social networking sites, the information that exists regarding LGBTQ youth and online use is more scarce. Within the context of understanding how and why LGBTQ youth utilize the online environment and social media spaces, the question is whether or not this new way of exploring, learning, and being actually promotes sexual literacy within this particular youth community and culture.

Sexual literacy is commonly defined as the knowledge and skills needed to promote sexual well-being, which is both the physical state, defined by positive health in the body, and a subjective or mental state, that is recognized by feeling joyful and positive about one's sexual life (Laumann et al., 2006). This essay will focus on how and why LGBTQ youth utilize the Internet and social media as well as discuss how sexual literacy is impacted by such utilization.

Purpose and Function of Internet and Social Media for Youth

By 2009, it was estimated that 93 percent of all teenagers had an online presence or engaged in regular online activity (Levine, 2011; Ralph, Berglas,

Schwartz, & Brindis, 2011). Within that 93 percent, 73 percent of those youth utilize social networking sites, such as YouTube, Facebook and Instagram to view photographs, connect with trending events, friends and family. In doing so, young people between the ages of 8 and 18 spend an approximate average of 45 hours per week in front of a computer, tablet, or smart phone (Kaiser Family Foundation, 2010). Approximately one-third of all youth have searched online for information on issues they express difficulty in talking with anyone about offline, including issues of sexuality and substance use (Borzekowski, 2006). The Internet is a useful way for young people to access sensitive health information or connect with potential offline resources and services (Gray, Klein, Noyce, Sesselberg, & Cantrill, 2005). Critical to many youth, the Internet and its various social networking sites allow the exploration and creation of online relationships that may or may not be available offline (DeHaan et al., 2013). Given these statistics and information, it is evident that we can no longer view the adolescent or their development, especially for LBGTQ youth that are in a stage of identity exploration, outside of the context of the online community. It is a central and integral part of their everyday lives, their connection to others and their own intrapersonal lives. The following sections will outline the two main ways in which youth, and specifically LGBTQ youth, engage with the online world: the pursuit of information and knowledge and the other—a place for self-expression, identity and community.

Information

As mentioned previously, a necessary component of sexual literacy is having the knowledge and skills needed to promote and protect sexual well-being. In terms of sexual knowledge, the Internet is a vast, valuable, albeit at times questionable, repository of information regarding sexual health and behaviors. Users get a huge amount of information of all kinds, factual and fake, online. Regarding sexual information, there is a wide variety of information available regarding sexual function and expression, body issues, intimacy and dating, sexual techniques, what is typical in terms of sexual behaviors, and what is quirky or highly individualized. It has also been established that young people utilize online resources often to gather this sensitive information and that the online environment is critical in the sexual socialization of young people (DeHaan et al., 2013).

Historically, sexual socialization was intensely private, largely restricted to the family and peers, and generally considered the province of personal morality (Gagnon, 2004; Kinsey et al., 1948; Irvine, 2000, 2002; Laumann et al, 1994; Regnerus, 2007). Where once it was hard to find certain kinds of sexual literacy in print form via newspapers or books in the library, these materials became more common as social media expanded. Magazines, for example, began to share images of bodies and related sexual health material, not all of which was accurate or based in research. The Internet hugely expanded the availability of such materials, including organizations, such as Planned Parenthood and the Sexuality Information and Education Council of the United States (SIECUS), and many popular online websites, such as Go Ask Alice, that made available sexual information to a large population of young people eager to receive such personal information. Online sexual socialization started out as a largely unacknowledged process to regulating and molding sexuality, especially for teens and young adults (Boyd, 2008; Carlsson, 2006; Ybarra & Mitchell, 2005). In the 1990s and early 2000s, a huge range of stories, images, and an increasing array of explicit adult sexual images all contributed to the shift from private to public sexual talk. Additionally, pornography became increasingly accessible and, in fact, difficult to avoid at times.

In regards to LGBTQ youth and the utilization of the Internet to increase knowledge and information, one study took a specific look at the interplay of online and offline explorations of identity, relationships, and sex (DeHaan et al., 2013). This qualitative study of 32 LGBTQ youth found that among the participants, there was a common need of having reliable resources, whether they came from online or offline sources. This finding was further broken down into four sub-themes or findings that highlight how LGBTQ youth weigh the relative reliability and authority of online and offline sources. The first sub-theme was that the Internet is not needed or desired when offline trusted sources are available (DeHaan et al., 2013). This study supported the popular and widely held notion that young people prefer to use trusted offline sources as their primary source of information. These trusted sources were defined as physicians and health professionals, counselors/therapists, teachers, family members, and friends as well as printed books and pamphlets. The second sub-theme was that the Internet was necessary when offline sources were unavailable, or could not be trusted such as sexual education programs at school that were solely focused on abstinence or failed to provide detailed sexual health information for their specific sexual information needs (i.e. LGBTQ sexual health and behaviors) (DeHaan et al., 2013). For these youth, online resources were quite valuable. The third sub-theme reported was that there is a bias toward being less trusting of online information. Simply, by virtue of being an online source, a number of youth in this study reported that while they used the Internet as a resource for sexual health information, they felt they could not trust the information completely. Much of this caution around the validity of online resources originated from the perception that unqualified people posing as qualified or authoritative figures are the creators of a large amount of online content. This concern relates to the final sub-theme in regards to the use of online information by LGBTQ youth, which was the convergence across online and offline resources. Many youth in this study felt that comparing online and offline resources for similarities and agreement was the best way to obtain the highest quality information as well as information that is specific to their LGBTQ identity (DeHaan et al., 2013).

For LGBTQ youth, having a space to research, gather information, and ask questions, is a critical component to their own self-awareness and identification of issues relating to their sexuality.

Self-Expression, Identity and Community

Facebook and related social media sites provide a context for new ways of expressing sexual individuality. Many LGBTQ people growing up and living in rural areas appear to be finding support online for the meaning and expression of their emotions and identity development (Gray, 2009). One Australian study found that many young gay and lesbian people use the Internet to develop six areas of their lives: identity, friendship, coming out, intimate relationships, sex, and community (Hillier & Harrison, 2007). Before the Internet, people had to run ads in newspapers and magazines to make romantic and sexual connections, and many people were quite unfamiliar with and uncomfortable with that way of meeting. Today, online dating provides a totally different way for people to connect sexually and romantically. Likewise, men and women may locate online a much broader array of potential partners, potential sexual expressions, and potential sexual communities than they may have previously imagined. This kind of sexual information may also deepen emotional literacy in the sexual expression of feelings, and the availability of other people to connect to in the search for meaning in sexual life.

While adolescence is a critical time in the formation of identity and roles, there are specific challenges and considerations to understand when discussing identity development among LGBTQ youth. Classic theories in human development look at adolescence as a time where many young people experience identity moratorium—which is the period of time where people actively engage in processes to find their sense of self—searching for one's occupational, religious, ethnic and sexual identity (Marcia, 1991). The exploration of a sexual identity often occurs within the context of the "presumption of heterosexuality" (Herdt, 1989) that exists in American culture. Heterosexual adolescents spend little or no time considering their sexual identity as anything but heterosexual, due to its prevalence in the world around them. However, the same is not necessarily true for LGBTQ adolescents. In American culture, alternate sexual identities and orientations are often degraded and stigmatized. This cultural context makes forming a sexual identity for the LGBTQ adolescent more challenging than for a heterosexual adolescent. Following the pattern of identity development in general, LGBTQ adolescents may experience a period of confusion and exploration before accepting and committing to their sexual identity. Regardless of orientation, the development of a clear sexual identity is important for the holistic well-being of the individual. Some adolescents become overwhelmed by the task of identity development and neither explore nor make commitments. This describes Marcia's (1991) diffusion status, in which adolescents may become socially isolated and withdrawn. The online environment has the potential to help serve as communities where these youth can turn to find information, encouragement and support in their search for their sexual identity, ultimately helping them move into identity achievement as it relates to their sexuality. It is important that considering the extensive utilization of online sources and communities by youth, that we get a clear picture of just how it is these communities contribute to the identity processes of young LGBTQ people.

Older theories and observations of online behavior suggested that youth, in general, often created a separate and disconnected identity in their online environments compared to the persona displayed in offline relationships and in daily life (Subrahmanyam & Smahel, 2011). For individuals who lack the freedom of true self-expression and identification in their offline worlds, there is evidence to show that one's true self can be more easily accessed online (Bargh, McKenna, & Fitzsimons, 2002). The true self, as defined by Davis (2011), "constitutes personal traits that individuals believe they possess but do not feel able to express in everyday social settings" (p. 637). It appears that the more anonymous one feels they can be online, the more one feels able to both access and express the true self. While achieving and maintaining anonymity online is becoming a more daunting task, the reality is that many people feel a sense of anonymity when they share of themselves online and this may encourage the user to embrace a greater sense of freedom from the constraints they may endure in other social contexts, resulting in a more disconnected and multi-faceted online identities (Davis, 2011; Kennedy, 2006).

For LGBTQ youth, this is important to understand. As many move through adolescence and begin to recognize and identify with a sexual orientation, that for many is not as common in their immediate surroundings as heterosexual attitudes, behaviors, and attractions, the online environment provides a seemingly safer and anonymous space to find people with whom they share similarities in their sexual attractions, desires and feelings. While it would be easy to end this discussion here with the hope that the online community can fill various needs for LGBTQ youth in the discovery and expression of their true identities, there are other issues to consider. It is important to understand and investigate whether having disconnected online and offline identities and multi-faceted online personas really lead to increased sexual literacy and social connectivity for LGBTQ youth or if this kind of disconnected and multi-faceted identity online and offline is really a reflection of heterosexual privilege, whereby heterosexual youth are allowed to be congruent and develop an identity that coordinates the multiple facets of oneself into a coherent whole, while many LGBTQ youth are more likely to have separate and disconnected identities and personas due to the fact that representation of their coherent, true self could lead to offline social disconnection, abuse and estrangement from family and community.

More recent work, in fact, suggests that youth are not necessarily forming separate, distinct personas online but that their online persona is very intertwined with their offline experiences (Davis, 2011). It seems that authenticity and reflection of reality is an important priority for the online lives of many youth. Traditionally, the more open and anonymous space of social media sites and the Internet, has been viewed as somewhat of a positive medium for LGBTQ youth to find spaces where they feel safe and comfortable expressing their identities. Communities have celebrated this kind of possibility for multiplicity because it does allow an individual who may be limited in their offline relationships and community an increased level of freedom online. The challenge in this is that it can be somewhat difficult to monitor all of one's multiple selves in multiple contexts (Davis, 2011). Even in online spaces, context characteristics between gaming sites (i.e., World of Warcraft), social media sites (i.e., Facebook) and blogging sites (i.e., LiveJournal) can be quite distinct from one another and online users may have very separate and distinct selves in each of these spaces despite the fact they exist all online. The problematic issue that is raised with some of these more recent conclusions is that LGBTQ youth may not be afforded the same privilege of congruence between their online and offline personas and lives. As mentioned previously, many LGBTQ youth do utilize the Internet as a space to not only explore their identity, but as a safe platform from which to express elements of the self they lack the freedom to in their offline lives (Pullen & Cooper, 2010). Sexual literacy and well-being for individuals means being able to find congruence between online and offline identities so that the support, information and community found online can, ideally, transfer to offline spaces. It must be acknowledged that, for many LGBTQ youth still, congruence in their online and offline lives is a privilege they do not have access to. It must be further acknowledged that this lack of privilege is an additional element that can lead to difficulty both intrapersonally as well as interpersonally.

The importance of the online social environment for young people can be seen when access is taken away, just as much as the importance can be seen when it is added to a young person's experience. The recent suicide of

Leelah Alcorn is a tragic event that highlights how critical the online identity and activity of young LGBTQ people is. Leelah was a 17-year-old transgender woman who left a suicide note on Tumblr detailing her difficulties trying to be herself within a family and community that would not accept her. In her suicide note, she explained that she knew since she was four years old that she was a girl but did not know how to express that in words. When she was 14, she discovered the term "transgender" and felt relief knowing there was a way to describe her long and deeply held beliefs about her gender identity. Leelah utilized social media to connect with others and find support. In a CNN media report, it was stated that Leelah's mother, at one time, took away her access to all social media (Fantz, 2015). Leelah described in her suicide note what it was like to not have social media to connect with friends. She wrote, "This was probably the part of my life when I was the most depressed, and I'm surprised I didn't kill myself. I was completely alone for 5 months. No friends, no support, no love. Just my parents' disappointment and the cruelty of loneliness" (Alcorn as cited in Fantz, 2015). These haunting and honest words describe, from one youth, just how critical having a connection on social media can be for discovering information, finding community and a safe place to express true identity.

One of the important issues to acknowledge as a result of the tragic suicide of Leelah is the important ways in which online activity and membership in social media can provide social capital for those youth who are lacking social connection and webs of support and membership in their offline lives. Social capital is the notion that individuals accrue benefits from personal associations with other individuals and groups (Drushel, 2010). Further the classification of social capital can be further broken down into three different types. *Bridging social capital* is a series of loose connections between individuals that may provide differing perspectives or information that is useful but it does very little in the way of establishing interpersonal social support (Putnam, 2000). In contrast, *bonding social capital* exists between individuals who are involved in emotionally intimate relationships that can include family and friends (Putnam, 2000). *Maintained social capital* is another form which describes the ability to stay connected to individuals with whom one has shared in a previously inhabited community (Ellison et al., 2007). It has been shown through research that LGBTQ youth often have fewer opportunities to acquire social capital in their offline lives. Social networking sites seem to be of particular value to gay, lesbian, and bisexual teens and young adults for the ways in which they provide opportunities to acquire social capital (Drushel, 2010).

One study attempted to look at the relationships between the amount bridging, bonding and maintained social capital from the networks of "friends" on MySpace for a number of youth identifying as a sexual minority.

The results supported the idea that many of these youth having a presence on social media were successful in accumulating both bridging and bonding social capital (Drushel, 2010). For example, of users self-identifying as gay, each had an average of 129 "friends." Of these friends, 60 percent were geographically located in an area nearby to the user. In addition, approximately one-third of the users' friends had left at least one comment on the profile page which supports the idea that maintained capital was attained as well. Users who identified as bisexual had a much larger average number of "friends" at 254, with about 50 percent living nearby but had only 10 percent of those individuals leaving personal messages, so bridging and bonding capital was evident but there was less maintained capital. Straight users had similar numbers of "friends" as those who identified as gay with similar percentages of those individuals posting on their personal profile pages suggesting a similar acquisition of bridging, bonding and maintained social capital (Drushel, 2010).

In terms of understanding the benefits of social capital, further research needs to examine these various types of social capital more closely to look at which ones seem to offer the greatest benefit to young people—i.e., is having a lot of individuals who share similar ideation but not necessarily a personal connection per se (bridging social capital) more relevant or useful for LGBTQ youth than acquiring other forms of social capital? When we are able to understand how these various forms of online social capital contribute to health and well-being of LGBTQ youth, then we can better direct efforts to connect young people to those individuals and resources that can be most effective and powerful.

These online sites also pose challenges for sexual safety. On the one hand, online sexual expression may cut down on being bullied or harassed physically, allowing people who are "trying out" new desires or who belong to a group that is generally not accepted by society to feel safer going online to find sexual partners than finding them in the real world. In this way the Internet is more democratic and allows for freer expression than some real world spaces (Hillier & Harrison, 2007). However, on the other hand, there are now so many well-known cases of online sexual bullying and intimidation, blackmail, and virtual violence that have even contributed to suicide, due to the public humiliation and reaction, that the risk is real. Some experts believe that the anonymity of the Internet allows people to actually more openly express hate, prejudice, and emotional rants that single out people because of their personalities or individual sexuality, gender, or other features. Glover (2007) found that 80 percent of people who play online sexual games had experienced homophobic speech, such as "Dude, you're a fag!" (Pascoe, 2007). It still may be safer than the real world, however, especially for people who feel marginalized in their sexual cultures and communities. But for people who live in sexually disapproving communities that censor and thwart sexual expression, the Internet can be a safe and supportive way to find sexual expression in a largely sex negative environment (Pascoe, 2011). Of course some of these same cultures and communities may exercise censorship even online to restrict sexual desires, identities, behaviors, and relationships.

Geography in the Real World

While the online world exists relatively separate from any one specific geographic position in the world, the reality is that participants in this global space *are* physically located within a community somewhere. In order to fully understand the online experiences and expressions of LGBTQ youth, it is important to examine how their geographic location and offline community intersect with their online experience, activity and expression.

Gray (2009) asked a particularly important question regarding youth in geographic locations that do not have offline supports that can help young people organize outside of online contexts.

> What happens to kids who read these online resources in places that don't have the capacity to organize and coordinate with youth services and the broader infrastructure of support one takes for granted living three blocks from the Castro? Were these youth able to do much more than read what we post? They have access to representations that are affirming, but, at the same time, none of these images reflect their local surroundings [xiii].

Gray's realization and subsequent question is a critical one for LGBTQ youth communities. The realization is that many youth-driven models of organizing in an online forum relied very much on an existing urban-based organizations for spaces to meet, access a computer to find resources and/or post online. In addition, there seems to be a presumption that online forums are central and necessary to do the work of connecting youth and providing resources (Gray, 2009). Gray's research set out to connect with a group of rural LGBTQ youth in order to understand how they engage with mass media and whether or not new media is playing as central a role to identity and community that many scholars assume to be the reality.

The findings and discussion of this piece of ethnographic work tend to move away from the question of whether or not LGBTQ youth are utilizing online media but how are they and others putting media engagements to use in their individual lives. In addition, we have to understand how this utilization translates into offline life for LGBTQ youth in rural areas (Gray, 2009). Gray's work illustrated that young people experience media engagements as possibilities of different ways of being. However, most notably for these youth, these possibilities are always intersecting with the actual physical and material conditions of their lives. When rural LGBTQ youth scan resources online, they do find resources that may affirm their identity or resonate with their own personal narrative.

> When they scan mass media and the Internet for materials to incorporate into their queer sense of self, a politics of LGBTQ visibility comes up on the screen. These representations organize recognition of queer difference through a grammar of narrowly defined LGBTQ Identities, a "visible minority," underwritten by capital of urban counterpublics that have no equivalents in rural areas [Gray, 2009, p. 168].

This is such a critical issue and outlines a very important element to what it means to be a rural LGBTQ youth trying to connect an online discovery and identity narrative to their offline world. Urban LGBTQ youth have the ability, in many cases, to live in their online spaces and then walk or transport in some way to a nearby gay bookstore, support center or coffeehouse where they find continued membership in community and subsequent resources. They are able to participate in LGBTQ communities—again, the issue and privilege of congruence being central—in an offline setting. In contrast, rural LGBTQ youth must address similar needs and desires of LGBTQ visibility and community membership while negotiating and balancing needs to fit in to their existing everyday structures. They have to negotiate being in an online space that often affirms who they are while at the same time feeling out of place in a physical environment that either fails to see them or recognize their specific needs (Gray, 2009).

Socially, politically, and even academically, it needs to be recognized that often the tools utilized by LGBTQ youth online such as listservs, social networks, and even online personal ads are seen as reflections of queer reality rather than objects and interactions that are mediated by the social, political and economic realities of rural communities (Gray, 2009). Understanding the nested social climate and context of LGBTQ youth is central to an even greater awareness of how online media is utilized by these youth in their own personal and sexual narrative and identity negotiation.

Conclusion

There are few things known for sure in regards to LGBTQ youth and their online presence. Fortunately, researchers are not completely in the dark and it seems there are a couple of important known pieces of information. First is the reality that identity must be examined within the context of online discovery, expression and communities. No longer is the online environment just an external source of information or merely a tool in aiding the finding of others with which to identify with. The online community and environment have now become central to the process of discovering identity and sharing that identity with the global world. It has become an inextricable part of the narrative of who we are and how we portray ourselves to the rest of the world, whether we are connected offline or not. Secondly, the online context is rapidly changing and our understanding of the benefits and drawbacks of online communities and activity needs to at least attempt to keep current with social and user trends online (Gilliam, Allison, Boyar, Bull, Guse, & Santelli, 2011).

The title of this essay asks whether or not the Internet and social media are a help or hindrance for LGBTQ youth on their journey towards sexual literacy. Like most investigations into these kinds of questions, we come out with many more questions than were answered. It does appear, through an examination of literature, that LGBTQ youth utilize online sources to equip themselves with information and they seem to be increasing in their discernment of the quality of online information, which are both positive and show that youth are increasingly taking responsibility for being an active agent for their own personal and sexual health—which leads to sexual literacy in their own lives. Of course, as online sites and portals of information increase exponentially every day in the online world, it is critical that sexual education and health professionals stay abreast of the kinds of resources that exist online and monitor the accuracy of information so that those who are seeking information are equipped with the most accurate information available. In addition, it is important to remember that even though widely utilized, not all youth and, specifically, sexual minority youth have access to these online sources and attempts must still be made to provide readily accessible resources to all youth.

In terms of identity, the question of whether online environments and social media contribute positively or negatively to sexual literacy is murkier and in desperate need of both further and specific investigation. Traditional research held that the opportunity for anonymity and the ability to present a multi-faceted or even distinct self online was a powerful, safe, and effective way for questioning youth to discover other narratives of identity and allow a safe space for research, wondering and reaching out to those they may not have exposure to in their offline lives. More current research suggests that youth who are have a more connected and fluid online presentation of the self, tend to experience better outcomes in terms of identity and even in perception by their peers. In addition, there may be a disparity in the kinds of social capital gained online by LGBTQ youth, which can have a lasting social impact as well.

More and more, adolescents are integrating online tools and experiences into their offline worlds (Subrahmanyam & Greenfield, 2008) and, for this reason, research needs to examine online and offline worlds not as separate entities, but as intertwined realities that may manifest into a variety of outcomes and expressions given the social, political and geographic context of any particular young person. The undertaking of this kind of research is extremely difficult given the rapidly changing nature of online media but the reality is upon us, that to truly understand how the intersection of LGBTQ youth and online resources and communities, contributes to or erects barriers to sexual literacy for this population. Further, understanding the role of online sources and communities for youth needs to actively extend beyond the superficial celebration or exaggerated moral panics that often seem to accompany any context where youth and online resources or social networks are collectively discussed (Buckingham, 2008).

But what is clear is that these online environments are integral to the establishment and sustainability of a virtual community that contributes to and helps youth develop not only a sense of self, but also a set of mores that transcends context. This new cultural context is worthy of the exploration and investment of time, resources and energy of those who desire to walk with youth as they move forward in their journeys toward identity, community, and sexual literacy.

References

Bargh, J. A., McKenna, K. Y. A., & Fitzsimons, G. M. (2002). Can you see the real me? Activation and expression of the "true self" on the internet. *Journal of Social Issues, 58*(1), 33–48.

Borzekowski, D. L. (2006). Adolescents' use of the internet: A controversial, coming-of-age resource. *Adolescent Medicine Clinics, 17,* 205–216. doi: S1547–3368(05)00065–3[pii]10.1016/j.admecli.2005.10.006.

boyd, d. (2008). Social networking sites: Definitions, history, and scholarship. *Journal of Computer-Mediated Communication, 13*(2), 210–230. doi.10.1111/j.10836101.2007.00393.x.

Brooks-Gunn, J., & Donahue, E. H. (2008). Introducing the issue. *The Future of Children, 18*(1), 3–10.

Buckingham, D (2008). Introducing identity. In D. Buckingham (Ed.), *Youth, identity, and digital media.* The John D. and Catherine T. MacArthur Foundation Series on Digital Media and Learning. Cambridge: MIT Press, 2008. 1–24. doi: 10.1162/dmal.9780262524834.001.

Carlsson, U. (2006). *Regulation, awareness, and empowerment: Young people and harmful media content in the digital age.* Goteberg: Nordicom and Goteberg University.

Davis, K. (2011). Tensions of identity in a networked era: Young people's perspectives on the risks and rewards of online self-expression. *New Media & Society, 14*(4), 634–651.

DeHaan, S., Kuper, L. E., Magee, J. C., Bigelow. L., & Mustanski, B. S. (2013). The interplay between online and offline explorations of identity, relationships and sex: A mixed-methods study with LGBT youth. *The Journal of Sex Research, 50*(5), 421–434. doi: 10.1080/00224499.2012.661489.

Drushel, B. E. (2010). Virtually supportive: Self-disclosure of minority sexualities through online social networking sites. In C. Pullen & M. Cooper (Eds.), *LGBT identity and online new media.* New York: Routledge.

Ellison, N. B., Steinfield, C., & Lampe, C. (2007). The benefits of Facebook "friends": Social capital and college students' use of online social network sites. *Journal of Computer-mediated Communication, 12*(4), 1143–1168.

Fantz, A. (2015, January 4). An Ohio transgender teen's suicide, a mother's anguish. *CNN: U.S. Edition.* Retrieved from http://www.cnn.com/2014/12/31/us/ohio-transgender-teen-suicide/.

Gagnon, J. (2004). *An interpretation of desire.* Chicago: University of Chicago Press.

Gilliam, M., Allison, S., Boyar, R., Bull, S., Guse, K., & Santelli, J. (2011). New media and research: Considering next steps. *Sexual Research and Social Policy, 8,* 67–72. doi: 10.1007/s13178-011-0035-4.

Glover, K. (2007). *The acceleration of just about everything.* New York: Vintage.

Gray, M. L. (2009). *Youth, media, and queer visibility in rural America.* New York: New York University Press.

Gray, N. J., Klein, J. D., Noyce, P.R., Sesselberg, T. S., & Cantrill, J. A. (2005). Health information-seeking behavior in adolescence: The place of the internet. *Social Science & Medicine, 60,* 1467–1478. doi: 10.101016/j.socscimed.2004.08.010.

Herdt, G. (1989). Introduction: Gay and lesbian youth, emergent identities, and cultural scenes at home and abroad. In G. Herdt (Ed.), *Gay and Lesbian Youth.* New York: Harrington Park Press,

Herdt, G., & Polen-Petit, N. C. (2014). *Human sexuality: Self, society and culture.* New York: McGraw-Hill.

Hillier, L., & Harrison, L. (2007). Building realities less limited than their own: Young people practicing same-sex attraction on the internet. *Sexualities, 10*(1), 82–100.

Irvine, J. (2000). *Disorders of desire: Sexuality and gender in modern American sexology.* Philadelphia: Temple University Press.

Irving, J. (2002). *Talk about sex.* Berkeley: University of California Press.

Kennedy, H. (2006). Beyond anonymity, or future directions for internet identity research. *New Media & Society, 8*(6), 859–876.

Kinsey, A., Pomeroy, W., & Martin, C. (1948). *Sexual behavior in the human male.* Philadelphia: W.B. Saunders.

Laumann, E. O., Gagnon, J. H., Michael, R. T., & Michaels, S. (1994). *Social organization of sexuality: Sexual practices in the United States.* Chicago: University of Chicago Press.

Laumann, E. O., Paik, A., Glasser, D. B., Kang, J. H., Wang, T., Levinson, M., & Gingell, C. (2006). A cross-national study of subjective well-being among older women and men: Findings from the Global Study of Sexual Attitudes and Behaviors. *Archives of Sexual Behavior, 35,* 143–159.

Levine, D. (2011). Using technology, new media, and mobile for sexual and reproductive health. *Sexual Research and Social Policy, 8,* 18–26.

Marcia, J. (1991). Identity and self-development. In R. Lerner, A. Peterson, & J. Brooks-Gunn (Eds.), *Encyclopedia of Adolescence (Vol. 1).* New York: Garland.

Pascoe, C. J. (2007). *Dude, you're a fag.* Berkeley: University of California Press.

Pascoe, C. J. (2011). Resource and risk: Youth sexuality and new media use. *Sexuality Research and Social Policy, 8,* 5–17. doi: 10.1007/s13178-011-0042-5.

Putnam, R. (2000). *Bowling alone: The collapse and revival of American community.* New York: Simon & Schuster.

Ralph, L. J., Berglas, N. F., Schwartz, S. L., & Brindis, C. D. (2011). Finding teens in their space: Using social networking sites to connect youth to sexual health services. *Sexual Research and Social Policy, 8,* 38–49. doi: 10.1007/s13178-011-0043-4.

Regnerus, M. D. (2007). *Forbidden fruit: Sex and religion in the lives of American teenagers.* New York: Oxford University Press.

Subrahmanyam, K., & Greenfield, P. (2008). Online communication and adolescent relationships. *The Future of Children, 18*(1), 119–145.

Subrahmanyam, K., & Šmahel, D. (2011). *Digital Youth: The Role of Media in Development.* New York: Springer Science+Business Media.

Ybarra, M., & Mitchell, K. J. (2005). Exposure to Internet pornography among children and adolescents: A national survey. *Cyber Psychology & Behavior, 8*(5), 473–486. doi: 10.1089/cpb.2005.8.473.

Youth Adult Partnerships
Re-Mixing Communities through Youth Popular Culture

JOHN A. OLIVER *and* WILLIE S. ANDERSON

Popular culture and media are interwoven threads in the American fabric. From popular art icon of the 1960s, Andy Warhol to new millennium social media conglomerate, Facebook, popular culture and media have historically intersected daily with the lives of youth. Both act as a socializing force on youth that both resist and reproduces mainstream ideologies and discourse. At times, the dissenting voice of youth is amplified through popular culture. As such, it provides opportunities for youth to speak truth to power. At other times, popular culture facilitates societal occurrences that dictate how individuals interact and express their lived experiences. To accomplish the above, various mediums serve as the canvas for the depiction of these lived experiences, i.e., computers and the Internet, video games, film, music, and fashion. These diverse media are used to represent popular conventions of gender, race, sexuality, disability, class, religion, and nationality. Additionally, they serve as indicators of simultaneously, fluid, flexible, and fixed realities of society, culture, and youth in particular. Ultimately, popular culture is directly connected and positively correlated with the influences of consumerism, political ideology, and educational outcomes.

The above outcomes are inextricably linked to culture. They form our understanding of cultural production, which is a collective effort that encompasses the skills and practices of individuals which allow them to engage as social actors who (a) make sense of their lives, (b) articulate a sense of self-identity, and (c) serve as a form of active resistance. These endeavors are articulated with a distinct level of creative energy that dictates how individuals interact in structured social conditions. It is the cultivation of these varied skills and practices that allow individuals to cultivate and participate in ever-expanding global phenomena known as youth popular culture.

Understanding Youth Popular Culture

Youth popular culture is somewhat of an enigma to adults. The very nature of culture requires that it be understood based on the expression and definition of those that create it and consume it. Generally speaking, adults are absent from those roles. Therefore adults seeking to understand youth popular culture naturally oscillate between their adult schema, and thus operate from opposing forces to youth: that of cultural containment and cultural resistance. Tensions exist as adults struggle to develop the necessary level of sophistication and complex ambiguity required to understand youth popular culture. Understanding youth popular culture requires a synergistic perspective that is free flowing, or ability to "freestyle" (freestyle is a term used in Hip-Hop culture to indicate the ability to create and articulate complex storylines with the a syncopated rhythm, delivered spontaneously—often under pressure and challenge of a peer). The ability to go with the flow thus enables individuals to effectively overlap multiple spheres, i.e., youth—adult, mainstream—counterculture, or the formally educated—global student. Additionally, youth popular culture informs how youth harness their skills, talents and capacities for, agency, self-expression, resistance, and social critique.

Intersection of Youth Popular and Hip-Hop

One key element of youth popular culture is its embrace of "alternative cultures" like hip-hop culture. A purview of the brief 40-year history of hip-hop culture provides insight of an environment that was both oppressive and innovatively creative. Present day hip-hop culture continues in this tradition, although within a different landscape. Now, hip-hop culture weaves messages that address injustice and oppression, as much as it celebrates the accumulation of unbridled wealth and prosperity. As such, current day participants of youth popular culture no longer fit neatly into stereotypical demographics. Instead, youth popular culture participants span varied races and ethnicities, genders, and geographic locations.

During the mid–1970s, hip-hop emerged as the premier voice for marginalized youth. During that time, to adults, it was largely an unknown phenomenon. At best, it was understood as a passing urban artistic movement (Dimitriadis, 2009). To the dismay of many adults, hip-hop grew in popularity and influence. In fact, early hip-hop pioneers represented the voices of their community. Many of these communities were faced with challenging environmental issues, rife with gang violence and plagued with crime. Youth were simultaneously challenged with escaping and changing their community environments. They were faced with both grave limitations and high expectations. In fact, individuals began using hip-hop music to address societal and environmental concerns, such as urban disfigurement, joblessness, racial tension, gang activity, and lack of community infrastructure. The musical expression lead to surges in communal resistance that created socio-political climates that exposed the historically exacerbated relationships between marginalized youth and adult-centered policy (Chang, 2005).

The fabric of hip-hop was interwoven into the pre-millennium decades of youth popular culture. Threads of hip-hop music, art, and fashion, permeated superficial societal surfaces and bled into embedded social fabrics. For youth, hip-hop served as a way and fact of life. In other words, the influence and confluence of hip-hop culture were inextricably linked to youth popular culture. This intersection led to profit driven commercialization of youth popular culture. The commercialization undoubtedly expanded the boundaries and enhanced artists' desire and ability for self-expression (Rose, 2008). Additionally, the advancements in technology widely increased the availability and affordability of music in particular. In fact, there was a proliferation of web and satellite-based music and file sharing applications (Jenkins, 2011). There was also increased availability of digitally enhanced and enabled devices. The enhancements in technology essentially made music "free," and portable. Another factor that increased access to hip-hop culture was the increased popularity of cable and online video services. These technological developments were ushered in alongside the traditional media outlets of radio and television.

While hip-hop enjoys as much praise in certain circles as it is maligned in others (Rose 2008), this essay purposefully chose to highlight the positive aspects by emphasizing an assets approach that presents opportunities and possibilities presented and provided to youth popular culture through hip-hop culture. This approach provides space to present hip-hop culture as a mediating force for deconstructing cultural content and various dynamics that emphasize personal growth and development, increased positive community and societal change, and need for addressing social injustices (Petchauer 2011a, b; Tyson et al. 2012; Prier & Beachum 2008a; Clay 2006; Veltre & Hadley 2012; Viega 2012; Emdin 2010; Seidel 2011).

Impacts of Hip-Hop Culture as a Mediating Factor for Social Change

Initially, hip-hop served as a coping mechanism to counter the effects of noxious socio-political climates. Ultimately, youth embraced hip-hop culture as a way of life, a vehicle for social change, and tool for economic mobility. By the turn of the new millennium, hip-hop became the embodiment of youth lived experiences within their communities (Chang, 2005; Emdin, 2010). In essence, hip-hop was woven into the layers and epistemological fabric of youth popular culture.

Hip-hop culture contains specific components that serve as forms of youth voice. Maston (2015) identified these components or artifacts of hip-hop as dj'ing (art of playing music for audiences), bboying (energetic dance form), mc'ing (interaction with listening audience while speaking over music) and graffiti (creative artistic expression that usually includes specific abstract elements). These artifacts formed the foundational building blocks of hip-hop and were utilized for expression of youth lived experiences. These artifacts created an avenue for youth popular culture and hip-hop to intersect. It provided a vehicle for youth to frame their story of contributions to their communities and society in general. Their story continues to till a societal landscape that spans the grassroots level and ascends to a bird's eye view of youth popular culture. On the surface, it positions youth popular culture as a function and source of pleasure and entertainment. More importantly, it provides insight of a nuanced context that explicates a form of patterning, developing, and sustaining youth cultural and ideological perspectives (Chang, 2005; Emdin, 2010).

There are clear historically underpinnings that indicate hip-hop's contributions and chronicling of empowerment messages, specifically through music. Hip-hop music espoused a belief in the ability of individuals to meet challenges and prevent victimization (Travis & Bowman, 2011). As such, hip-hop was a primary force for empowerment through community mobilization and social action (Flores-Gonzalez, Rodriguez, & Rodriguez-Muniz, 2006). It affirmed youth identity and formed pathways for positive youth development within the United States and internationally (Altschul, Oyserma, & Bybee, 2008; Mitchell, 2002). Travis and Bowman (2011) explain that hip-hop created empowerment capital gained through engaging through listening, creating, and listening to hip-hop music (Bowling & Washington, 1999; Elligan, 2004; Kobin & Tyson, 2006; Travis and Bowman, 2011; Tillie-Allen, 2005 and; Tyson 2002, 2003).

Empowered Youth Popular Culture: Hip-Hop as a Source of Capital

Empowerment in relation to hip-hop and youth popular culture is defined as both a process and outcome. It acts a bridge for healthy development of individual resilience that ultimately positively impacts communities (Guitierrez, 1995; & Freire, 1990). Travis and Deepak (2011) accurately describe this interactive positive development as Individual and Community Empowerment. They express that this form of empowerment is interrelated and mutually reinforcing. In its simplest iteration, empowerment places emphasis on the personal and interpersonal development of individuals to actively control and/or improve life situations and circumstances (Gutierrez, 1990). At more complex levels, empowerment has added value for all marginalized individuals within high stress environments (Freire, 1990). Even in stressful environments, there are possibilities of empowerment, especially when individuals in these stressful environments locate and identify with others experiencing similar perspectives. These possibilities create opportunities for individuals to develop specific skill sets and capacities and engage in change of a collective nature (Gutierrez, 1995). The collective nature of hip-hop culture embraces opportunities for successful individual empowerment and in turn leads to empowered communities. Successful individual empowerment can help empower the collective community, and an empowered community can help maintain environments that are more conducive to individual empowerment (Travis & Bowman, 2011).

The Youth Popular Culture Struggle Is Real

Youth popular culture has its most direct intersection within youth experiences in educational settings. In fact, exploring youth popular culture within the context of educational settings provides a promising opportunity to create a vehicle for youth and adults to work as partners to traverse the terrain of school improvement, social movements, and community change. Educators could incorporate youth popular culture so that it creates opportunities for youth to participate in the democratic process and receive authentic political representation, provide access to economic capital, and control, produce and distribute the various forms of media they consume. To achieve the above goal would require a paradigm shift and thus a very real struggle.

The youth struggle explicates a certain reality; that youth live in an increasingly complex world where they are viewed as commodities. The unfortunate reality is that youth are viewed as big business. As such, advertisers, media conglomerates, industries (sports, fashion, and entertainment), faith-based organizations, health care providers, community-based organizations, and even governmental entities (local, state, and federal) vie for control of youth spheres of influence. Yet these very entities exclude youth from full participation in such markets. Unfortunately, due to age, lack of fiduciary capacities, and limited access to civic arenas, youth are systematically and systemically eliminated from directly profiting in the very markets in which they are commodities. As a result, youth find themselves increasingly marginalized and disproportionately vulnerable to political, social, and economic shifts that invariably erode their quality of life and flattens their life trajectories.

Youth Popular Culture and Social Construction

Fortunately, youth are "Digital Natives" who in some aspects, function as both producers and consumers of media and technology (Prensky, 2001). Their knowledge and expertise perfectly positions them to amplify their voices through popular culture. Their voice could be amplified with the assistance of adults. Adult assistance requires that adults engage youth in authentic and responsible ways. Adult engagement with youth should move beyond the mentor to mentee relationship. Instead, it should include opportunities for youth and adults to be responsible and accountable to one another. This interaction would amplify rather than stifle or silence youth voice. Additionally, it would help to merge two distinct and divergent modes of operation for both youth and adults. Rather than adult perspectives framed on a depiction of youth as individuals experiencing a dark and stormy period in life where they lack motivation and concern for the well-being and development of their communities, it would shift their perspective to highlight the vary manners in which youth work willingly and collaboratively with adults (Lerner, Almergi, Theokas, & Lerner, 2005). There is clearly a need to broaden the discussion and depictions of youth. In fact, academic and community scholars suggest that a broader and more current understanding of youth as co-creators a social ecology. This ecological framing includes virtual spaces that encompass social media and technology.

The power and magnitude of youth as co-creators is not new to world. Youth have been at the forefront of many social change efforts. For example, youth organizations with foci on student identity were crucial to the American civil rights movement (e.g., Southern Student Organizing Committee, Students for a Democratic Society, and Student Nonviolent Coordinating Committee). These organizations were at the forefront and the storefronts when they staged sit-ins, Brown-outs, and other non-violent protest activities. Additionally, hundreds of students played integral roles to secure voting rights for African Americans.

Students were also literally on the frontlines of the Vietnam War as well as on the frontlines in its protest. College campuses were integral for war protest, sit-ins, and other types of demonstrations. Youth led organizations at the helm of these protest included Young Americans for Freedom, Students Peace Union, and the Student Libertarian Movement. More recently, youth played important roles in the Arab Springs. Technology and media played integral roles in each of the above-mentioned protest. Television, radio, newspapers, and magazines were the precursors for social media (e.g., Twitter, Instagram, Facebook, Vine, etc.).

Expanding Possibilities through Partnerships

Youth popular culture has the potential to promote positive youth development and thus outlines a transformational process for academic scholarship and communities (Granger, 2002). As such, a broadened scholarship could then advance from positive youth development to a more progressive and emerging approach of youth adult partnerships. This is an important step that would acknowledge that many youth need adult assistance and resources. Conversely, it speaks to adults' need for youth assistance with media and other technologies. However, to reach youth requires an appropriate message. But, first, adults must be culturally competent and relevant to youth popular culture and willingly incorporate youth knowledge and experience as a foundation for their education and information dissemination in their outreach strategies.

Creating sustainable partnerships between youth and adults is one component for correcting negative life trajectories for youth, as well as revitalizing adult trajectories. These partnerships also improve and renew the outlook adults have about youth; thus reviving their commitment to youth and the communities in which they live. Youth adult partnerships generate a synergistic environment for authentic youth participation in all aspects of society. Additionally, it harnesses the energy and expertise found in the clusters of individuals working in local communities across the country to bridge multiple gaps of race, culture, class, faith, sexual orientation, and disability. In essence, these individuals work to improve the conditions and the quality of life for all members of society and for youth in particular.

The youth-adult partnerships also benefit adults' ability to positively and effectively communicate with youth. Specifically, developing a working knowledge of youth popular culture helps adults understand the information that youth possess and youth processes. However, adult's understanding of youth popular culture is only a start. Adults must also embrace the collective nature embedded within youth popular culture. That is to understand that youth popular culture expresses a particular worldview, one that builds on collective perspectives shared by youth for an enhanced future.

Youth Popular Cultural Competence

The need for youth popular cultural competence needs to be addressed with greater urgency. Societal emphasis and importance to understand and accept youth popular culture should mirror that of other cultural groups. There is need to demonstrate greater sensitivity to understanding youth, their approach to life, and how they interact and interpret their environment. The embrace could begin with educators. By embracing youth popular culture, educators could form a greater understanding of how to teach various methodologies that will create greater cultural responsiveness, relevance, and significance throughout society, particularly in educational settings. The current occurrences in society indicate that educators cannot operate as usual. Unfortunately, traditional approaches to pedagogy continue to be uncreative in their approach and willingness to engage youth in activities that link youth competencies, interest, and varied life and learning experiences. When pedagogies engage youth in this manner, they create meaningful relationships between educators and students and thus enhance the learning experiences of youth. Ultimately, these pedagogies increase youth potential for successful educational outcomes and increased life trajectories.

Youth popular culture helps youth make sense of the world. Sense making is particularly important when things around youth seem deafening and chaotic; hopeless and scary; and constantly faced with frustrating and unjust outcomes. Youth popular culture helps link words with thoughts and thoughts with action. It allows youth to consider the historical context of society and identify their place within it. It creates opportunities to investigate, interrogate, and create a reality that is meaningful for and to youth. It provides a venue for youth to express their voice through avenues of film, television, music, and digital media. It provides context to historical events and insight for current events and frames possibilities for the future. Youth popular culture competence provides space and creates venues for youth to speak truth to power.

Youth Popular Culture and Radio Broadcast Production

Few would disagree that good teachers ground their curriculum with the lives of their students. As such, the remainder of this essay focuses on curriculum that incorporated multiple aspects, components, and approaches highlighted previously in this essay. Specifically, the following sections present aspects of a youth adult partnership centered curriculum used to develop and broadcast a youth radio program on a community radio station. Additionally, sections provide insight of how adults worked with youth to integrate social media into the radio broadcast. Specifically, responses from listeners via social media were used to determine various topics addressed on the radio broadcast. Most importantly, the sections highlight the challenges and opportunities for youth adult partnerships and the potential for those partnerships to have pragmatic impacts on the development of youth journalism skills.

KAZI 88.7 FM, a community radio station located in Austin, Texas, offers a plethora of news, music, and information. Music genres include Gospel, R&B, Hip Hop, Jazz, Neo Soul, Zydeco, and Reggae (kazifm.org, 2014). The platform also includes aspects that solicit interaction from the listening audience. Over a two week period, KAZI engaged an active curriculum to explore how youth integrate public radio and social media to effectively produce and promote a radio magazine grounded in youth popular culture.

The curriculum purposefully engaged youth in online training activities, face-to-face instruction, and reflective journaling to develop participants' journalism acuity, production techniques, and interviewing skills. A particularly unique aspect embedded within the curriculum was the opportunity to create authentic partnerships between the community radio educator, Ms. Anderson and the youth volunteers. Over the course of 20 years, Ms. Anderson shared that she learned the importance of purposeful development and cultivation of relationships. She considered them to be bedrocks in the industry. Therefore, she included similar opportunities to build relationships and create bonds with the youth volunteers. She expressed that although the youth volunteers had regular interactions with adults at the radio station, it was clear that the youth had developed their own cultural dynamic within the KAZI radio community. Therefore she wanted to begin their interactions in a manner that assured the youth that she was "cool." She further explained that being "cool" was about letting them know that she cared about them, as she put it, "youth don't care what you know, until they know you care."

Developing Students' Journalism Skills

Prior to 2013, KAZI was the only radio station—public or private that served a primarily African American community as the target audience. In fact, KAZI is still the oldest community radio station of any kind in Austin. As such, historically, most of the youth participants for the station have been of African American descent and they represent a wide range of socioeconomic backgrounds. However, due to the eclectic music programming and diverse coverage of news and opinion, the station's listening audience has remained multicultural and diverse.

Ms. Anderson used a purposeful sample to identify youth to participate in the curriculum. She identified youth based on their availability and frequency of volunteering at the station. Additionally, she invited youth that previously expressed interest in expanding their journalism skill sets. This admission was a welcomed revelation, as she often listened to youth produced radio shows on several stations and could indicate moments when youth were "winging it." Ms. Anderson admits that there are moments were being able to speak "off the cuff" is necessary, however, she differentiated that from "winging it," because "winging it" was a sign of inadequate preparation. She stressed the importance of being properly prepared to prevent poor performance. As such, she assured that the curriculum included purposeful preparation strategies.

The curriculum also included insightful ways to effectively integrate social media into public radio broadcast platforms. Students posed questions via social media and framed their broadcast topics based on the trending responses. This approach allowed them to incorporate the interactive component many youth find valuable in their daily interactions. A few of the most popular trending topics included (a) journalism ethics in covering social unrest, (b) over-militarization of Black communities, and (c) cyber bullying or online etiquette. Ultimately, youth were able to consider the power and accompanied responsibility in deciding "newsworthy" topics for their broadcast and online communications. This lesson also helped them reflect on current media practices and the inadequate and inaccurate coverage of youth and marginalized individuals.

Online activities were also a key component of the curriculum. The online activities allowed students to complete designated readings, view and listen to content (e.g., Meet the Press, Respect the Mic, Democracy Now, and Consider Your Source), and record reflective audio journals about their perspectives. Each week students were expected to complete online activities on journalism skills, on-air presence, media and online ethics. Each activity included a detailed rubric that provided the guidelines and expected outcomes. Students also participated in focus group discussions with Ms. Anderson prior to producing their radio broadcast. The rubric and discussions allowed students to self-assess their progress and provided additional opportunities to reinforce areas in need of clarity or improvement. Finally, Ms. Anderson conducted performance evaluations based on her analysis of the recording of the radio broadcast.

Outcomes and Implications for Future Broadcast

The curriculum actively engaged both youth and adults for successful radio broadcasts. The curriculum was successful in many aspects. Youth expressed that they felt better prepared when they hosted their show and reported they could flow a lot smoother as a result of participating in the activities. Ms. Anderson reported her satisfaction with the curriculum, as there were fewer broadcasting errors, such as utterances of "uhs," "ums," and "you knows." She was also pleased with the reduction of "dead air" or radio silence. Ms. Anderson shared that several adult volunteers noticed markedly differences in youth interactions and the display of professionalism. One news director stressed that even though he makes it a point to learn from youth, he was particularly impressed with the youth volunteers as a result of their participation in the curriculum. He continued by stressing that he learned a lot from the youth participants. She directly attributes the changes to the online assignments and the follow-up discussions.

The success of the youth adult partnership for the development and broadcast of radio magazine provides encouragement for future youth adult interactions. It supports the idea that although youth benefit from mentors in the industry, the necessity of "Oprah Winfrey" or "Peter Jennings" was lessoned because the broadcast were based on youth generated topics, youth lead discussions, on youth produced shows. A music director at the station shared, "I don't think they have to always follow the adult example. This is something they are creating for themselves and their peers. We just need to guide them a little and get out of the way."

Lessons Learned and Steps Moving Forward

The media of previous generations included newspapers, magazines, and books. Whereas, today's media also includes the previous, it places emphasis in online networking systems. Additionally, the music culture has moved beyond music consumption only to include musical exchange, marketing and selling music as a form of culture, lifestyle and the byproduct of each. In consideration of the above, the question arises *What should we do with youth popular culture and its intersection with media?* The simplest and yet most comprehensive answer is to embrace it. One way to embrace it is to include it in the educational process in a purposefully authentic manner.

Youth Popular Culture and Education

Educators could drastically improve the life trajectories of youth and thereby improve the positive outcomes for society by simply beginning the development of curricula from the premise that what matters to youth matter to everyone. The "popular" aspect of youth culture is present in every classroom each and every day. In our current society, it is unacceptable both socially and politically to oppress any cultural group in public spaces, particularly educational settings. The same should be true for the treatment of youth popular culture. Critiquing the current system or the media is not enough. There is need for universal shift in the intellectual activity that takes place in educational settings. Educators must realize that the embrace or oppression of youth popular culture is inherently political. As such, shifting the paradigm of thought requires a larger stance and resistance against the status quo. As with every movement in history, when adults stand with students in protest of injustices, change occurs. Educators can no longer remain "neutral." In fact, education by its very nature is political. Therefore, educators must utilize their positions of power, privilege, and resources to help amplify the voice of marginalized cultures. This shift will not occur with consequence. It will not happen without struggle. However, struggle is a daily occurrence in the learning process. Just as educators embrace the struggle that accompanies learning, they must also embrace the struggle to create meaningful, purposeful, and authentic dialogue first with students, then with other educators, and finally they must facilitate conversations between youth and adults, about politics of youth popular culture.

How Can Teachers Shift Pedagogical Practices?

In order to shift pedagogical practices, teachers must first resist the corporate interests that have crept into educational settings. Once teachers fully understand the complex social histories and the struggles of identity development, they will also understand the importance of expelling corporate interest from educational settings. For example, the complex social histories associated and directly related with segregation, genocide, and military interventions have direct links or connections to corporate interest. However, rather than embracing the complex nuances of each issue, educators are instead pushed to reorganize curricula into diluted reorganized or simple dichotomies of good and evil. Such simplistic and distorted representations of complex historical phenomenon support the oppressive thought, particularly against marginalized cultures. Instead, there is need for critical examination of the production and circulation of media and an accompanying analysis of the motivations and profits generated as a result of its distribution.

As stated in various sections of this essay, youth popular culture has the embedded capacity to critique and speak truth to power. This critique could be honed in educational settings so that youth learn to rethink connections among race, class, gender, sexuality, ability, social economic status, and various educational levels. Understandably, this paradigm shift will not happen in one fell swoop. Instead, to make the shift sustainable, it should occur in parts. The parts could be as follows: *What is the relationship: Youth, education, and corporations; Youth popular cultural critique: Reframing historical events; Youth popular culture and marginalized communities; Partnerships in educational settings: Educators, students, and communities; Social justice or social just us; and Youth popular culture as a vehicle for change now.*

Explicating Relationship Between Youth, Education and Corporations

There is a thin line between education and corporate interest. Unfortunately, that line becomes increasingly blurry with each policy and the change of each administration. Drawing attention to the strategies utilized by corporations to define youth perspectives is key. Schools are recurring targets for advertising campaigns. As such, it is important to teach students about the ploys used to "teach" them brand loyalty (e.g., free copies of "popular" magazines, free samples of products, label collection, etc.). Many schools are complicit in these advertising campaigns as they receive income by entering into exclusive product sales agreements. Teachers and students are often bombarded by advertisements on school Internet services, product placements and within the interior of the school itself. Many schools find it hard to decline such offers, especially as they undergo budget cuts and reductions in force.

Youth Popular Cultural Critique: Reframing Historical Events

Youth popular culture is a natural match for the critique of historical and political occurrences and the seemingly undeniable and seemingly straightforward storyline, neatly manicured plots, interesting characters, and iconic images. However, the accuracy of each occurrence is dependent upon the perspective and point of view. For example, the "historical" accounts of enslaved Africans of the transatlantic slave trade differs from those of the slave catcher, or the "historical" accounts of incarcerated prisoners of Auschwitz concentration camp complex differs from the Nazi solider. There are countless "historical" events that deserve critical critique.

Youth Popular Culture and Marginalized Communities

Society and culture are inextricably designed to reproduce themselves. Therefore, popular culture and media also engage in a relentless reproduction process. As such, examination of existing dominant ideologies and their action upon or against marginalized groups is worthy of explication. Cultural inequities can only be leveled and differences erased when the perverse existence of sexist, racist, classist, and the remnants of colonization or exposed and universally viewed as deviant and counterproductive to the human sustainability. The ideas about race, class, and gender can no longer masquerade as a fixed and inflexible paradigm.

Partnerships in Educational Settings: Educators, Students and Communities

There is need to reframe relationships between educators, students and the community. Current social text present particular anxieties about youth adult interactions and thus hold teachers up to be the "saviors" or "missionaries" for "helpless" youth. The caring protagonist or heroine is usually a white woman prepared to "save" students from their underserved conditions. Conversely, the children are often depicted as uncivilized, uneducated, and vulnerable. The critique of this popular narrative could draw attention to the political nature and inherent difference between education and schooling as an ideological realization for just societies.

Social Justice or Social Just Us

Teachers and students can take positive actions in the classroom and within the community. Providing educators and students with plausible resistance strategies against corporate assault on their everyday occurrences and lived experiences is paramount. Youth popular culture and media can be utilized to examine issues of violence, exploitation, marginalization, power, and privilege to expose the hypocrisy and inequities. Specifically, through the use of critical media literacy, individuals develop a social justice orientation necessary to move beyond being politically correct and neutral. Instead, individuals learn the necessity of taking a purposeful stance for justice and inclusion of marginalized populations in the classroom and within the communities they live and serve.

Youth Popular Culture as a Vehicle for Change Now

Examining how youth popular culture and media can create the space and resources necessary to change the social and political landscape is key. Utilizing technological advancements and social media platforms creates an entry point for marginalized groups to participate. However, there is necessity for revision of mainstream storylines and recomposed mainstream images. The use of poetry, art, film, and music provides opportunities for educators to teach about artistic resistance.

Conclusion

Youth popular culture is a viable and vibrant vehicle for youth to express and articulate their voice. It provides the canvas for them to depict their lived experiences. It provides the amplification of their voice. It provides opportunity to resist the status quo. It pushes the boundaries of pragmatism. Youth popular culture is necessary for the healthy existence of society. It provides a necessary balance through critique, revision, and reframing of society. It provides the space for students and educators to produce, and consume media. It provides spotlight that shines equally on all regardless of their position life.

REFERENCES

Altschul, I., Oyserman, D., & Bybee, D. (2008). Racial-ethnic self-schemas and segmented assimilation: Identity and the academic achievement of Hispanic youth. *Social Psychology Quarterly, 71*(3), 302–320.

Bowling, L., & Washington, P. (1999). Rap music videos: The voices of organic intellectuals. *Transcultural Music Review, 4.* Retrieved from http://www.sibetrans.com/trans/trans4/dee.htm.

Chang, J. (2004). *Can't stop won't stop: A history of the hip-hop generation.* New York: St. Martin's Press.

Clay, A. (2006). "All I need is one mic": Mobilizing youth for social change in the post-civil rights era. *Social Justice, 33*(2), 105–121.

Dimitriadis, G. (2009). *Performing identity/performing culture: Hip hop as text, pedagogy, and lived practice.* New York: Peter Lang.

Elligan, D. (2004). *Rap therapy: A practical guide for communicating with young adults through rap music.* New York: Kensington Publishing.

Emdin, C. (2010). *Urban science education for the hip-hop generation.* Rotterdam, NY: Sense.

Flores-Gonzalez, N., Rodriguez, M., & Rodriguez-Muniz, M. (2006). From hip-hop to humanization: Batey Urbano as a space for Latino youth culture and community action. In S. Ginwright, P. Noguera, & J. Cammarota (Eds.), *Beyond resistance: Youth activism and community change.* Oxford: Routledge.

Freire, P. (1990). *Pedagogy of the oppressed* (trans. Myra Bergman Ramos). New York: Continuum.

Granger, R. C. (2002). Creating the conditions linked to positive youth development. *New Directions for Youth Development, 95,* 149–164.

Gutierrez, L. (1995). Understanding the empowerment process: Does consciousness make a difference? *Social Work Research, 19*(4), 229–237.

Gutierrez, L. M. (1990). Working with women of color: An empowerment perspective. *Social Work, 35,* 149–153.

Jenkins, T. (2011). A beautiful mind: Black male intellectual identity and hip-hop culture. *Journal of Black Studies, 42*(8), 1231–1251.

Kazifm.org. (2014). *Kazi 88.7.* Retrieved from http://www.kazifm.org/.

Kobin, C., & Tyson, E. (2006). Thematic analysis of hip-hop music: Can hip-hop in therapy facilitate empathic connections when working with clients in urban settings? *The Arts in Psychotherapy, 33,* 343–356.

Lerner, R. M., Lerner, J. V., Almerigi, J. B., Theokas, C., Phelps, E., & Bobek, D. L. (2005). Positive youth development, participation in community youth development programs, and community contributions of fifth-grade adolescents: Findings from the first wave of the 4-H study of positive youth development. *Journal of Early Adolescence, 25*(1), 17–71.

Matson, A. C. *Spiritualizing Hip Hop with I.C.C.: The poetic spiritual narratives of four Black educational leaders from Hip Hop communities.* Ph.D. dissertation, Texas State University, May 2014.

Mitchell, T. (2002). *Global noise: Rap and hip-hop outside the USA.* Middletown, CT: Wesleyan University Press.

Petchauer, E. (2011a). Knowing what's up and learning what you're not supposed to: Hip-hop collegians, higher education, and the limits of critical consciousness. *Journal of Black Studies, 42*(5), 768–790.

Petchauer, E. (2011b). I feel what he was doin': Responding to justice-oriented teaching through hip-hop aesthetics. *Urban Education, 46*(6), 1411–1432.

Prensky, M. (2001). Digital natives, digital immigrants part 1. *On the Horizon, 9*,(5), 1–6. Retrieved from http://dx.doi.org/10.1108/10748120110424816.

Prier, D., & Beachum, F. (2008). Conceptualizing a critical discourse around hip-hop culture and black male youth in educational scholarship and research. *International Journal of Qualitative Studies in Education, 21*(5), 519–535.

Prier, D. C. (2012). *Culturally relevant teaching: Hip-hop pedagogy in urban schools.* New York: Peter Lang.

Rose, T. (2008). *The hip-hop wars: What we talk about when we talk about hip-hop.* Philadelphia: Basic Books.

Seidel, S. (2011). *Hip hop genius: Remixing high school education.* New York: Rowman & Littlefield.

Tillie Allen, N. (2005). Exploring hip-hop therapy with high-risk youth. *Praxis, 5,* 30–36.

Travis, R., & Bowman, S. (2011). Negotiating risk and promoting empowerment through rap music: Development of a measure to capture risk and empowerment pathways to change. *Journal of Human Behavior in the Social Environment, 21,* 654–678.

Travis, R., & Bowman, S. (2012). Ethnic identity, self-esteem and variability in perceptions of rap music's empowering and risky influences. *Journal of Youth Studies, 15,* 455–478. doi:10.1080/13676261.2012.663898.

Travis, R., and Deepak, A. (2011). Empowerment in context: Lessons from hip-hop culture for social work practice. *Journal of Ethnic & Cultural Diversity in Social Work, 20,* 1–20.

Tyson, E. (2002). Hip-Hop therapy: An exploratory study of a rap music intervention with at-risk and delinquent youth. *Journal of Poetry Therapy, 15*(3), 131–144.

Tyson, E. (2003). Rap music in social work practice with African American and Latino youth: A conceptual model with practical applications. *Journal of Human Behavior in the Social Environment, 8*(4), 1–21.

Tyson, E., Detchkov, K., Eastwood, E., Carver, A., & Sehr, A. (2012). Therapeutic uses of rap and hip-hop. In S. Hadley & G. Yancey (Eds.), *Therapeutic uses of rap and hip-hop* (pp. 99–114). New York: Routledge/Taylor & Francis Group.

Veltre, V., & Hadley, S. (2012). It's bigger than hip-hop: A hip-hop feminist approach to music therapy with adolescent females. In S. Hadley & G. Yancy (Eds.), *Therapeutic uses of rap and hip-hop* (pp. 79–98). New York: Routledge/Taylor & Francis Group.

Viega, M. (2012). The hero's journey hip-hop and its applications in music therapy. In S. Hadley & G. Yancy (Eds.), *Therapeutic uses of rap and hip-hop* (pp. 57–78). New York: Routledge/Taylor & Francis Group.

FaithFull Youth

How Religious Youth Live in the
Tension Between Faith Culture
and Popular Culture

BRYAN CURRIE

FaithFull Youth: They Are All Around Us

Whether a youth leader interacts with gifted students in an afterschool leadership program, coaches young athletes for a soccer team, or teaches theology to a church youth group, the young people s/he leads in these programs exist in a system where each of their identities influences the other and none can be fully understood apart from the whole. The students in our care do not exist with dozens of separate identities, each piled independently on top of the other. Instead, these youth see themselves as having only one identity, with dozens of interacting components. There is no such thing as a youth who is a musician and a computer programmer and a Christian and a fashion diva. There is only a Christian musician computer programming fashion diva.

Almost 70 percent of youth are now or previously have been involved in a religious youth group (Smith, 2005), and at least half of the youth in our schools and community programs say faith is important in their lives. Studies show that these faithFull youth—the religiously-interested majority who invest time in spiritual activities—are considerably more likely than their non-religious peers to also be actively involved in volunteer programs, sports teams, school clubs, and other organized youth activities outside the church (Smith, 2005). In other words, even non-faith-based youth programs are extremely likely to attract faithFull youth. It is critical that youth leaders in a variety of settings understand how adolescents' interaction in faith systems may also impact their interactions in the broader world. After all, a youth's faith identity influences far more than just how s/he spends time within the sacred space of a church, mosque, or temple. It also impacts the way they interact with family, peers, concerned adults, community programs, and popular culture.

It is important, therefore, that youth development professionals understand that for the faithFull teenagers in their care, faith systems are often not only a way of interacting with the divine; they are also a way of interacting with culture. Obviously, not all religions view popular culture in the same light. Every religion—and the hundreds of sects, congregations, and communities therein—have different values that inform how their followers interact with the broader culture. It should be noted, however, that many sects within the world's major faith traditions (including Christian, Jewish, and Muslim) are driven by a belief that popular culture is a "stumbling block" to be either avoided or highly scrutinized by the faithful. These traditions sometimes (if not often) protect the purity of their followers by attempting to keep them uncontaminated by the broader culture. For many of these groups, fearless pro-sex anthems streamed online, shameless displays of flesh by pop divas, moral relativism preached by Hollywood storylines and starlets, violence glorified in must-see blockbusters, lust and greed role-modeled by reality TV stars, and the vulgarity of often-imitated stand-up comics all threaten to undermine the highest values of the faithful.

While many youth see pop culture as an integrated part of their everyday life, faithFull youth may see their faith culture and popular culture in desperate tension. These two worlds exist on a binary scale, where one is often at odds with the other. Considering that many teenagers engage with popular culture (music, movies, Internet-based media, etc.) not only as a form of entertainment, but also as a way of establishing identity and bonding with their peer group, faithFull youth may feel forced to make a difficult choice as to which culture (religious or popular) they will identify with and engage in on a daily basis. Many feel they can either actively engage with popular culture and find themselves at odds with their faith tradition, or they can reject popular culture and fully embrace their faith identity. Each option presents faithFull youth with potential estrangement. Will they sacrifice coveted social standing and peer relationships for the security and identity they find in being faithFull? Or, will they put themselves at odds with family, faith leaders, and faithFull peers in order to explore and engage with the forbidden fruit of popular culture? Given that both popular culture and faith culture have the potential to provide incredible supportive and developmental resources, is disengaging from either a good option?

In the discussion that follows, the beliefs of all faith traditions are held in the highest regard. This discussion is not a critique of religion, but rather an attempt to shed light on the tension that faithFull youth may feel surrounding the interaction of their faith and popular culture. Since many youth development professionals consider working knowledge of pop culture (and perhaps active engagement in pop culture) to be an important element of their ability to work effectively with teenagers, it seems critical that these concerned adults understand how the faithFull youth in our care interact with popular culture. After all, a majority of the teenagers who make up youth football teams, after school programs, model UN delegations, Scout troops, student councils, and leadership clubs consider "faithFull" an important part of their identity. How can they be supported in their journey?

Who Are FaithFull Youth and How Do They Interact with Popular Culture?

Does it come as a surprise that youth are interested in matters of faith and spirituality? In the midst of chemistry tests and Friday night football games, are youth really thinking about philosophy, theology, and the mysterious nature of g/God? Apparently they are. According to a nationwide, random-digit-dial telephone survey of 3,370 teenagers conducted by the National Study of Youth and Religion (NYSR),[1] more than 80 percent of teenagers believe in God, and about half report that faith is very or extremely important in their lives. Nearly four in ten U.S. adolescents are actively involved in a religious youth group, with many claiming they would like to attend religious services even more often than they currently do (Smith, 2005). Among other things, these youth identify as Protestant, Catholic, Jewish, Muslim, Hindu, Wiccan, and Buddhist. Many are connected to the faith of their family. A few are not.

Notably, the NYSR reports that three quarters of U.S. youth identify as "Christian" with the next largest group (16 percent) being the minority who consider themselves "not religious" (Smith, 2005).[2] The discussion that follows will, therefore, examine faithFull youth and pop culture through the statistically sizable lens produced by Christian youth groups, churches, and para-church organizations. It should be noted, however, that this conversational boundary is not intended to diminish the experience of faithFull non-Christian youth. Rather, many readers who are familiar with non-Christian religious traditions (Islam, Judaism, etc.) may notice striking parallels between how these important traditions and Christianity teach their youth to interact with popular culture.

Although many non-clergy Christians may not be familiar with the name H. Richard Niebuhr, those more versed in academic Christian theology will recognize Niebuhr as a dominant voice in conversations about how

Christians typically interact with culture. In his seminal book *Christ and Culture*, Niebuhr (1951) defines culture as the "artificial, secondary environment which [humanity] superimposes on the natural" (p. 32). By defining culture as "artificial" and "secondary," Niebuhr presents "a distinctive contrast between Christ, who demands complete loyalty to the sovereign God, and culture, with its humanly constructed system of competing values and ideas…. Thus, the Christian is caught in between these two competing ideals—Christ and culture—and by necessity, must respond" (Erwin, 2010, p. 171). Even without studying formal theology, many faithFull youth are intimately familiar with the idea of religion and popular culture being cast in opposing roles.

Most faithFull youth find themselves (sometimes unknowingly) fitting neatly into one of Niebuhr's five models of how Christ-followers likely interact with popular culture. Some Christian youth choose to stand *against culture,* believing that faith and culture are irreconcilable, and that the faithFull must choose one over the other. Some Christian youth feel that their faith is *of culture,* meaning that they see Christ as the ultimate fulfillment of culture's highest—if not yet realized—ideals. Other faithFull youth see their faith as being *above culture,* believing that everything good and beautiful within culture is a gift from God. Still others experience faith and culture *in paradox.* These youth believe that culture is "infected with godlessness" (Niebuhr, 1951, p. 154), but that they are nevertheless called to work within this system as agents of light. Finally, a fifth group of the faithFull feel their faith is the *transformer of* culture, ultimately bringing it from what it currently is into a more perfected state (Niebuhr, 1951).

Whichever of these beliefs a faithFull youth might subscribe to, it is not difficult to see that each work from a premise that faith and culture are fundamentally separate. While their less faith-involved peers casually cruise the Internet, listen to music, attend movies, watch TV, and bond together over the common cup of popular culture, faithFull youth may not be able to absorb culture as casually as their friends do. Their faith may require them to either keep popular culture at arm's length or reject it altogether. But even when a faithFull youth does not personally find this necessary, their faith community, church youth leaders, parents, and faithFull friends may encourage them to think more critically about—and possibly reject—popular culture.

These youth find themselves in a difficult position. On one side they feel an incredible need and desire to connect with their peers, often over whatever is most widespread in popular culture at the moment. On the other, their religious communities—which have been shown to be richly supportive and protective spaces for youth (Regnerus, 2003)—may be pulling them away from popular culture and into a more insulated community. Each culture, both popular and religious, provides rich soil for the youth's growth. But what happens when they stand in tension? And why might youth feel forced to choose one over the other?

FaithFull History: The Choice Between Secular or Sacred

As "adolescence" grew into a new category of both development and culture in the early twentieth century, churches began to organize young people into their own Christian sub-culture to train them in the Christian faith. The earliest Christian youth leaders saw their mission as one of promoting "Christian citizenship" among youth and building a generation of young people resistant to the forces of secular culture. In these leaders' opinions, the years after the second World War found the United States in a "crisis of civilization" where the dominant culture's values—as expressed through its music, media, and licentious habits, threatened to undermine the purity of the moral (i.e., religious) minority (Bergler, 2012).

As a result, the early and mid-twentieth century saw various Christian denominations founding youth organizations such as the United Christian Youth Movement, Youth for Christ, Young Life, and Young Christian Students to help youth address this culture crisis and combat the evil influences of the world. Young Life, for example, began holding sizable youth rallies in the 1940s to help establish Christian youth as a viable counter-culture. Some of these organizations' earliest leaders, including a young Billy Graham, stressed to a growing generation of faithFull youth that following Christ required absolute separation from "the world." To use Niebuhr's paradigm, these early Christian youth programs stood *against culture*, and encouraged young people to do the same. In the idiom of the day, they were trying to save the nation by saving its youth (from culture) (Bergler, 2012, p. 24).

From Elvis to MTV and beyond, faithFull youth have been consistently called to rally against the forces of culture; and it seems that contemporary youth ministries may be following suit. Just as the Christian youth movement began as a rally against popular culture, many of the church-based youth groups that 38 percent of millennial teenagers are actively involved in (Smith, 2005) take an *against culture* stance. This theological tendency can be seen not only at the grassroots level, but also as a theme in the writings of many Christian cultural analysts. For example, in a lecture at Princeton University, Dr. William Romanowski (2012), author of several notable Christian critiques of popular culture, affirms this *against culture* tendency by saying that "the fact that entertainment media play a role in the enculturation process has long been a source of irritation to parents, social, educational, and religious leaders who have all worried about the effect that such a diffusion of authority might have on the young and impressionable, and also on the vitality of family, church and school" (p. 1).

Likewise, Walt Mueler, a widely published cultural analyst who provides training, resources, and education for faith-based youth workers, writes extensively about the ways Christian youth interact with pop culture. His opinions about the dangers faithFull youth potentially expose themselves to when interacting with pop culture may be representative of many faith-based youth leaders, and have certainly influenced the thousands of professional youth leaders he trains every year. Mueller, like many Christian youth leaders, sees pop culture as an embodiment of a moral relativism that threatens many churches and faith communities. For example, Mueller (2006) warns faith-based youth workers that pop culture robs youth of a much-needed barometer of right and wrong, encourages boundary-less sexuality, and normalizes behavior that should be considered abnormal. The intent of this critique, of course, is a noble encouragement for youth to practice healthy sexuality, make sound moral choices, and define their identity in productive, empowering ways. In doing so, however, it also calls youth to examine how they will interact with pop culture—often with a cautionary tone. The choices presented by Mueller, Romanowski, and others seem to be for youth to either think critically and proceed cautiously (Niebuhr's *culture in paradox* with faith), or protect themselves through disengagement (Niebuhr's *faith acting against culture*).

Just as the "culture wars" of the 1990s divided political opinions into "secular" and "traditional" camps (Hunter, 1992), many faithFull youth are encouraged to divide culture into safe (faith-based) and unsafe (pop culture) categories. It should be noted that reporting on the opinions of cultural analysts like Romanowski and Mueller is in no way meant to critique their theology, but instead to highlight a prevalent worldview that heavily influences many faithFull youth. While other youth feel the freedom to enjoy pop culture, and even shape it, many faithFull youth are instead encouraged to isolate themselves from pop culture in an effort to protect their faith and purity. How do these youth respond to living in the tension between faith and culture?

Faith or Culture? Make Your Choice

FaithFull youth may be deeply invested in systems that encourage them to choose between their faith and the music, movies, personalities, and other elements of pop culture that vie for their loyalty. If youth workers, pastors, and concerned adults understand these youth only as products of their faith systems, they might be tempted to believe that faithFull youth are trapped in an either/or world. FaithFull youth do not, however, live only within the confines of the church. They are not solely influenced by youth pastors and faith-based programs. It seems, therefore, that in addition to understanding these youth as faithFull, youth workers must also understand them as products of their generation and wider culture. These faithFull *millennial* youth are the product of a generation that resists black and white propositions; they enjoy they gray space between. As millennials, these youth generally value choice and embrace the free exchange of ideas. They do not want to be told "you must believe this OR that." They want to explore both.

As evidence, consider the disparity between how different generations view popular culture. In 2007, a majority of the Baby Boomer generation said that the content of music and movies was a major problem facing America; but only one third of millennials agreed. Research suggests that this disparity occurred for a mix of two reasons: millennials either did not care about the values expressed in the media, or they did not notice (Kinnaman & Lyons, 2007, p. 126). While faithFull youth may be taught by their faith communities that holiness requires choosing the sacred over the secular (i.e., choosing faith over pop culture), it is possible that not all millennials are convinced. Once upon a time, preachers could stand in their pulpits and talk about the evils of culture (i.e., "the world") because the church was the primary shaper of culture. Millennials now see, however, that the church does not stand at the center of culture. Many of these youth are tired of the church viewing culture as the enemy. Some faithFull youth may question whether the goal of Christian living is to escape the evils of culture and remain untainted by "the world" (Powell, 2014).

The reason(s) faithFull youth may feel uneasy drawing a line between their faith and their participation in culture (rather than allowing both to occupy the same space) might not only be theological and generational, but also developmental. In his discussion of an ethnographic study exploring the life experience of middle adolescents, researcher Chap Clark (2011) asserts that

> Adolescents have the ability to apply abstract thought and reflective action within a given realm, or "self," of life. But once a midadolescent has moved on from a self—be it a relationship, a role, an expectation, or an activity—he or she creates a different, almost totally unique conceptualization process in the new self and then applies abstract thought and processing in that context as well. This has always been true of adolescents who have the ability to actualize abstract and nuanced thought processes. But what is new is the lack of ability to construct bridges between one self and another. The inability to see contradictions as contradictions and the ability to easily rationalize seemingly irreconcilable beliefs, attitudes, or values are but two of many markers that may be pointing to an emerging phase of adolescent development and may provide a key indicator of the essence of midadolescence [p. 28].

Clark (2011) suggests that youth (and especially midadolescents) may apply different decision-making processes to various sectors of their lives.

They may think abstractly and critically about a variety of subjects (i.e., faith and culture), but may not be able to build bridges to connect their insights. While older youth can see where the conclusions of one thought process might have implications for a seemingly unrelated thought process, midadolescents may have trouble making these connections. They "are fully capable of penetrating and insightful dialogue regarding a variety of topics and issues, but when it comes to applying the conclusions reached during these discussions to a relationship or social reality, especially in a different social context, they cannot see the connection" (Clark, 2011, p. 45).

This developmental context becomes incredibly relevant for faith-based youth leaders attempting to understand (and possibly influence) the way youth interact with popular culture. For example, a faithFull youth might learn from church leaders that her faith prohibits sex outside of marriage because the exclusivity of the husband/wife relationship is a symbol of God's desire for an exclusive relationship with God's people ("Thou shall have no other gods before me"[3]). That same youth might be able to talk intelligently about why a reality TV star's sexual exploits are immoral or degrading to women. But when a youth leader says, "You shouldn't watch that show because it's important for Christians to keep their minds pure," it is possible that the youth will not understand. She might not immediately see the connection between her exposure to sexually charged TV shows and her church's teaching about sexual purity. Each idea lives in a separate space. As a result, the way youth interact with their faith community and the way they interact with popular culture may be completely disconnected.

The idea that faithFull youth have separate "compartments" for the way they interact with faith and popular culture may be supported by the findings of the National Study of Youth and Religion (NSYR). According to this groundbreaking study, about half of youth claim that faith is very or extremely important to them. It seems, however, that many of these faithFull youth's religious beliefs do not bleed over into other areas of their lives. Religion is important, but only in the religious sector. For example, data from NSYR reveal that most U.S. teenagers who participate in religion do so either because of the way it makes them feel or because of how it helps them resolve problems. Very few claimed, however, that their religious participation involved disciplined practice or asked them to adhere to an ethical standard (Smith, 2005). Apparently, even the youth who report that faith is "very" or "extremely" important to them feel no need to let their faith influence their thinking about things such as relationships, dating, school, and sexual activities. These youth seem to have distinct compartments for their "religious life" and their "other" life. Much to the chagrin of their pastors and church youth leaders, these faithFull youth may see no tension between being fully engaged in a faith community and also fully engaged in the broader culture.

Why would one need to contradict the other? For faithFull millennial youth, each live in separate spaces.

Many faithFull youth, therefore, may feel a disconnect with their church's opinion that they should *separate from* or *stand against* popular culture (to use Niebuhr's paradigm). Whether because of a theological bias against the church's teaching, a generational dissatisfaction with being asked to make this choice, or a developmental inability to connect the church's stance with its cultural application, a significant number of faithFull youth may hear their faith-community's call to disengage from popular culture … and simply not respond. But what about the rest? What happens when a faithFull youth decides to abandon popular culture in order to fully engage with the faith community? Or, what happens when a youth is ostracized from her church because her immersion in popular culture makes her too "worldy"?

Connecting to Faith Culture … Retreating from Popular Culture

How often has a young teenage boy put on his headphones when his mother starts yelling through the house that it is time for him to turn off his game station and help wash the dishes? How often has an adolescent girl pretended not to hear her stepfather telling her to quit chatting online and finish her homework? The boy will eventually help his mother. The girl will eventually do her homework. These teenagers are not choosing one or the other. They have simply decided that the choice is not immediately important. The same thought process might come into play with faithFull youth who are asked to choose between engaging with their faith and engaging with popular culture. They simply decide that the choice is not important, ignore the request to choose, and engage in both. Other faithFull youth, however, find themselves genuinely wrestling with whether their faith and popular culture can cohabitate in peace. Perhaps insulating themselves in the safe confines of spirituality—and a faith community—feels comforting and secure. Perhaps they're afraid to challenge the authority of their tradition. Or maybe they obey willingly because questioning the norm never occurs to them. Whatever the reason, many faithFull youth choose to retreat from popular culture in an effort to either better connect with their faith or conform to its standards.

Faithfull youth who came of age in the 1980s and 1990s (many of whom are now parents of millennial teenagers) may remember youth meetings spent talking about hidden Satanic messages in popular music[4] and the need to remain pure by not "following the things of this world." Although it might seem foreign to those whose youth was not immersed in church culture, it was not uncommon for the most zealous faithFull youth to become so convicted by these conversations that they pulled the tape out of their "secular" cassettes (or later, broke their CDs), put on a Christian t-shirt, and vowed to never listen to "ungodly" music again. Fortunately, a burgeoning Christian music industry provided plenty of alternatives, many of which closely imitated the style of their secular counterparts.

FaithFull youth who have come of age in the first decades of the 21st century may not share these exact experiences (after all, deleting a series of "secular" MP3s is not nearly as cathartic as snapping a CD in half), but many may understand the motivations behind them, including the strong sense of identity associated with being faithFull. As such, faithFull youth whose identity, reputation, and sense of self rely on their faith association may more strongly feel the need to disassociate from popular culture in order to protect that identity. This assertion seems to be reflected in the habits of faithFull youth. The National Survey of Youth and Religion affirms that "the most religiously involved American teens appear to watch less television during the week and on the weekends and are much less likely to watch R-rated movies. They are also less likely to use the Internet to view pornographic Web sites and... spend considerably less time playing action video games" (Smith, 2005, pp. 222–223).

FaithFull youth may avoid popular culture not only because their faith community asks them to, but also because of qualities intrinsic to religious youth. It is possible that youth with certain "hard-wired personalities" may be drawn to religion, such as those who are risk averse, joiners, or are especially conventional, conformist, and/or clean-living (Smith, 2005). When youth with these personality traits become invested in a faith tradition, they may be more inclined to both deeply invest in the faith's culture and also disengage from popular culture. It may also be true, however, that rather than simply drawing youth who are predisposed to traits like conformism and conventionality, religion gives faithFull youth the eye, ear, and training to more carefully evaluate the popular culture around them. Instead of living as blind consumers, these faithFull youth are "healthy eaters" who carefully read the labels on their pop culture diet. While some youth may be drawn to religion because of their nature, others may be nurtured by their faith in ways that make them especially sensitive to the messages of popular culture. But, whether nature or nurture is the prominent force in their growing worldview, the end result seems to be the same; many faithFull youth segregate themselves from popular culture in order to maintain their own standard of purity and meet the requirements of their faith.

Many well-intentioned youth pastors and faith-based youth leaders direct the youth in their care away from popular culture. Whether these concerned adults hold to a belief that popular culture may lead youth away from faith, may pollute their faith, or stands in defiant opposition to their faith, they believe they are doing youth a service by protecting them from a potentially dangerous outside force. Protecting youth is a noble goal, and comes from a place of genuine concern and compassion. Is it possible, though, that as these youth are insulated from popular culture, they are also insulated from important sources of resilience, socialization, and support? Is it possible that popular culture may have the ability to facilitate important development in young people, including positive socialization, healthy identity formation, and the ability to better understand and make decisions within their rapidly changing world? When faithFull youth make the choice to honor their faith by abstaining from popular culture, are they denying themselves access to important developmental tools?

Socialization

It will likely come as a surprise to few that adolescence is a time when youth distance themselves from their parents and feel a gravitational pull toward their peers. Multiple studies show that during adolescence youth transition from spending more time with their parents to spending more time with their friends (Larson, Moneta, Richards, & Wilson, 2002; Buhrmester & Carbery, 1992), and also begin to depend more on these friends for intimacy (French, Rianasari, Pidada, Nelwan, & Buhrmester, 2001; Nickerson & Nagle, 2005; Updegraff, McHale, & Crouter, 2002). But why do youth have such an intuitive drive to connect with their peer community? Clark (2011) points out that one of the possible reasons millennial youth feel the need to bond with their peer community is that they feel cut off from the rest of society. Even though these youth are separating themselves from the adult world in order to form their own identity, they feel betrayed by the adults who are allowing them to "leave." These youth feel a tremendous need to build powerful relationships to survive in the new, uncharted pre-adult territory in which they find themselves (Clark, 2011; Delaney, 1995; Lashbrook, 2000).

The relationships youth form during this time exist in an intricate and sophisticated world—a world built as an underground society completely distinct from the world of adults (Clark, 2011). In this underground society, pop culture often serves as the secret handshake that lets the youth in, the operating language that connects them with others, and the social currency that mediates their standing in a group. A common interest in popular music, TV shows, films, Internet sites, and social networks often gives adolescents a sense of being connected to their subculture and provides social cohesion. It also helps emphasize what group a youth belongs to, and perhaps just as important, what group s/he does not belong to (Savage, Collins-Mayo, & Mayo, 2006). And because much of commercial popular culture is aimed at giving youth what *they* want (as opposed to what parents, teachers, faith leaders, and other adults want them to have), the youth who immerse themselves in these influences find themselves in control of their own socialization. They get to choose the music they will listen to, the movies they will watch, the commercials they will respond to, the messages they will internalize, and the culture they will build with their peers as a result. They are able to access popular culture as a source of information about sex, politics, religion, etc., that their parents are unwilling (or unable) to provide (Arnett, 2010). In other words, popular culture gives youth the opportunity to jump from the nest of adult-controlled socialization and fly together in a free sky of their choosing.

If popular culture is such an important socialization tool for youth, is it possible that faithFull youth who feel unsafe engaging with this culture may also find themselves pushed outside peer groups that bond over popular culture? If familiarity with pop culture is the handshake that lets youth in, are these youth left out? If the language of pop culture is the common tongue, are these youth able to engage? If pop culture savvy is the currency of social standing, where do these faithFull youth fall in the hierarchy? During a developmental stage when connecting with a friend group is not only a form of socialization, but also a (perceived) method of survival, how might faithFull youth be handicapped when they disengage from popular culture?

Because of their connection to churches and faith-based youth programming, faithFull youth often have a community of other faithFull youth that they socialize with regularly. Even so, when faithFull youth feel the need to disengage with popular culture, are there ways youth development professionals and other concerned adults can help them reap the rewards of a broader range of friendships they might be forfeiting because of their convictions?

Identity Formation

Perhaps one of the most stereotypical—and perhaps accurate—perceptions of adolescence is that it is a time when youth work to "find themselves," constantly developing an identity of their own. Noting this, the developmental psychologist Erik Erikson defined adolescence as a period when youth must examine the person they have become under their parents' influence and take responsibility for shaping themselves into the adult they want to grow into.[5] Just as adolescence is a time of pulling away *socially* from parents and connecting more intimately with peers, it may also be a time of pulling away from the *values* of parents and toward the *values* of peers, thus forming an independent identity. David Elkind (1994) argues that "identity formation requires a kind of envelope of adult standards, values and beliefs that the adolescent can confront and challenge in order to construct and test out her own standards, values and beliefs…. Today, however, adults have fewer standards, values and beliefs and hold on to them less firmly than was true in the past. The adolescent must therefore struggle to find an identity without the benefit of this supportive adult envelope" (p. 197). As youth naturally pull away from the adults in their lives, is it possible that that the common language, images, stories, and sounds of popular culture they share with their peers may provide an important "envelope of standards" they use to form their identity in their strange new adult-free world?

Of course, certain types of media may be more useful than others in this process of identity formation, or may help youth form identity in different ways. When a youth connects with the messages found in her favorite song, for example, those messages can be important for shaping identity. Interestingly, researchers have found that music holds a greater power for *reinforcing* identity than in actually *shaping* it (Savage et al., 2006). It seems that youth most readily connect with lyrics and themes that echo either their actual reality or a reality they have already imagined for themselves. They connect with music because they see themselves in the songs, and the songs reinforce the youth's growing identity. Television and film may act in a contrasting way, however. Instead of reinforcing existing self-image, the characters youth find on television and in the movies become a menagerie of potential selves they can use to model who they do and do not want to become (Savage et al., 2006). In this way, the media "provides adolescents with information that would otherwise be unavailable to them, and some of this information may be used to help construct an identity" (Arnett, 2010, p. 340).

If faithFull youth are sheltered from media that show lifestyles, values, and decision making processes foreign to their faith-culture, are they being given a full range of identities to either accept and reject? Are they being limited to an existing "envelope of adult standards"? If faithFull youth who avoid pop culture only see images that reflect the reality they currently know, are they handicapped by not being exposed to characters and storylines that might expand their sense of who they might become? By disengaging with pop culture, are they also inadvertently disengaging with a valuable identity development workshop?

Many of these faithFull youth are actively involved in their wider community. How can concerned adults in this community help them form their identity while still respecting their beliefs?

Understanding Their World

Puberty sends young people into the holding cell between childhood and adulthood. Although the young adolescent might occasionally sneak back into childish amusements, they are no longer children. And even though older teenagers might experiment with adult attitudes and lifestyles, they are not yet adults. In many ways, these youth are on their own, preparing themselves for an adult world they know looms ahead, but do not yet fully understand. If, as Clark (2011) proposes, youth perceive themselves to be abandoned by adults and thus truly on their own, what will be the textbook, language guide, or classroom that they will consult to lead them from adolescence into adulthood?

It has been proposed that popular culture (especially television and film) may "provide a rehearsal space [for youth] to engage with the complexity of life in a manageable way" (Savage et al., 2006, p. 41), and give youth a peek into what they expect the adult world must look like. Research suggests that storylines in television and film give youth an opportunity to reflect on real people, experiences, and world around them. And, when youth personally identify with the conflicts in these storylines (even when these conflicts are expressed in very unrealistic or fictionalized ways), they feel comforted by the sense that they are not alone in their problems (Savage et al., 2006). After all, if the characters youth see on television or in the movies experience the same struggles and feelings that they do, then someone (even if only a Hollywood producer) must understand their struggles. And, when youth see conflicts resolve, even in the most fictionalized and/or horrific programs, the message they receive is often a reassuring one that "no matter how dreadful things look, there is really nothing to fear" (Clark, 2005, p. 47). It seems, therefore, that popular culture (especially television, movies, and story-based media) may even give adolescents a means through which to problem solve their own conflicts. Through popular culture, youth learn from the successes, failures, and escapades of the fictional adults they emulate, and expand their worldview to better understand the ways people with diverse backgrounds (socio-economic, ethnic, religious, etc.) live, love, and deal with challenges (Savage et al., 2006).

If youth use popular culture as a venue for problem solving ways to deal with the emerging conflicts of adulthood, are faithFull youth handicapped when they do not access this resource? Is it possible that because faithFull who choose not to consume "secular" television and movies are not given the opportunity to see how people from diverse cultures, socio-economic backgrounds, and religions deal with life's dilemmas, that they have fewer role models (both positive and negative) to learn from? And, if adolescents are able to feel less alone when they personally connect with the conflicts, emotions, and relationships they see in the media, is it possible that faithFull youth my feel unnecessarily secluded—unaware that the wider world understands what they are going through?

Many faithFull youth have the benefit of being in relationship with caring pastors, youth leaders, and other adults who serve as important role models.

While respecting their boundaries, are there ways non-faith-based youth workers can expand these youths' worldview and help them learn from the lived experience of people in diverse situations and from diverse backgrounds?

Connecting to Pop Culture ... Retreating from Faith Culture

Some faithFull youth see no tension between their faith and popular culture, and happily engage in both. Others feel the expectations of their faith community require them to limit how they interact with popular culture and happily comply. It seems, though, that some faithFull youth do not respond well to being asked to limit the music they listen to, the movies they watch, the television programs they enjoy, and the personalities they emulate. They do not want to be told that they cannot watch a television program because it features a gay couple or listen to music because of the language it uses. A 2007 study by the Barna Group (a leading research group that explores the intersection of faith and culture) indicates that 36 percent of young churchgoers disparagingly call their faith "old fashioned," and 32 percent say it is "out of touch with reality" (Kinnaman & Lyons, 2007, p. 34). These youth apparently find a sheltered faith unappealing, and many of them end up leaving the church as a result. Could it be that when a faith community stands stolidly *against culture,* faithFull youth find it old fashioned and out of touch with reality?

Popular culture may, it seems, be a means through which some youth process spiritual ideas in a way that seems relevant to them. It may be a vehicle through which they engage with religiosity without committing themselves to a specific church or belief system (Collins-Mayo & Beaudoin, 2010). Some theories even suggest that youth often imbibe pop culture with religious significance, transforming it into a form of "invisible" or "implicit" religion (Savage et al., 2006). For example, these youth use the Internet to find support and form like-minded communities that they the local church lacks (Campbell, 2003). They express their beliefs through music, and use music to connect to the beliefs of others. They use the storylines in movies and television to better understand their world and workshop ethical responses to issues they face. For faithFull youth, popular culture is an important "space" where their faith is expressed and explored. When faithFull youth feel their religious tradition is "out of touch with reality" and asks them to sacrifice an important medium through which they experience religious ideas and community, they often abandon it.[6]

Faith-Based Resources ... What Are They Running From?

The purpose of this discussion is neither to defend religion nor to promote popular culture. Where a youth's development is concerned, each has both merits and downfalls. Even so, it is important for adults who serve teenagers to understand what faithFull youth may give up when they walk away from their religious community. Even though engaging in popular culture may give youth important socialization opportunities, venues for identity formation, and a means through which to better understand their world, these youth may lose equally important protective measures when they sacrifice their faith-involvement to engage with popular culture. For example, youth who frequently attend religious services and experience high levels of spiritual support report the lowest scores on the Beck Depression Inventory (Wright, Frost, & Wisecarver, 1993). Likewise, studies have shown an important negative correlation between religious identity and depression in college students (Koteskey, Little, & Matthews, 1991); and data from the 2001 National Longitudinal Study of Adolescent Health show that boys who hold a religious identity are considerably less likely to attempt suicide (Borowsky, Ireland, & Resnick, 2001). It seems, therefore, that religious involvement might be a significant protective force against both depression and suicide.

While religious involvement has been shown to support youth resilience against negative forces such as psychological and emotional distress, it also seems to promote important positive outcomes. Not only have religious youth been shown to display higher social adjustment (Mosher & Handal, 1997), they may also be more physically and psychologically healthy (Chiswick & Mirtcheva, 2013). Data from the High School Effectiveness Study indicates that faithFull youth—especially those who are "intensely religious"—hold higher educational standards for themselves and score better on standardized tests (Regnerus, 2000; Regnerus & Elder, 2003). Likewise, just as the National Study of Youth and Religion showed that religious youth are more likely to participate in non-faith-based extracurricular activities (Smith, 2005), it seems that faithFull youth are also more likely to volunteer and participate in community service projects (Trusty & Watts, 1999). In fact, nearly 74 percent of faithFull youth report that they participate in monthly community service, compared to only 25 percent of non-religious youth (Youniss, McLellan, & Yates, 1999).

Why might religion have such positive impacts on faithFull youth's physical, psychological, and social health, and why might this be an important consideration in a discussion about pop culture? The correlation is actually quite natural. While researchers theorize that religion's positive impacts may come from its *regulative mechanisms* (i.e., programs, doctrine, etc., that discourage unhealthy behavior) and/or its *spiritual mechanisms* (i.e., beliefs, rituals, etc., that give meaning to life and improve self-esteem), religion's *social mechanisms* are also an important component in its contribution to overall health. Since religious participation often takes place in group settings and promotes social relationships, religious participation is able to facilitate social development, give vehicles for family interaction, and support youth during difficult times (Chiswick & Mirtcheva, 2013; Hawe & Shiell, 2000). It seems that just as interaction with pop culture has the potential to activate positive outcomes through the community it promotes, so religion may protect against depression, promote academic success, encourage community service, and build healthier youth because of its social nature.

If youth abandon religious communities that seem "old fashioned" or too confining because they encourage disengagement from popular culture, might they be walking away from communities that also provide tremendous long-term resources? If, as research suggests, a greater involvement in religious communities yields greater psychological and physical health (Chiswick & Mirtcheva, 2013), might youth be handicapping themselves when they disengage in religious communities to satisfy their attraction to pop culture? When they disengage with these faith systems, are youth cutting themselves off from important sources of encouragement and support? In the midst of this struggle, are there ways culturally savvy adults can help discouraged youth carefully count the cost before walking away from these communities that hold such potential for support?

Conclusion

A significant subculture of youth identify as faithFull. These youth's belief systems shape more than just how they view the divine and internalize spiritual ideas. Their beliefs are also a significant part of a system of self that affect the way youth interact with the rest of his/her world. Religion challenges faithFull youth with abstract thought, gives them a sense of purpose and value, and connects them to a community of concerned adults. It shapes their family interactions, peer groups, and concept of self. It provides both protective measures (e.g., against depression and suicide) and encourages positive outcomes (e.g., school success and volunteerism). When outside influences (such as popular culture) interact, and possibly interfere, with this important system, the effects can be widespread.

What happens when faithFull youth's religious community encourages them to disengage from popular culture? When happens when popular culture becomes more attractive to them than their faith tradition? Do they lose something important when they choose either over the other? The faithFull youth affected by these questions are actively involved not only in faith communities, but also in the same non-faith-based community and school programs other youth enjoy. "FaithFull" is, therefore, an important identity marker for many (perhaps 70 percent) of the youth in our care. It is vital that adults who work with adolescents in a variety of settings be aware of how these faithFull youth are uniquely affected by the popular culture that surrounds them. Popular culture directly influences a youth's faith—sometimes supporting and enhancing it, but sometimes causing tremendous tension in their belief system, in their family system, and between them and their faith community. When youth experience this tension, they often choose to resolve it by disengaging from either pop culture or their faith culture. Given that both have the potential to give youth important developmental resources, is either a good option?

After all, faithFull youth might not need to be converted from either popular or religious culture to its counterpart, or pulled away from one so they can benefit from the other. They may instead need to be supported by caring adults who understand the tension they live in—the tension between faith and culture.

NOTES

1. A full report of this survey's findings can be found at http://youthandreligion. nd.edu/research-findings/reports/.

2. Smith (2005) reports that the top five religious groups that American youth identify with (not including the 16 percent who identify as "not religious") are:
- Christian (both Protestant and Catholic): 75 percent
- Mormon: 2.5 percent
- Jewish: 1.5 percent
- Jehovah's Witness: 0.6 percent
- Muslim: 0.5 percent

3. Exodus 20:3.

4. This idea was explored in the Christian documentary film *Hell's Bells: The Dangers of Rock 'n' Roll*, which has been used widely in evangelical youth ministries.

5. In Erickson's theory, this psychosocial stage is generally referred to as "identity vs. role confusion."

6. In his research into why young Christians are leaving the church and rethinking faith, David Kinnaman (2011) found that church-going youth report three notable dissatisfactions that drive them away from religion:
1. Christians demonize everything outside the church, implying that every non-Christian thing is "bad."
2. Christians are afraid of pop culture, especially movies and music.
3. Christians maintain a false separation of sacred and secular.

REFERENCES

Arnett, J. (2010). *Adolescence and emerging adulthood: A cultural approach* (4th ed.). Upper Saddle River, N.J.: Pearson Prentice Hall.

Bergler, T.E. (2012). *The juvenilization of American Christianity*. Grand Rapids: William B. Eerdmans.

Borowsky, Iris W., Ireland, M., and Resnick, M.D. (2001). Adolescent suicide attempts: Risks and protectors. *Pediatrics, 107,* 485–493.

Buhrmester, D., & Carbery, J. (1992, March). *Daily patterns of self-disclosure and adolescent adjustment.* Paper presented at the biennial meeting of the Society for Research on Adolescence, Washington, D.C.

Campbell, H. (2003). Approaches to religious research in computer-mediated communication. In J. Mitchell & S. Marriage (Eds.), *Mediating religion: Conversations in media, religion and culture* (pp. 185–198). London: T&T Clark.

Chiswick, B., & Mirtcheva, D. (2013). Religion and child health: Religious affiliation, importance, and attendance and health status among American youth. *Journal of Family and Economic Issues, 34*(1), 120–140.

Clark, C. (2011). *Hurt 2.0: Inside the world of today's teenagers.* Grand Rapids: Baker Academic.

Clark, L. (2005). *From angels to aliens: Teenagers, the media, and the supernatural.* Oxford: Oxford University Press.

Collins-Mayo, S., & Beaudoin, T. (2010). Religion, pop culture, and "virtual faith." In S. Collins-Mayo & P. Dandelion (Eds.), *Religion and youth* (pp. 17–23). Burlington, VT: Ashgate.

Collins-Mayo, S., & Dandelion, P. (Eds.). (2010). *Religion and youth.* Farnham, Surrey: Ashgate.

Delaney, C.H. (Winter 1995). Rites of passage in adolescence. *Adolescence, 30*(120), 891–897.

Elkind, D. (1994). *A sympathetic understanding of the child: Birth to sixteen.* Boston: Allyn & Bacon.

Erwin, P. (2010). *A critical approach to youth culture: Its influence and implications for ministry.* Grand Rapids: Zondervan.

French, D.C., Rianasari, J.M., Pidada, S., Nelwan, P., and Buhrmester, D. (2001). Social support of Indonesian and U.S. children and adolescents by family members and friends. *Merrill-Palmer Quarterly, 47,* 377–394.

Hawe, P., & Shiell, A. (2000). Social capital and health promotion: A review. *Social Science and Medicine, 51,* 871–885.

Hunter, J. D. (1992). *Culture wars: The struggle to control the family, art, education, law, and politics in America.* New York: Basic Books.

Kinnaman, D. (2011). *You lost me: Why young Christians are leaving church ... and rethinking faith.* Grand Rapids, MI: Baker Books.

Kinnaman, D., & Lyons, G. (2007). *UnChristian: What a new generation really thinks about Christianity ... and why it matters.* Grand Rapids: Baker.

Koteskey, R. L., Little, M.D., & Matthews, M.V. (1991). Adolescent identity and depression. *Journal of Psychology and Christianity, 10,* 48–53.

Larson, R. W., Moneta, G., Richards, M. H., & Wilson, S. (2002). Continuity, stability, and change in daily emotional experience across adolescence. *Child Development, 73,* 1151–1165.

Lashbrook, J. (Winter 2000). Fitting in: Exploring the emotional dimension of adolescent peer pressure. *Adolescence, 35,* 747–57.

Mosher, J. P., & Handal, P.J. (1997). The relationship between religion and psychological distress in adolescents. *Journal of Psychology and Theology, 25,* 449–457.

Mueller, W. (2006). *Engaging the soul of youth culture.* Downers Grove, IL: InterVarsity Press.

Nickerson, A. B., & Nagle, R. J. (2005). Parent and peer attachment in late childhood and early adolescence. *Journal of Early Adolescence, 25,* 223–249.

Niebuhr, H. R. (1951). *Christ and culture*. New York: Harper & Brothers.

Powell, F. (2014, June 25). 10 reasons churches are not reaching millennials. Retrieved November 18, 2014, from http://frankpowell.me/ten-reasons-church-absent-millennials/.

Regnerus, M. (2000). Shaping schooling success: A multi-level study of religious socialization and educational outcomes in urban public schools. *Journal for the Scientific Study of Religion, 39*, 363–370.

Regnerus, M. (2003). Religion and positive adolescent outcomes: A review of research and theory. *Review of Religious Research, 44*(4), 394–413.

Regnerus, M., & Elder, G. (2003). Staying on track in school: Religious influences in high and low risk settings. *Journal for the Scientific Study of Religion, 42*(4), 633–649.

Romanowski, W. (2012, April). Gotta cut loose: Youth culture and entertainment media. Retrieved November 21, 2014, from http://www.ptsem.edu/lectures/?action=tei&id=youth-2012-04.

Savage, S., Collins-Mayo, S., Mayo, B., & Cray, G. (2006). *Making sense of generation y: The world view of 15-25-year-olds*. London: Church House.

Smith, C. (2005). *Soul searching: The religions and spiritual lives of American teenagers*. Oxford: Oxford University Press.

Steele, J.R., & Brown, J.D. (1995). Adolescent room culture: Studying media in the context of everyday life. *Journal of Youth & Adolescence, 24*, 551–576.

Trusty, J., & Watts, R.E. (1999). Relationship of high school seniors' religious perceptions and behavior to educational, career, and leisure variables. *Counseling & Values, 44*, 30–40.

Updegraff, K. A., McHale, S. M., & Crouter, A. (2002). Adolescents' sibling relationship and friendship experiences: Developmental patterns and relationship linkages. *Social Development, 11*, 182–204.

Wright, L.S., Frost, C.J., & Wisecarver, S.J. (1993). Church attendance, meaningfulness of religion, and depressive symptomatology among adolescents. *Journal of Youth and Adolescence, 22*, 559–568.

Youniss, J., McLellan, J.A., & Yates, M. (1999). Religion, community service, and identity in American youth." *Journal of Adolescence, 22*, 243–253.

Body Art Among Transgender Youth

Marking Social Support, Reclaiming the Body and Creating a Narrative of Identity

JENIFER K. MCGUIRE
and ALISON CHRISLER

In the past 50 years, tattooing and piercing, often referred to as "body art," has gone through a transformation or "renaissance" (Rubin, 1988). During the 1980s and 1990s, body art became more artistic and the practice broadened from marginalized populations to readily include adolescents and young adults, as well as women and middle-class individuals (Adams, 2009; Armstrong, Koch, Saunders, Roberts, & Owen, 2007; Armstrong, Owen, Roberts, & Koch, 2002; Atkinson, 2002; Deci, 2005; Irwin, 2001; Rubin, 1988). Tattoos and body piercings are most often completed by a professional and require parental consent if the individual is under the age of 18 years. When youth are unable to obtain such consent, they may receive body piercings or tattoos, referred to as "stick and poke," from peers or even complete it themselves (Armstrong & Murphy, 1997). Another form of body art, "scarification," refers to when designs are cut or burned into the skin. Because stick and poke and scarification are completed by an inexperienced and unlicensed professional, these forms of body art are often perceived as being more risky than tattoos or body piercings obtained in a tattoo parlor.

When asked about obtaining body art, youth provide a variety of reasons. Self-expression is most commonly reported (Armstrong & Murphy, 1997; Ferreira, 2009; Gold, Schorzman, Murray, Downs, & Tolentino, 2005; Kang & Jones, 2007), while other reasons include wanting to obtain a "beauty mark" (Deschesnes, Demers, & Fines, 2006); wanting to be unique (Kang & Jones, 2007; Preti et al., 2006); a way to cope with past trauma (Preti et al., 2006); wanting to commemorate a past event (Irwin, 2001; Kang & Jones, 2007); and a way to gain or maintain group membership or social bonds (Kang & Jones, 2007; Silver, VanEseltine, & Silver, 2009).

Tattooing and piercing also communicate gender messages (Adams, 2009; Deschesnes, Demers et al., 2006). For example, piercings tend to be more common among females; whereas, tattoos are more prevalent among males (Antoszewski, Sitek, Fijalkowska, Kasielska, & Kruk-Jeromin, 2010; Armstrong, Roberts, Owen, & Koch, 2004a). As a result, some women acquire tattoos as a way to defy gender expectations and male dominance and assert more independence (Adams, 2009; Kang & Jones, 2007; Makkai & McAllister, 2001; Riley & Cahill, 2005). When considering differences among race/ethnicity and socioeconomic status, adolescents from low-income families are more likely to acquire tattoos when compared to peers from higher-income families (Silver et al., 2009). Additionally, black and Hispanic youth are also more likely to obtain a tattoo when compared to their White and Asian counterparts (Silver et al., 2009). Within queer culture, body art among all genders is about double that of the general population (Sever, 2003). In the following section, we provide an overview of the body art literature. First, we outline the risks associated with body art and then examine how a resiliency framework has been used to examine body art.

Overview of Body Art Literature

Risks Associated with Body Art

Much of the body art literature focuses on the health aspects of tattooing and piercing, primarily the risks associated with obtaining body art. The physical risks often associated with body art are infections at the site and contracting an infectious disease, such as hepatitis B and C (Cetta, Graham, Lichtenberg, & Warnes, 1999; Chismark, 2013; Deci, 2005; Griffith & Tengnah, 2005; Koch, Roberts, Cannon, Armstrong, & Owen, 2005; Larzo & Poe, 2006). Common complications include skin irritation for piercing and bleeding for tattoos (Armstrong & Murphy, 1997; Armstrong et al., 2004a). Often, adolescents and young adults do not consider the health risks associated with body art (Carroll & Anderson, 2002; Huxley & Grogan, 2005). Additionally, males tend to be less knowledgeable of infection diseases related to body art when compared to their female counterparts (Cegolon et al., 2010; King & Vidourek, 2007).

The vast majority of research on tattoos, especially those among young people, have framed tattooing as a risk behavior and correlated it with other risk behaviors. Having a tattoo has been correlated in research studies with alcohol use (Braithwaite, Robillard, Woodring, Stephens, & Arriola, 2001; Brooks, Woods, Knight, & Shrier, 2003; Ekinici et al., 2012; Roberts, Auinger, & Ryan, 2004; Roberts & Ryan, 2002); cigarette smoking (Ekinici et al., 2012; Roberts et al., 2004; Roberts & Ryan, 2002); illicit drug use (Braithwaite et al., 2001; Brooks et al., 2003; Carroll, Riffenburgh, Roberts, & Myhre, 2002; Deschesnes, Fines, & Demers, 2006; Ekinici et al., 2012; Roberts et al., 2004; Roberts & Ryan, 2002); increased and/or unsafe sexual activity (Carroll et al., 2002; Roberts & Ryan, 2002); poor academic achievement (Ekinici et al., 2012; Roberts & Ryan, 2002; Silver, Silver, Siennick, & Farkas, 2011); disordered eating (Carroll et al., 2002); and suicidality (Carroll et al., 2002; Roberts et al., 2004). Tattoos and/or piercings among adolescents have also been linked to deviant behavior (Silver et al., 2011); self-perception of riskiness (Armstrong & Murphy, 1997); and impulsivity (Gunter & McDowell, 2004). Some researchers argue that tattooing among youth is frequently impulsive and leads to regret and future removal of body art (Benjamins et al., 2006; Houghton, Durkin, Parry, Turbett, & Odgers, 1996). Though there appears to be a vast amount of literature that focuses on the risk associated with body art, researchers have begun to investigate the positive aspects of body art.

Resiliency Associated with Body Art

An emerging body of literature focuses on how body art can be used to demonstrate resiliency. Though some researchers argue that impulsivity often accompanies the acquirement of body art (Fisher, 2002; Gunter & McDowell, 2004; Manuel & Sheehan, 2007), others have examined the intentionality of body art (Armstrong et al., 2004a; Forbes, 2001; Koch et al., 2005) and how body art can also be used to reclaim the body (Hicks, 2005; Kang & Jones, 2007). The most common resiliency process associated with body art focuses on identity development. For some individuals, they use their body as a "canvas" to communicate to others their identities and personal transformations (Kang & Jones, 2007; Riley & Cahill, 2005; Schildkrout, 2004; Selekman, 2003). For lesbian, gay, bisexual, and transgender (LGBTQ) persons, elements of resiliency, such as social support, emotional openness, and future orientation, support individuals in reducing reactivity to prejudice (Kwon, 2013). It is possible that for some youth, body art serves as a mechanism to display and/ or promote these resilient processes. For instance, using a tattoo to mark an identity helps communicate to others with that identity, thereby increasing opportunities for like-minded social contacts.

Intentionality. The motivations behind tattooing are much more than just acting in an impulsive nature; rather, individuals who decide to get a tattoo or piercing are deliberate and report having spent time planning the tattoo design (Armstrong et al., 2004a; Caliendo, Armstrong, & Roberts, 2005; Forbes, 2001; Koch et al., 2005). After careful consideration, some individuals may decide against obtaining body art. Such reasons may include not knowing what the tattoo will look like when they are older, not wanting a permanent marking, cost, contracting an infectious disease, parental disapproval, and pain (Armstrong & Murphy, 1997; Armstrong et al., 2004a; Forbes, 2001). For some individuals, religious beliefs may prevent them from obtaining body art (Armstrong et al., 2004a), while for others, non-affiliation with a religious organization may increase the likelihood of obtaining body art (Laumann & Derick, 2006; Stirn, Hinz, & Brahler, 2006). Thus, choosing to get a tattoo (or not) can be both an intentional and thoughtful act that reflects the personal beliefs of the individual.

Reclaiming the body. A more qualitative analyses of body art has begun to reveal tattooing as a means to reclaim the body in psychological and physical ways from an event that was seen as an assault on the body (Kang & Jones, 2007). From this perspective, the human body can be viewed as an aesthetic construction of the everyday mundane world (Hicks, 2005). To create this aesthetic, the human body is a resource rather than a destiny (Rich, 1976). Breast cancer survivors have reported using tattoos as a way to reclaim their chest after radical mastectomy (Mifflin, 1997), but also as a way to promote a more realistic looking reconstruction (Kiernan, 2014). Women have also reported tattoo use as a means of recovery from sexual assault (Kang & Jones, 2007). Youth report using tattoos as "a provocative symbol of their right to do as they please with their own bodies" (Hicks, 2005, p. 6), but also as vehicle to mark adulthood, define social connections, and mark transitions (Kang & Jones, 2007). Finally, tattoos and the act of getting it can serve as spiritual experiences and metamorphic rites (Kang & Jones, 2007). They are tools to counter the body dissociation associated with trauma or even transition.

Identity. For adolescents, obtaining body art is a way to gain control and certainty during a time when they feel their world around them is constantly changing (Kang & Jones, 2007; Koch et al., 2005; Selekman, 2003). Tattoos are also a way for adolescents to create a visual narrative of their lived experiences (Atkinson, 2002; Selekman, 2003). For example, in one study, an individual explained how her tattoo (an image of a Pegasus with spread wings on its hind legs) communicated to others her ability to become more confident after breaking away from the self-hatred she had for her body (Kang & Jones, 2007). Interestingly enough, researchers have also found that as individuals experience personal growth, the interpretations of their body art change as well (Kang & Jones, 2007; Springgay, 2003).

Many researchers have found body art to be associated with positive self-ratings of image and identity (Koch, Roberts, Armstrong, & Owen, 2010; Swami, 2011; Tate & Shelton, 2008). Similarly, individuals with tattoos perceive themselves as being "more creative, artistic, and adventurous" (Drews, Allison, & Probst, 2000, p. 480). In other studies, body art has been associated with lower ratings of anxiety, depression, conformity, and impulsivity, as well as higher ratings of body appreciation, attractiveness, autonomy, self-esteem, and uniqueness or need for uniqueness (Drews et al., 2000; Forbes, 2001; Iannaccone et al., 2013; Manuel & Sheehan, 2007; Swami, 2011; Tate & Shelton, 2008; Tiggemann & Golder, 2006; Tiggemann & Hopkins, 2011).

Although body art is now widely accepted among a variety of social groups, it retains its status as a marker of cultural identity among queer identified youth. Even among queer youth, sub-groups such as transgender youth develop norms and practices around body art and modification that both mark a cultural group membership and serve resilient functions for personal identity development. Conceptually, there are a variety of lenses through which to examine body art. In this essay, we use a queer cultural lens to examine the queer elements that emerge from the image of the body art and the act of getting the tattoo. Additionally, we root our interpretations in a resiliency framework, focusing on how transgender youth use body art to create meaning out of ambiguity.

Theoretical Underpinnings

The notion of applying a queer lens to culture and society was cultivated and described by Eve Sedgewick (1985, 1990) who argued for the examination of the potential queer nuances in literature. We apply her ideas to body art, both in examining the potential queer elements of the image of body art, but also in the process and reason for obtaining the body art.

Eve Sedgewick focused on the use of words rather than images or body art, but her message to examine the potential queer nuances of literature provides context for an examination of body art as well. When we examine body art, we consider the elements of the art, both the image and the process of obtaining it and how it reveals a queer identity or concept. A complementary queer theoretical approach, espoused by Judith Butler (1990), describes the performance of gender as opposed to the essential (inborn) nature of gender. These concepts have particular relevance for those who are gender nonconforming or seek to alter or switch their gender identity as the process of gender change involves both internal identity-based processes of understanding one's essential gender, as well as outward process of altering the way one presents oneself. In Butler's philosophy, gender is created through its performance. In the consideration of body art, body art for transpersons can serve both performativity and essentialist functions. For instance, tattoos may be used to mark an identity that an individual may experience as essentially derived. On the other hand, use of body art can create an image that in itself performs and establishes a gender expression.

In our analyses of transgender youth's body art, we incorporate these multiple perspectives and focus our interpretation on the narrative created upon the body by transgender youth. In her theory of ambiguous loss, Boss (1999) describes the need to make meaning out of chaos and the use of narrative as a tool to create meaning. Over and over again, young people in this study described their body art as documentation of their changing relationships with their physical and psychological selves. In her work, Boss describes strategies for resiliency when dealing with ambiguous changes (losses).

Boss frames the ambiguity through distinction of physical and psychological presence, with an unknown outcome or process in one of those dimensions. In the case of a person in gender transition, the changes definitely take an ambiguous form. That is, changes in both the physical and psychological self are likely to accompany any kind of gender transition, and their process and outcome is often unknown or unclear, regardless of whether or not specific medical interventions occur. Physically, a person may change in their outward expression using things like hairstyle, clothing, or makeup. They may make semi or permanent body modifications with things like piercings, tattoos, or other body art, and they may make medically supported changes through hormones or surgery. Psychologically, a person may change the gender roles they take in interactions (e.g., speaking first or loudly), use different pronouns, and display social characteristics of the experienced gender (e.g., competitiveness, nurturance).

Boss describes a resilient response to ambiguity to involve meaning-making. One process of meaning-making is to create a narrative from chaos. It is this aspect of meaning-making, we focus most closely on in our analyses of transgender youths' descriptions of their own body art. When considering body art, there is a need to consider both the content of the art, as well as the process of obtaining it. We asked youth to explain their body art and to give any context to the meanings it had for them. In this process, most described when and how they got the body art and their plans for future body art. It was the planful and thoughtful process of obtaining body art, coupled with the clear meanings for marking identity and documenting a narrative that compelled us to use a resiliency-based framework in analyzing youths' body art descriptions.

Method

Participants

Data analyzed for this study are pulled from a larger study of wellbeing among transgender-identified youth. The larger sample consisted of a total of 90 transgender participants from eight different cities in United States, as well as young people from Ireland and Canada (respectively 83 percent, 11 percent, and 6 percent from each country). Assigned genders at birth were reported to be 42.2 percent male and 57.8 percent female. Participants currently identified as male (F-M; 30 percent), female (M-F; 34 percent), third gender (32 percent), or same as natal sex (4 percent). About half of the participants described themselves as gender queer, whether or not they also retained a binary gender identification.

Participants ranged in age from 15–30 ($M = 22.56$; $SD = 2.9$), although only two were over age 26 and seven were under 18 years of age. Overall, the study was ethnically and culturally diverse. From the United States, 54 percent of participants were White, 14 percent Latino/Hispanic, 11 percent African American, 7 percent Native American, 6 percent Asian, and 8 percent another ethnic/racial background. All of the youth from Canada and Ireland identified as Caucasian.

Procedures

We recruited through LGBTQ youth centers, trans-advocacy organizations, a website, and the use of email listservs. We visited support groups and worked with center staff and community organizers to identify potential participants, with an eye for diversifying the range of participants. Participants were compensated 20 U.S. or Canadian dollars or 15 Euros to for their time and inconvenience.

The Institutional Review Board of Washington State University provided approval for the study and questionnaire prior to any of the interviews. Participants used a pseudo name, and identifying information was never collected. Participants answered questions about variety of topics including family, body image, religion, mental health, and community involvement. This study represents a coding of the responses regarding body art. Interviews were recorded and transcribed, then coded using Nvivo and open coding procedures.

Coding Procedures

Each interview was reviewed for references to body art and tattoos, both in response to that specific question, as well as throughout the interview. Relevant portions were cut into separate documents and imported into Nvivo as a distinct body art dataset. Open coding procedures were used. We identified conceptual categories and linkages among them (Braun & Clarke, 2006; Strauss & Corbin, 1990). Once the categories were established, we coded each idea segment in Nvivo and computed a Kappa on a subset of participants to confirm inter-rater reliability (Hruschka et al., 2004; Kuper, Coleman, & Mustanski, 2013). If Kappa was below .95, the idea segments were discussed and recoded until reaching 99 percent reliability.

Results

In this study, participants were asked about their body art, such as a tattoo, piercing (not including single ear piercing), stick and poke, and/or scarification. About one-third were not asked this question, as the body art question was added after several participants spontaneously discussed the meaning of their body art. Another 24 of the participants (27 percent) did not have any type of body art beyond simple ear piercing. However, 36 youth reported having some form of body art. Thirty of the participants (33 percent) reported a tattoo(s), and 23 youth (26 percent) had scarification or piercing(s), including piercings that were recently closed up. Seventeen participants (19 percent) had both piercing(s) and tattoo(s). Participants were asked by the interviewer to discuss their body art and whether it had any relationship with their gender and/or transition status.

In analyzing the body art descriptions of participants, we apply a queer lens to an activity that has long been viewed as counter-cultural, risk motivated, and/or impulsive. We examine body art as markers of resilience among youth and an effort to reclaim a body that has in many cases been the source of incongruence between one's psychological sense of self and the perceptions that others have. We begin with a documentation of the limited (albeit still present) nature of risk and impulse as factors in contributing to body art for trans* youth. We then examine resilience through pathways, such as social support, reclaiming the body, and using the body to create a narrative of the gender experience.

Risk

Adolescent risk-taking. A risk perspective is by far the most-developed lens taken on adolescent and young adult body art. Our participants did describe some elements of risk (n=9), such as "liking the feeling of getting pierced." Consistent with the research on body art as beautification (Claes,

Vandereycken, & Vertommen, 2005; Forbes, 2001), seven youth described their body art as "beautiful," "sexy," or "the prettiest part of me." Several also described elements of adolescent development that seemed unrelated to gender such as "I love the ocean" or "I play music." It was quickly obvious that a risk perspective with this population would yield a shallow and incomplete examination of the complicated nature of body modification through art among transgender youth. In this section, we touch on the elements of risk raised by our participants and work to frame the context of the body art in an effort to better understand potential risk-seeking motives.

Self-made body modification. Four participants discussed their "do it yourself" tattoos, often referred to as stick and poke. Two participants merely stated they had a stick and poke tattoo with little explanation as to why they performed it themselves. Another teen stated that she used to give herself piercings. When reflecting on that experience, she said, "I don't think it was a good idea. I was never successful in giving myself piercings" (River, 24, White, Male-Feminine). Though stick and poke tattoos are often done by adolescents because they may be unable to obtain parental consent to purchase a tattoo at a parlor (Armstrong & Murphy, 1997) or may not have the resources to pay for a trained tattoo artist. Cost and parental consent were not mentioned as factors in the use of stick and poke methods in this sample, and both participants with stick and poke were over 18 when they did it. In both cases, stick and poke tattoos, much like the artist created tattoos in the rest of the sample, were described as markers of social relationships and identity. One youth said that a few weeks after she turned 18, she got a stick and poke tattoo as a way for she and her friend to be with one another no matter the distance. Another participant created a stick and poke of a trans symbol at the age of 18. Why adolescents chose this method is certainly worth further explanation, but in these cases did not seem to be due to the most typically cited reasons of lack of parental consent or lack of finances. In the sample, a large number of youth also described engaging in self-injury behaviors such as cutting. Links between self-injury and self-made tattoos or piercings bear further exploration in the research because of their common feature of self-inflicted breaking of the skin.

Regret. Only three of the participants discussed how they regretted their body art, largely because of the meaning or the circumstances of obtaining it. Being under the influence of substances when getting a tattoo was one risk-based reason for regretting a tattoo named by a couple of participants that is consistent with the risk-based literature (Varma & Lanigan, 1999). For example, one participant said, "Um, so I got that one and then I have a gecko that's on my butt and that was a bad drunk decision" (Thaloneous Hughes, 21, Native American, Female-Masculine).

Research suggests people shift the meaning behind body art as their identities change (Kang & Jones, 2007; Springgay, 2003). One participant contradicted this sentiment when voicing her regret: "Uhm, yeah, but I regret all of those meanings" (Clark Kent, 23, White, Female-Male). However, several other youth described developing new meanings for old body art or modifying images to represent new identities that still incorporate the identity represented when the image was first created. For instance, one youth had a "Jesus fish" tattoo that no longer represented his religious worldviews (Thaloneous Hughes, 21, Native American, Female-Masculine). Instead of voicing regret, he planned to build upon it, incorporating other religious traditions that had developed more meaning for him over time.

Risk-taking as an underlying process was evident in some participants. However, it was neither pervasive nor common in the sample. Based on participant responses, two elements of risk-taking may be worth further exploration specifically among transgender youth. The first area of exploration should consider links between self-injury and self-made body art. The second area of exploration should explore transgender youth's capacity for reframing the meaning of body art obtained prior to initiating transition.

Resilience

For most of the youth in the sample, descriptions of body art were framed as markers of resilience processes. Youth described tattoos as a way to mark and solidify social relationships, build and communicate personal identity, and make meaning through a narrative of the transition.

Social support. Social support is an integral part of resilience. People who are embedded in a supportive environment report greater capacity to recover from setbacks (Egeland, Carlson, & Sroufe, 1993). Tattoos were described as a way to solidify social relationships, communicate membership in a group, or invite social connections with others regarding shared interests or identities. Relationships and social support are well established in research as among the most significant of resilience processes (Walsh, 2006). The capacity to develop and maintain supportive social relationships is among the most protective of capacities that youth can access to overcome difficulties encountered as byproducts of the process of gender identity transition. Body art was a way of remaining connected to peers or loved ones who had died (Firmin, Tse, Foster, & Angelini, 2008; Martin, 2000). It also served as a way to designate intimacy. In this section, we describe tattoos as markers of specific social relationships with known relationships as opposed to markers of an identity status (like queer or trans*) that we discuss later in the identity section.

Social group. Of the 30 participants with tattoos, five adolescents discussed how their social or peer group influenced their decision to get body art (Adams, 2009; Armstrong, Roberts, Owen, & Koch, 2004b; Koch et al., 2005). For example, one youth said, "My close friends at the time, we all got a lightning bolt to mean that we have the power to do anything in our—close to our, like, at hand kind of thing" (Turbo, 21, White, Female-Feminine). Two youth discussed getting body art to remain connected to a peer, while another youth pointed out that his tattoo was the handwriting of a friend who had died. Tattoos as memorials to persons who died offer a sense of permanence (Martin, 2000) and can be a source of resilience for those mourning the loss of a loved one.

Another teen discussed how coincidentally he and his childhood friend got the same tattoo:

> I think this is my favorite one, the pinky promise. Just me and a really close friend of mine both got it done. But the thing was we got it done at the same time in different states without knowing we were doing it. It's really weird. We kind of freaked out about it. But we both did it for the same reason—kind of just a reminder of childhood and how important that was. It really meant a lot to make a pinky promise as a kid, like you can't break it! Kind of a call back to the innocence of that time [Dylan, 21, Native American, Female-Third Gender].

In this example, the participant discussed how the tattoo evoked memories of their long-standing friendship.

Partners. Two youth discussed getting a tattoo with their romantic partners. For example, one teen discussed how he and his partner got a tattoo together to celebrate their one-year anniversary. Rather than get their names written on one another, the teen said:

> I convinced him for us to both to get the equality symbol in the same place. I was like, you know, we can get a similar tattoo in the same place so that maybe if we don't last or if, you know, things are bad or if we are having conflict, you won't look and be like fuck him because his name is on me. But I mean it represents equality it represents something good, I mean, it's ... it's a positive thing [Jason, 23, White, Male-Third Gender].

Though this represents positivity in a relationship, another youth discussed that when he got his tattoo, he was in a relationship that was not going well. He recalls how the relationship "pretty much changed who I was and who she was. Really horrible. I was initially going to get a different tattoo but I was like no I want those words right there" (Dylan, 21, Native American, Female-Third Gender). As evidenced by the literature, tattooing is a way to commemorate both good times and bad times (Irwin, 2001; Kang & Jones, 2007).

Family. Five youth discussed how their families influenced the design of their body art. Three youth got tattoos of their parents' names and of those three, one youth said he and his brother got the tattoo together to commemorate the death of their father (Firmin et al., 2008; Martin, 2000). Two youth discussed how their tattoos reminded them of their childhood. For example, one teen said that he has his home state on his foot. Another adolescent said the reason he has a ginkgo leaf tattoo is because it is his grandmother's favorite tree.

In all of these cases, tattoos provided a physical marker of a tangible relationship and gave a focal point to permanently link individuals over time. Most of the tattoos described as linked to social relationships did not also incorporate queer identity content, although some were designating links in queer relationships or utilizing queer symbolism. Family member tattoos are especially poignant among transgender youth because so many youth report family rejection, thus enhancing the relational value of an accepting family. For a trans* youth to create a permanent marker of this bond signifies a rare degree of family connectedness, that is empirically shown to be protective (Ryan, 2009).

Reclaiming the Body

One element of developing a strong identity includes a sense of psychological ownership of one's body. This is especially relevant in the case of transgender youth, who by definition experience some incongruence between the sex they were assigned (based on their body) and the gender they feel most closely represents their true self. For many, the body is a source of dysphoria and self-hatred. Body art is one element of reclaiming a body that does not fundamentally reflect the gender the participant most identifies with. One participant eloquently explained:

> My tattoos help me, or at least in the way I see them, help me reclaim my body in a way I feel I haven't been given the opportunity. I feel a lot of people have been born into their bodies and feel comfortable in them, I feel my tattoos are me taking my body back from the image this world had for my body and making it into my own and kind of beautifying myself that way [Jax, 21, White, Female-Masculine].

Although many participants described beginning medical transition therapies (e.g., hormones) as associated with "a new sense of, uhm, just feeling okay with my body not feeling that huge disconnect" (Girlfriend, 30, White, Male-Female), others acknowledge the limits of those treatments and how body art can mitigate the gap. Another participant explained body art as "my way reclaiming my body" (Casey, 24, White, Male-Feminine). The participant went on to say the following:

> I do not have a lot of power to mold my body into what I want but I can with tattoos. I can decorate my body how I want to. It lets me take on meaning that I want instead of what people see.

Within the context of body reclaiming, participants described the territorial value of body art for asserting ownership or control over the body, as well as the pragmatic functionality of body art for shaping and artistically enhancing vestiges of the sex transition process, such as surgical scars on the chest.

Asserting ownership and control. A number of participants (n=7) specifically described the notion of taking ownership or controlling the body with body art as a counterpoint to the lack of body control they have around gender and sex. Body art was described as something "I can control about my body." One transgender male said the following:

> The tattoos and stuff that is very much about me being able to take ownership over my body. So being able to like see tattoos or scars on my body and be able to like have a sense of who I was, or where I have been, at that time is really important to me [Justin, 26, White, Female-Third Gender].

For some, the expression of body ownership extended to things that "aren't even necessarily gender-related but I think they have helped me to own my body more in a sense. So that's good" (Ray, 22, White, Female-Masculine). Another youth discussed how having tattooed forearms communicates to others that "you know, like, I don't want anyone to touch my forearms ever. Ever!" (Dee, 25, White, Female-Masculine). Another participant explained how his tattoo served as a reminder that he owned his body:

> It's a song lyric, and it was this reminder that like the way that I own my body and the way I survive is by owning my body, I have to do that in order to survive. And tattooing is this really positive way to do that so to get this tattooed on there was really good [Justin, 26, White, Female-Third Gender].

The concept of body ownership has unique relevance for people with gender incongruence. In the sample, many participants reported dissociation from their bodies, specifically around body elements that may reveal assigned gender like body shape, shoulders, or hand size (McGuire, Doty, Catalpa, & Ola, under review). Body art appeared, at least for some, to be a way to take ownership over some elements of the body, in counterpoint to the many things that cannot be controlled in the body.

Covering or reshaping surgical scars. For some (n=3), body reclaiming took a very pragmatic form, and body art was used as a way to cover or reshape surgical scars associated with gender reassignment surgeries, especially on the chest. For example, one participant covered a hysterectomy scar with a tattoo. Another participant explained his reasoning for getting a chest tattoo:

> A lot of my dysphoria was around my chest and so now that I don't have to deal with that anymore. I actually just completed a really big chest piece tattoo, it feels really good, I feel really good about my body [Jax, 21, White, Female-Masculine].

Finally, piercings can be used to complement surgical approaches and create visual effects (see Cameron, 1996 for photographic examples) with surface or skin level foci:

> I got my nipples pierced for my one year on T [testosterone] anniversary. It was actually after my top surgery and I don't know what happened it healed weird, one of my nipples was kind of funky and inverted so it was very much to fix that, which helped a lot and then also doing something physical to commemorate the one year anniversary [Todd, 23, White, Female-Masculine].

In this way, the body art becomes a part of the physical transition, turning what otherwise may look like surgical wounds or scars into a self-determined artwork.

Narrative of Identity

One of the most profound themes to emerge from the data suggested a form of meaning-making that involved using body art to create a narrative of the evolving gender identity. The process of transition can be lengthy, taking a minimum of one to two years. For this sample, youth's transitions were co-occurring with late adolescent and young adult body changes that are dramatic on their own, such as solidification of a more masculine or feminine shape, weight gain, entrenchment of adult body hair distribution and density. Adding cross-sex hormones to this mix can contribute to a physical and psychological experience that may feel chaotic and difficult to control. Many transgender persons describe the experience of first taking cross-sex hormones as "like a second puberty." For this sample, most of them were within ten years of the onset of their first puberty. Very few of this sample (n=3) had access to puberty suppression, which is more commonly prescribed for younger teens and among youth with a higher socio-economic status than this sample (this is especially true in the United States, wherein health policies typically do not cover puberty suppression). For these participants, response to increased cross-sex hormones existed within the context of a body that was still in recalibration from the influx of increases in naturally occurring sex hormones. Physical and psychological responses to cross-sex hormones are documented in the literature. In this section, we focus on the use of body art as a tool of meaning-making regarding the physical and psychological transition. Getting tattoos was described as a process intertwined with the developing gender identity. Several participants had multiple tattoos, each representing another element of the transition (e.g., coming out, starting hormones). Others used tattoos as ways to remake or in some cases, cover elements of identity that had been altered or abandoned (e.g., old religious symbols, representations of a prior gender expression). Finally, the content of tattoos was often carefully selected to represent either literally or metaphorically a transgender persons status.

Marking the (anticipated) journey. Tattoos and piercings as markers of the process of gender transition were quite common and a major theme for almost all of the youth with body art. One youth explained, "I thought this is a way I can ... kind of mark my journey" (Jason, 23, White, Male-Third Gender). One participant described her multiple tattoos and the point at which she obtained each one:

> The first is a phoenix for rebirth at the beginning of my transition. The second is a yin-yang to symbolize balance. It is a symbol of duality and forms of strength. It spoke to me and told me I needed it because it encompassed the duality of masculine and feminine. I am experimenting more with queer and got the third tattoo- a coyote, shape shifter for metamorphosis [Casey, 24, White, Male-Feminine].

Another youth concurred with the meaning of tattoos in relation to the transition timeline by stating, "I guess this one kind of is because, uh, I got that one when I was quite young, so it was kind of when I discovered myself [my trans status] first" (Clark Kent, 23, White, Female-Male). One youth marked the date of legal name change with a tattoo, while another youth described the redefinition of her prior name tattooed on one arm:

> I have one tattoo of my name. Um, it's on my arm, it was the first tattoo I got. It kind of like reminds me who I am at times. Some people ask me who is that on your arm? You got your boyfriend's name on your arm and I be like, yeah, my boyfriend, he died [Layla, 24, African American, Male-Third Gender].

Five youth discussed waiting to get a tattoo or obtaining additional tattoos until they had taken certain steps in their transition process. For example, one teen said, "I would like to be covered in ink. Especially once, once I can get on hormones and my body fat repositions, that's when I really want to start getting tattooed" (Emma, 24, White, Male-Feminine). Another teen echoed a similar sentiment, discussing how she wanted a half-sleeve tattoo "as soon as I lose a little bit of weight and stuff" (Maggie, 24, Other, Male-Third Gender), while another teen talked about waiting to get more tattoos once starting "hormones cuz I know that my muscle mass will get bigger and I'm scared whatever tattoos I'll have, I'll get now it'll stretch out" (Habib, 18, White, Female-Masculine). One teen discussed how she wanted to get a tattoo of a fairy because "is has to do with becoming more feminine" (Mirror, 18, Native American, Male-Feminine).

Remaking the meaning of old symbols. Body art was a way to express gender and create a new meaning from prior elements of life. For example, one youth reflected on an old tattoo of her prior name:

> I like having a reminder of having my name changed to be my chosen name, that's kinda like my tattoo of that time and reminding myself of what it means to be, or what I feel like when it comes to being transgender [Dana West, 24, White, Female-Third Gender].

Other youth discussed how their body art emphasized their gender expression. A couple of youth discussed how their body art reminded themselves of their past. For example, one teen said, "I did get this one, it was my first tattoo, and it is an old lesbian sign. And when I got it, I was like, I know it's not going to be a way that I identify as forever and I want myself to remember that it has been a really important part of my life" (Batboy, 23, White, Female-Third Gender). Another youth discussed his scarification by saying, "I experienced a lot of uh physical abuse as a child and earlier this year uh I was in a situation where um memories of that were very strongly triggered for me" (Chuck, 24, White, Female-Masculine). Though scarification is commonly viewed as a risk behavior, for Chuck, etching the Hebrew word "hesed," which means love and kindness, into his chest and arm was a way to cope with his past trauma. When reflecting on his past experiences, Chuck remarked on how these experiences made him want to be "kinder to people" and helped him realize "how incredibly fragile people can be."

Two youth foresaw getting future tattoos to cover up a "janky" tattoo, while another teen discussed wanting to get additional tattoos on his foot such as "a star of David and some other religious symbols near it like the Islamic moon and stuff so that it's more like all encompassing" rather than just having a "Jesus-fish" on his foot (Thaloneous Hughes, 21, Native American, Female-Masculine). For this youth, he got a "Jesus-fish" on his foot when he was young. However, now he feels it does not fully encompass his identity so making modifications would more clearly communicate his religious identity.

Designation of status. Tattoos served as markers of the duality of transgender lives. The markers often took the form of animals associated with mythical transformations (e.g., chameleon, phoenix, coyote, octopus, Japanese fox) or spiritual symbols that represent duality (e.g., yin-yang, two-spirit figures). One participant described the process of defining and artistically representing the duality of gender queer identity:

So I kind of like just talked through with the artist the things about a um, a female identity that I kind of gravitated towards and enjoyed. Um ... and the things about the masculine or male identity that I kind of, you know, gravitated towards or enjoyed. And then I just gave him a picture of me and just asked him to draw me as my two-spirits [Jason, 23, White, Male-Third Gender].

Three participants had chosen the phoenix, a mythical creature who rises from its own ashes, as the basis for pieces of body art. Some had elements of the phoenix spread across the body, others had a phoenix embedded in other pieces of art, and a couple had a single phoenix somewhere on their body. Some described tattoos that incorporated self-reflection about how they had one view of themselves in stark contrast to others' view of them (e.g., shape-shifters, symbols embedded or hidden within pictures). For example, one participant said, "I really identify with the phoenix 'cause it's like, no matter what happens, you can always ... reborn-rebirth yourself" (Emily, 22, White, Female-Third Gender). Another participant said the following:

> I can imagine the man in the bear hat saying, 'I'm a bear" and everybody hearing, "You're a man in a bear hat" and everybody hearing that the other thing is actually a bear. Like the sort of essentialist versus constructionist embodied in a strange art piece [Rain, 22, Latino, Female-Masculine].

Another participant reflected on the imagery associated with an octopus:

> For me it's just a [symbol] of my own life. I mean, just signifies my own.... I guess ... the octopus is a very ... dynamic creature, it has chameleon like properties, it can change color, camouflage and all that and really that just signifies my own need to change and my multifaceted change [Maggie, 24, Other, Male-Third Gender].

Finally, a number of youth had explicit transgender symbols, either readily visible or embedded in other art or piercings that designate queer status. One youth described an embedded trans* symbol as a "subtle way of branding myself with negative space" (Casey, 24, White, Male-Feminine). Another youth described the discreteness of the tattoo:

> If you look at it you're not going to actually see what it is unless you know what you're looking for. But it's kind of just a testament to, you know, I am a male with a female history and, you know, I have no reason to erase that. I can't erase it [Allen, White, 24, Female-Masculine].

One youth embedded a trans* symbol within a religious symbol and explained, "I am Trans, I am male, I am Jewish" (Dee, 25, White, Female-Masculine). Another youth described the desire for a discreet tattoo by saying, "It's a Trans symbol, right there, sort of near my crotch. [laughing] So it's, you know, easily hideable if I want it to be, but it's also um, a permanent symbol of Trans identity" (Rain, 22, Latino, Female-Masculine). For these youth, body art served as a reminder of the duality of their gender identities.

Conclusion

Tattooing among adolescents has been often viewed as impulsive and risky in the public health literature. In this study, some participants described their body art in ways that were consistent with this perspective, specifically indicating issues like health risk, impulsivity, and regrets. However, even among participants with those partial narratives, a deeper notion of the tattoo especially as something that represented a process of adaptation was very clear. Participants, for the most part, engaged in a thoughtful and planful process when deciding on their tattoo(s) and what it represented. For most of the youth in the sample, body art was intentionally placed as permanent reminders of social relationships (e.g., a family member's name), processes (e.g., a phoenix rising from the ashes to represent transformation), and identities (e.g., a trans* symbol). For many, the act of body modification served as a mechanism to claim (or reclaim) the body after a period of feeling incongruent or dissociated. Body art not only enabled transgender youth to visually represent their identity transformations, it served as a mechanism for youth to create a narrative of a dualistic and at times chaotic sense of gender identity development.

REFERENCES

Adams, J. (2009). Bodies of change: A comparative analysis of media representations of body modification. *Sociological Perspectives, 52*(1), 103–129.

Antoszewski, B., Sitek, A., Fijalkowska, M., Kasielska, A., & Kruk-Jeromin, J. (2010). Tattooing and body piercing—what motivates you to do it? *International Journal of Social Psychiatry, 56*(5), 471–479.

Armstrong, M. L., Koch, J. R., Saunders, J. C., Roberts, A. E., & Owen, D. C. (2007). The hole picture: risks, decision making, purpose, regulations, and the future of body piercing. *Clinics in Dermatology, 25*(4), 398–406.

Armstrong, M. L., & Murphy, K. P. (1997). Tattooing: Another adolescent risk behavior warranting health education. *Applied Nursing Research, 10*(4), 181–189.

Armstrong, M. L., Owen, D. C., Roberts, A. E., & Koch, J. R. (2002). College tattoos: More than skin deep. *Dermatology Nursing, 14*(5), 317–2323.

Armstrong, M. L., Roberts, A. E., Owen, D. C., & Koch, J. R. (2004a). Contemporary college students and body piercing. *Journal of Adolescent Health, 35*(1), 58–61.

Armstrong, M. L., Roberts, A. E., Owen, D. C., & Koch, J. R. (2004b). Toward building a composite of college student influences with body art. *Issues in Comprehensive Pediatric Nusing, 27*(4), 277–295.

Atkinson, M. (2002). Pretty in ink: Conformity, resistance, and negotation in women's tattooing. *Sex Roles, 47*(5/6), 219–235.

Benjamins, L. J., Risser, W. L., Cromwell, P. F., Feldmann, J., Bortot, A. T., Eissa, M. A., & Nguyen, A. B. (2006). Body art among minority high school athletes: Prevalence, interest and satisfaction; parental knowledge and consent. *Journal of Adolescent Health, 39*(6), 933–935.

Boss, P. (1999). *Ambiguous loss.* Cambridge: Harvard University Press.

Braithwaite, R., Robillard, A., Woodring, T., Stephens, T., & Arriola, K. J. (2001). Tattooing and body piercing among adolescent detainees: Relationship to alcohol and other drug use. *Journal of Substance Abuse, 13*(1–2), 5–16.

Braun, V., & Clarke, V. (2006). Using thematic analysis in psychology. *Qualitative Research in Psychology, 3*(2), 77–101.

Brooks, T., Woods, E. R., Knight, J. R., & Shrier, L. A. (2003). Body modification and substance use in adolescents: Is there a link? *Journal of Adolescent Health, 32*(1), 44–49.

Butler, J. (1990). *Gendger trouble: Feminism and the subversion of identity.* New York: Routledge.

Caliendo, C., Armstrong, M. L., & Roberts, A. E. (2005). Self-reported characteristics of women and men intimate body piercings. *Issues and Innovations in Nursing Practice, 49*(5), 474–484.

Cameron, L. (1996). *Body alchemy: Transsexual portraits.* Pittsburgh: Cleis Press.

Carroll, L., & Anderson, R. (2002). Body piercing, tattooing, self-esteem, and body investment in adolescent girls. *Adolescence, 37*(147), 627–637.

Carroll, S. T., Riffenburgh, R. H., Roberts, T. A., & Myhre, E. B. (2002). Tattoos and body piercings as indicators of adolescent risk-taking behaviors. *Pediatrics, 109*(6), 1021–1027.

Cegolon, L., Miatto, E., Bortolotto, M., Benetton, M., Mazzoleni, F., & Mastrangelo, Giuseppe. (2010). Body piercing and tattoo: Awareness of health related risks among 4,277 Italian secondary school adolescents. *BMC Public Health, 10*(1), 73–81.

Cetta, F., Graham, L. C., Lichtenberg, R. C., & Warnes, C. A. (1999). Piercing and tattoing in patients with congential heart disease: Patient and physician perspectives. *Journal of Adolescent Health, 24*(3), 160–162.

Chismark, A. (2013). Oral piercing and body art-21st century realities and safety issues. *CDHA Journal, 28*(1), 16–34.

Claes, L., Vandereycken, W., & Vertommen, H. (2005). Self-care versus self-harm: Piercing, tattooing, and self-injuring in eating disorders. *European Eating Disorders Review, 13*(1), 11–18.

Deci, D. M. (2005). The medical implications of body art. *Patient Care for the Nurse Practitioner, 39*(4).

Deschesnes, M., Demers, S., & Fines, P. (2006). Prevalence and characteristics of body piercing and tattooing among high school students. *Canadian Journal of Public Health, 97*(4), 325–329.

Deschesnes, M., Fines, P., & Demers, S. (2006). Are tattooing and body piercing indicators of risk-taking behaviours among high school students? *Journal of Adolescence, 29*(3), 379–393.

Drews, D. R., Allison, C. K., & Probst, J. R. (2000). Behavioral and self-concept differences in tattooed and nontattooed college students. *Psychological Reports, 86*(2), 475–481.

Egeland, B., Carlson, E., & Sroufe, L. A. (1993). Resilience as a process. *Development and Psychopathology, 5*(4), 517–528.

Ekinici, O., Topcuoglu, V., Sabuncuoglu, O., Berkem, M., Akin, E., & Gumustas, F. O. (2012). The association of tattooing/body piercing and psychopathology in adolescents: A community-based study from Istanbul. *Community Mental Health Journal, 48*(6), 798–803.

Ferreira, V. S. (2009). Youth scenes, body marks and bio-sociabilities. *Young, 17*(3), 285–306.

Firmin, M. W., Tse, L. M., Foster, J., & Angelini, T. (2008). Christian student perceptions of body tattoos: A qualitative analysis. *Journal of Psychology and Christianity, 27*(3), 195–204.

Fisher, J. A. (2002). Tattooing the body, marking culture. *Body & Society, 8*(4), 91–107.

Forbes, G. B. (2001). College students with tattoos and piercings: Motives, family experiences, personality factors, and perception by others. *Psychological Reports, 89*(3), 774–786.

Gold, M. A., Schorzman, C. M., Murray, P. J., Downs, J., & Tolentino, G. (2005). Body piercing practices and attitudes among urban adolescents. *Journal of Adolescent Health, 36*(4), 352.e315–352.e321.

116   The Young Are Making Their World

Griffith, R., & Tengnah, C. (2005). Public health 3: Legal regulation of tattooing and body art. *British Journal of Community Nursing, 10*(12), 575–579.

Gunter, T. E., & McDowell, B. M. (2004). Body piercing: Issues in adolescent health. *JSPN, 9*(2), 67–69.

Hicks, L. E. (2005). Explorations of visual culture: Written on the body. *Culture Work, 9*(3), 1–13.

Houghton, S. J., Durkin, K., Parry, E., Turbett, Y., & Odgers, P. (1996). Amateur tattooing practices and beliefs among high school adolescents. *Journal of Adolescent Health, 19*(6), 420–425.

Hruschka, D. J., Schwartz, D., D. C. St. John, Picone-Decaro, E., Jenkins, R. A., & Carey, J. W. (2004). Reliability in coding open-ended data: Lessons learned from HIV behavioral research. *Field Methods, 16*(3), 307–331.

Huxley, C., & Grogan, S. (2005). Tattooing, piercing, health behaviors and health value. *Journal of Health Psychology, 10*(6), 831–841.

Iannaccone, M., Cella, S., Manzi, S. A., Visconti, L., Manzi, F., & Cotrufo, P. (2013). My body and me: Self-injurious behaviors and body modifications in eating disorders-preliminary results. *Eating Disorders, 21*(2), 130–139.

Irwin, K. (2001). Legitimating the first tattoo: Moral passage through informal interaction. *Symbolic Interaction, 24*(1), 49–73.

Kang, M., & Jones, K. (2007). Why do people get tattoos? *Contexts, 6*(1), 42–47.

Kiernan, C. (2014). *A tattoo that completes a new breast.* New York: New York Times. Available at http://well.blogs.nytimes.com/2014/06/02/a-tattoo-that-completes-a-new-breast/.

King, K. A., & Vidourek, R. A. (2007). University students' involvement in body piercing and adherence to safe piercing practices. *American Journal of Health Education, 38*(6), 346–355.

Koch, J. R., Roberts, A. E., Armstrong, M. L., & Owen, D. C. (2010). Body art, deviance, and American college students. *The Social Science Journal, 47*(1), 151–161.

Koch, J. R., Roberts, A. E., Cannon, J. H., Armstrong, M. L., & Owen, D. C. (2005). College students, tattooing, and the Health Belief Model: Extending social psychological perspectives on youth culture and deviance. *Sociological Spectrum: Mid-South Sociological Association, 25*(1), 79–102.

Kuper, L. E., Coleman, B. R., & Mustanski, B. S. (2013). Coping with LGBT and racial-ethnic-related stressors: A mixed-methods study of LGBT youth of color. *Journal of Research on Adolescence, 24*(2), 703–719.

Kwon, P. (2013). Resilience in lesbian, gay, and bisexual individuals. *Personality and Social Psychology Review, 17*(4), 371–383.

Larzo, M. R., & Poe, S. G. (2006). Adverse consequences of tattoos and body piercings. *Pediatric Annals, 35*(3), 187–192.

Laumann, A. E., & Derick, A. J. (2006). Tattoos and body piercings in the United States: A national data set. *Journal of American Academy of Dermatology, 55*(3), 413–421.

Makkai, T., & McAllister, I. (2001). Prevalence of tattooing and body piercing in the Australian community. *CDI Quarterly Report, 25*(2), 67–72.

Manuel, L., & Sheehan, E. P. (2007). Getting inked: Tattoos and college students. *College Student Journal, 41*(4), 1089–1097.

Martin, A. (2000). On teenagers and tattoos. *Reclaiming Children and Youth, 9*(3), 143–144.

McGuire, J. K., Doty, J. L., Catalpa, J. M., & Ola, C. (under review). Gender identity, body size, and body image: A qualitative analysis of transgender youth.

Mifflin, M. (1997). *Bodies of subversion: A secret history of women and tattoo*. New York: Juno Books.

Preti, A., Pinna, C., Nocco, S., Mulliri, E., Pilia, S., Petretto, D. R., & Masala, C. (2006). Body of evidence: Tattoos, body piercing, and eating disorder symptoms among adolescents. *Journal of Psychosomatic Research, 61*(4), 561–566.

Rich, A. (1976). *Of woman born: Motherhood as experience and institution*. New York: Norton.

Riley, S. C. E., & Cahill, S. (2005). Managing meaning and belonging: Young women's negotiation of authenticity in body art. *Journal of Youth Studies, 8*(3), 261–279.

Roberts, T. A., Auinger, P., & Ryan, S. A. (2004). Body piercing and high-risk behavior in adolescents. *Journal of Adolescent Health, 34*(3), 224–229.

Roberts, T. A., & Ryan, S. A. (2002). Tattooing and high-risk behaviors in adolescents. *Pediatrics, 110*(6), 1058–1063.

Rubin, A. (1988). The tattoo renaissance. In A. Rubin (Ed.), *Marks of civilization: Artistic transformations of the human body* (pp. 233–264). Los Angeles: Museum of Cultural History, University of California, Los Angeles.

Ryan, C. (2009). *Supportive families, healthy children: Helping families with lesbian, gay, bisexual & transgender children*. San Francisco: Marian Wright Edelman Institute, San Francisco State University

Schildkrout, E. (2004). Inscribing the body. *Annual Review of Anthropology, 33*, 319–344.

Sedgwick, E. K. (1985). *Between men: English literature and male homosocial desire (gender and culture)*. New York: Columbia University Press.

Sedgwick, E. K. (1990). *Epistemology of the closet*. Berkeley: University of California Press.

Selekman, J. (2003). A new era of body decoration: What are the kids doing to their bodies? *Pediatric Nursing, 29*(1), 77–79.

Sever, J. M. (2003). A third of Americans with tattoos say they make them feel more sexy. Rochester: The Harris Poll.

Silver, E., Silver, S. R., Siennick, S., & Farkas, G. (2011). Bodily signs of academic success: An empirical examination of tattoos and grooming. *Social Problems, 58*(4), 538–564.

Silver, E., VanEseltine, M., & Silver, S. J. (2009). Tattoo acquisition: A prospective longitudinal study of adolescents. *Deviant Behavior, 30*(6), 511–538.

Springgay, S. (2003). Cloth as intercorporeality: Touch, fantasy, and performance and the construction of body knowledge. *International Journal of Education & the Arts, 4*(5), 1–21.

Stirn, A., Hinz, A., & Brahler, E. (2006). Prevalence of tattooing and body piercing in Germany and perception of health, mental disorders, and sensation seeking among tattooed and body-pierced individuals. *Journal of Psychosomatic Research, 60*(5), 531–534.

Strauss, A., & Corbin, J. M. (1990). *Basics of qualitative research: Grounded theory procedures and techniques*. Newbury Park, CA: Sage.

Swami, V. (2011). Marked for life? A prospective study of tattoos on appearance anxiety and dissatisfaction, perceptions of uniqueness, and self-esteem. *Body Image, 8*(3), 237–244.

Tate, J. C., & Shelton, B. L. (2008). Personality correlates of tattooing and body piercing in a college sample: The kids are alright. *Personality and Individual Differences, 45*(4), 281–285.

Tiggemann, M., & Golder, F. (2006). Tattooing: An expression of uniqueness in the appearance domain. *Body Image, 3*(4), 309–315.

Tiggemann, M., & Hopkins, L. A. (2011). Tattoos and piercings: Bodily expressions of uniqueness? *Body Image, 8*(3), 245–250.

Varma, S., & Lanigan, S. W. (1999). Reasons for requesting laser removal of unwanted tattoos. *British Journal of Dermatology, 140*(3), 483–485.

Walsh, F. (2006). *Strengthening family resilience* (2nd ed.). New York: Guilford Press.

Dance as Youth-Adult Partnership
Promoting Transformation through Reflection and Embodiment in the Teen JUSTICE Project

ELIZABETH SHARP, DARLA J. JOHNSON
and NICOLE WESLEY

To speak, spoken, whisper like a ghost
Running so fast
Harnessing essence is elusive
But freeing
I make space for the words to
Drop, float, descend, swirl
They are so young and mostly untethered
Moving is the only way to process
Experiences that don't make sense
So we circle, we see, listen, dance
I am holding, rocking, shaping
Trying to let each one take form
Stories never dared told land
Heard in murmured nodding
And the circle tightens, shoulders, elbows, feet touching
Leaning in until
With urges and sniffles we levitate
Out of the floor more fully embodied
The listening has become space inside the self
To hold and encourage to make shape
Out of telling
To transcend pain,
Now the physical space holds us

Gives us the grace to continue
Moving the emotion into connection
Moving the emotion into form
Making way for the exhilaration of
Moving the story out into the open
Making way for more feeling, more movement.

This poem was written by Darla J. Johnson (co-director of the JUSTICE Project) as she reflected on her work with high school students as part of the JUSTICE Project—an immersive dance-making workshop. In the poem, she provocatively expresses the power of dance for youth, underscoring how movement facilitated connecting, shaping, clarifying, and telling never-before- told stories, all of which culminated in a transformative experience for youth (and for the directors). In this essay, drawing a dance-theatrical project among high school youth (The JUSTICE Project), we explore possibilities of dance as medium for positive youth development.

The current cultural backdrop surrounding youth is characterized by post-feminist, post-racist (i.e., widespread beliefs that gender and race equality has already been achieved; McRobbie, 2008), and neoliberalist sensibilities (i.e., focus on individuals, adhering to a capitalist-market place ideology; Gill, 2008). Teens are developing in fast-paced, technology-driven landscape, which promotes isolation, "soundbites" of information, and minimal face-to-face engagement within communities. As Darla observed from her work

Trio on the move (photograph by Anne Wharton).

with high school students in the JUSTICE Project over several months in 2014, "there is so much fragmentation, and so much distraction" in the youth's lives. In response, the JUSTICE Project offers a space for youth to deeply reflect on their communities, justice, their own lives, their classmates' lives, and to engage in the process of translating their life stories to dance. The dialogue exchanged and the dances created within that space are the "soul" of the JUSTICE Project. Unlike many places in contemporary society, the JUSTICE Project offers young artists the opportunity to embrace and express their vulnerable and authentic selves through dance.

What Is the JUSTICE Project?

The JUSTICE Project is an intensive dance workshop designed for small populations to celebrate thoughtful and authentic art making processes, encouraging participants to connect with themselves, their communities, and broader social justice issues. The project culminates in a live performance. Darla and Nicole co-founded the project in 2007. In another paper, Darla and Nicole explained the project by stating that the JUSTICE Project promotes

> practices of inclusion, collaboration, community building and genuine listening to what the participants share and express through their bodies and voices are what we believe creates a project with depth, authenticity, resonance and transformation for all involved. Social shifting takes place within the container created by respect, vulnerability and tolerance of the human search for justice. It is a place where all human beings are heard, accepted and validated for their uniqueness [Johnson & Wesley, 2013].

The JUSTICE Project was originally conceived as a way to create a deeper sense of community through dialogue, dance making, and collaboration. The premise of the work is to celebrate the authentic artistic voice and to embrace transformation that arises at the intersection of self and community, through dialogues of social, political and personal responses to justice. Exploring themes of justice through self-expression and creative processes in a community setting invites the participant to explore intimate realms of cultural, and personal experience. Darla and Nicole intentionally privilege the process of making dance over the (final) performance, and authentic dance-making over rigid dance techniques.

This essay explores the JUSTICE Project with a group of inner-city high school students who participated in the JUSTICE Project in the spring of 2014. Prior to working with teenagers, Darla and Nicole had previously staged commissions of the JUSTICE Project at several universities, including the University of Bedfordshire in Bedford, England; Spelman College in Atlanta, Georgia; Northumbria University in Newcastle, England; Texas State University in San Marcos, Texas; and Austin Community College in collaboration with the University of Trinidad and Tobago. All of these workshops produced transformative experiences and creative, authentic dance-making.

As Darla and Nicole have previously argued, "Each iteration of the JUS-TICE Project produces an experiential and community-centric performance work, created and developed collaboratively within diverse populations." Darla and Nicole had investigated the extent to which the authentic perform-ance practice of the JUSTICE Project influenced how participants artistically dialogue with themselves, with their community, and with the material they were investigating. Participants have expressed that

> [the JUSTICE Project offers an] environment in which the participants can fully explore themselves without fear. Students who have undertaken this project have deepened their self-knowledge, self-awareness, and compassion for others and this has contributed immensely to their growth as artists and community members.... The JUSTICE Project enables participants to come to value their own experiences as a precious and worthy resource.

Another participant expressed: "I value myself more now. I gained a new sense of humanity and community. People ARE nice, loving, and honest. I had forgotten that."

Extending their work to a younger group of participants, Darla and Nicole adapted the successful model of the JUSTICE Project from the University commissions to a group of high school students living in Austin, Texas. To write this essay, Elizabeth spent several hours interviewing Darla and Nicole together about their experiences. The interview was a dyadic interview (both Darla and Nicole were present) and the interview took place at Darla's house. Elizabeth, Darla, and Nicole also ate lunch together, helping to create an open and informal atmosphere. Elizabeth audio-recorded the interview and listened to it multiple times and transcribed portions of the interview. Additionally, Darla and Nicole gave Elizabeth all written material from the teenagers (e.g., reflections on articles given to students two weeks prior to the first session, index cards with responses from an activity, ideas for dances, etc.). Elizabeth read through the materials and portions of the material are used throughout the essay. Elizabeth was also given a video-recording of the "circle discussion," which was the closure session of the project, facilitated by Darla at the end of the JUSTICE Project. The circle discussion focused on participants' reflecting on their experiences and their (deepening) under-standing of justice, communities, and connecting to others. Elizabeth listened and watched the video a couple of times and took notes.

Trained as a social scientist, Elizabeth was especially interested in the JUSTICE Project because she has been working with choreographers and dancers for the past three years. She and her co-PI (Genevieve Durham-DeCesaro) have created a performance from Elizabeth's qualitative data sets (see Durham-DeCesaro & Sharp, 2014; Durham-DeCesaro & Sharp, 2013; Sharp & Durham-DeCesaro, 2015; Sharp & Durham-DeCesaro, 2013). Her work with dancers and choreographers underscored the transformative potential of dance, the rich interplay of ideas across disciplines, and has opened up a host of possibilities. As a feminist family scholar, Elizabeth is also highly invested in social justice issues (Sharp & Weaver, in press).

In this essay, we focus on how the JUSTICE Project informed teens' artistic vision, working strategies, dance making interests, and choreographic processes and helped them more deeply engage with themselves, each other, and larger issues of justice in their high school and communities. In so doing, we argue that the JUSTICE Project is a unique way to promote Positive Youth Development, especially within the current wider context. The Youth AP cornerstone principles of (a) authentic decision-making, (b) natural mentors, (c) reciprocal activity, and (d) community connectedness mapped on to practices used in the JUSTICE Project.

Components of the JUSTICE Project for High School Students

From February to April 2014, Darla[1] met with 16 high school female students at the Fine Arts Academy, associated with McCallum High School in Austin, Texas. The purpose of the work together was to create a dance performance to be performed to a live audience—the performance would be

Vine video section of the JUSTICE Project (photograph by Anne Wharton).

held at the high school on April 11 and 12 (three months after the JUSTICE Project began). With the goal of the live performance, deep connections in a short amount of time are forged. In addition to the scheduled live performance at the high school, the youth also were invited to a second performance, as part of a conference entitled "No Place for Hate" held at their high school on May 16, 2014.

The youth were aged 16 through 18 years old (sophomores through seniors), female, and all identified as dancers. Prior to the JUSTICE Project, dancers were selected by the academy faculty to participate in the pre-professional dance class. This class consists of the most advanced and mature students following the dance track at the academy. Students following this program audition and are placed in levels that reflect their training and experience in dance. One student had been dancing since she was two years old. The participants had varied backgrounds, including diverse racial/ethnicity identifications, SES levels, and several, like many youth, carried with them histories of personal trauma. The students and Darla met every other day for two hours during the regular school periods—they met an hour before school started and during their "first period dance" course.

Two weeks prior initial start of the JUSTICE Project, participants were asked to read and reflect on two community dance articles (i.e., Fitzgerald, 2008; Marion, 2008). The purpose of asking the participants to read ahead of time was to provide an overriding focus and common understanding of justice and community dance, to encourage a shared language about the issues, and for participants to carefully engage in an understanding of oppression and justice (including historical understandings) and to underscore how dance has powerful potential to promote justice. Entitled "Community Dance Reflection" assignment, participants were asked to write the main ideas of the articles and journal their reactions and their own experiences with oppressions and how others are oppressed. They were also required to prepare one-minute solo works based on their reflections. Darla collected the written comments at the first day of the JUSTICE Project. Some of the comments from the youth included:

> Beyond simple expression, dance can also help people learn how to better connection with others around them. Connection, be it other dancers or even just music, is fundamental in dance, and people who have had bad experiences or a poor home life can find connecting to the things around them very difficult, so this kind of outlet benefits them enormously … [dance] is a language without barriers, and for that reason it is possible to link people who would seemingly have no other connection. It is beautiful and powerful thing, and one that always deserves further exploration.

Another student wrote:

> It was fascinating to learn that students who had come from unstable home lives were the ones who took the most risk in their movement because of their extraordinary adaptive

skills. Often, in contemporary dance, some movements and steps can become very ingrained. But through community dance, a whole other movement vocabulary is born because of the collaborative nature of the projects brings together dancers from such vastly different backgrounds.

Structure of JUSTICE Project

Darla met with the youth during their first period class from mid–February to April 2014. This was part of the students' regular high school course schedule. Darla came to the high school and worked with the students in their space. The teacher, who is the head of the dance area, of "Dance Period 1" helped welcome Darla to the students and, in general, was in and out of the space—the teacher did not contribute to the dance making or the ongoing discussions and can be best characterized as a distant-observer.

The first task Darla and Nicole accomplished was to "facilitate a space of trust within the community by engaging in exercises encouraging mental and physical openness and vulnerability" (Johnson & Wesley, 2013, p. 3). They shook hands with each participant, made eye-contact, and sat in a circle. At the high school on the first day, Darla discussed the expectations of the project, the requirements of participants, including attendance at all rehearsals. Because the project was on a tight time schedule and the work was "intense and intimate," Darla and Nicole conveyed that "every moment, every conversation and every offering was crucial to the work. Missing rehearsals can cause disjointedness and close people off from allowing themselves to go deeper into the work." Darla also discussed the readings with the participants. After the discussion the students were asked to write down words and phrases that affected them emotionally and viscerally from the readings. From these words each dancer created a solo.

Generally, sessions began with physical warm-ups, consisting of a fusion of Pilates, Bartenieff Fundamentals, yoga, and Feldenkrais and improvisational dancing—all of these physical practices and philosophies reflect an understanding that action in the body comes from a very central and internal source. Darla explained that "having a traditional dance warm-up full of plies and tendus" was counterproductive to the larger goal of the JUSTICE Project which was to "practice movement forms that encourage authenticated responses." Nicole explained that the "movement presented should progress in a more organic sense so that the true self can begin to expose itself." When participants are in the realm of self-discovery, even within the warm-up, their latter investment tends to involve a more grounded and vulnerable focus. It is from that communal focus that work begins to reveal itself.

In addition to creation of solo dances, participants were also encouraged to create dances based on stories from the group and their own stories. A considerable amount of time was spent discussing, reflecting, and writing stories. Darla and Nicole helped the students translate the stories into movement. They were paired up and/or grouped together and instructed to combine their choreographies collaboratively This work helped to create the individual sections of the performance work.

Additionally, in response to working with youth, Darla and Nicole experimented with student created videos called Vine and were highly popular among youth at the time of the project. Vines were considered "collages" and represented salient issues to the youth. As part of their participation in the JUSTICE Project, the youth were required to create two separate vines and were instructed that the vines were to be "meaningful but not about themselves." Participants were given two prompts: (a) one was personal to and could include images of themselves in the video, and (b) the other prompt was a reflection of who they are based in their environment. Some students made abstract videos, others included animals, rain, etc. Nicole then created a video instillation with the vines. A student's reflection monologue that was developed into a poetry slam served as the sound score. Nicole's colleague, Seth Warren-Crow, was the music editor for the video montage. The vine video instillation was a section of the performance that included the ensemble moving in unison in front of the image.

The final performance from the JUSTICE Project consisted of eight sections and was approximately 22 minutes in length and was embedded with

McCallum student performing a monologue for the JUSTICE Project (photograph by Anne Wharton).

a larger performance (i.e., a group show with multiple choreographers, lasting about two hours). Feedback from the audience suggested that the Project JUSTICE performance was well-received, with considerable applause and responsiveness from audience members.

Mapping on to Youth-Adult Partnership Models: Promoting Positive Youth Development

As mentioned before, the social science research indicates that four central components of successful Youth-Adult Partnership models include (a) authentic decision-making, (b) natural mentors, (c) reciprocal activity, and (d) community connectedness (Zeldin, Christens, & Powers, 2013). The JUSTICE Project includes all of these principles seamlessly. The four principles operate together to promote a powerful, transformational experience for the youth. In this next section, we share examples of how the four major components of successful Youth Asset Program models were present in the JUSTICE Project.

Encouraging Authentic Decision-Making

One of the most salient themes Elizabeth heard when she talked to Darla and Nicole was their goal of having participants experience *authenticity* of their bodies and their minds. Darla and Nicole encouraged authentic decision-making throughout the entire project. They contrasted authentic dance-making with rigid, structured techniques often linked with dancing. In many instances, dancers learn movement based on a choreographer's and teacher's preferences and training. Dancers become very skilled in particular gestures, techniques, and alter their movements to adjust to the choreographer's demands/requirements. Performing dance based on choreographer's decisions and requirements (generally) does not require deep self-awareness, felt (authentic) embodiment, nor does it encourage intense reflection from the dancers and (fundamentally) censures and restricts dancers' movements. In contrast to this imperative, Darla repeatedly encouraged the young dancers *not* to censor their movement. She repeatedly told them that she wanted them to offer expression from their "unique location and their own sense of self." This does not mean that the dancers threw out their technique and training. Their foundations were used as a springboard to access their deeper movement and creative selves.

To encourage authenticity, Darla and Nicole engaged in a number of activities enabling the youth to share their stories (some participants shared stories they had never shared before) and were reassured that they "can't do it wrong." Over time, the deepening of the dialogue exchanged among the group members and increased feelings of trust helped facilitate risk-tasking.

As one participant shared at the end of the project: "the JUSTICE Project made me grow, ... it helped me tell never-told stories ... and [allowed] me to take freedom back within myself." This last portion of the quote is especially powerful, as the young women expressed her agency in "taking back" her own sense of autotomy within herself. She attributed the JUSTICE Project to stretching her and offering conditions such that she felt safe to be vulnerable to share stories she has kept only to herself.

There was one potent instance in Darla and Nicole's work with the youth when authenticity was called into question. After months of engaging in the discussions and practicing "raw" and uncensored movements and dance-making, a couple of the young women came to rehearsal in very skimpy outfits they intended to wear as costumes for the piece. As Darla and Nicole reflected, the dance did not match the choice of costumes. The costumes reflected trite, popular culture objectification of girls' bodies which is not altogether unsurprising as many scholars have argued that the "sexualization of the female body is taken for granted as normal and banal" in contemporary society (Ringrose, Harvey, Gill, & Livingston, 2013, p. 306). It was at this point in the project that Darla and Nicole stepped in and expressed to the girls that they would need to choose a less objectifying costume. Darla and Nicole explained that the costumes were inconsistent with the intent of the dance. Darla and Nicole were adamant in their standards that they would not allow dancers to be objectified. In reflections with Elizabeth, they pointed to the wider culture and some popular dance shows that hypersexual women dancer's bodies, as well as the music videos and pervasive representative of the sexualized, objectified bodies of dancers. The girls' desires for objectifying/sexualized outfits raises important questions about the limits of authenticity and manufactured images. How do teenage girls tease apart their desires from contemporary culture, especially when pole-dancing classes and the *So You Think You Can Dance?* television show are some of the most pervasive images of dance in the popular culture right now? And what the limits of authenticity and authority with teenagers? Did Darla and Nicole authority interfere with the girls' authentic decision-making?

Natural Mentors and Reciprocal Activity

The aforementioned example of Darla and Nicole stepping in and using their authority was rare throughout the JUSTICE Project. In fact, the costumes and one participant being late/missing rehearsal were some of the only times that Darla and Nicole engaged in prescriptive, hierarchical decision-making, not allowing the girls to make their own decisions. These instances were rare because using hierarchy was antithetical to the larger goals of the

JUSTICE Project. Indeed, a fundamental component of the JUSTICE Project is that Darla and Nicole fostered a unique, non-hierarchical relationship with the teenagers, creating conditions for natural mentoring relationships. This is especially the case because Darla and Nicole came into their lives for a period of several months with a focused task. As they incisively explained to Elizabeth, "we were not their teachers, but more like facilitators within the process." Rather than a one-directional relationship, Darla and Nicole created space for reciprocity—between themselves and the girls and among the girls. However, it was always clear from the beginning that Darla and Nicole would be artistically shaping the material into an overall performance work. Their job was to craft the material that the dancers created into a work that represented the concept and the voices of all of the participants. By creating trust and a balance of power from the beginning of the project, there was never any doubt about the roles that each person played within the group. Although dancers' ideas were always listened to, the overall structure and flow of the work was directed by Darla and Nicole.

Darla and Nicole worked to create inclusive, non-hierarchical relationships with all students. The non-hierarchical relationships and practices were intentional and foundational to the project and created a space where the teens were comfortable sharing vulnerabilities and aspects of their authentic selves. As Darla explained, "self-reflection becomes easier when you have

Group discussion with McCallum students. Students are taking performance notes on their mobile devices (photograph by Dennis Fagan).

support." Participants, Darla, and Nicole met in circles for discussions—keeping everyone at the same level (i.e., the adult was not standing in front of the teens), students called Darla and Nicole by their first names, and students were given considerable autonomy in the creation of the material within the project. In alignment with Community Youth Development, Darla and Nicole intentionally created a community, "whereby power was more even, the hierarchy dampened," which, they explained lead to "empower[ing] people [youth] at a deeper level to be authentic and they will start self-defining and asking questions of themselves- and working from a place of clarity of who they are, what they need, what they want to express."

Community Connectedness

The combination of the authentic-decision making, and the non-hierarchal relationships/natural mentorships helped foster a strong sense of connectedness. When listening to the girls verbally express their reflections about the JUSTICE Project in the "closure circle discussion" after the final performances, Elizabeth was struck by how many of the young women commented that the project evoked a heightened sense of connectedness. They expressed deeper connection among each other and how this sense of connectedness was also linked to larger communities and both personal and broader notions of justice. Many participants offered affective responses and commented on how sharing their stories and then making dances from these stories created a deeper connection within themselves, their bodies, and with each other. As one participant remarked, "Once we shared our stories, I was dancing for myself and for the other dancers." Another participant offered her epiphany: "Ohmygod—everyone has a story!"

The above quotes indicate a growing sense of closeness and accountability to each other as well as an acute awareness of the lives and the histories of those around them. This suggests that the JUSTICE Project is especially helpful in disrupting the egocentrism often linked with teenagers. Additionally, the closeness helped counter stereotypical images and high school cliques that had already formed among the girls in the "dance period one" class. As one participant explained in the circle discussion at the end of the JUSTICE Project, over time, "we got closer to each other ... and dismantled cliques.... [I first thought] 'disrespect was going on in that class' but [now] we have each other's back.... We are on the same wave-length ... that is very comforting." This participant indicates that there is a shared sense of understanding among the participants.

Another participant shared, "the JUSTICE Project made each other accountable for each other" and others gained "comfort ... knowing that others have gone through what you have gone through." Extending this line of thought, another participant said, "yeah ,… it is comforting knowing you are not the only one with awful things to have happened to you."

Another participant explained, "I had felt like I didn't belong in this class … but my input into choreography [with JUSTICE Project] made me feel like I actually belonged here." In this quote, we can see that the participant moved from feeling a sense of non-belonging/otherness to connectedness, in large part, she argues, because she helped create the dance. Her input was deemed as valuable and she had a stake in the processes. The function of having the responsibility to make decisions in the dance-making created a sense of connectedness to others that was not present prior to the JUSTICE Project.

Conclusion

When listening to Darla and Nicole reflect on the JUSTICE Project with the high school teenagers, at times, Elizabeth was moved to tears. She welled up because of their deep commitment to social justice and their descriptions of the powerful nature of their work with teenage girls. At a time when young girls are encouraged to disassociate from their bodies (Tolman, 2013), Darla and Nicole's work is especially needed to counter the disembodiment, manufactured images, and the "fractured"/disjointedness of a neoliberalist, postfeminist, post-racist area. Darla reflected, "I believe most of the work I did was in the realm of holding the space for them to authenticate themselves through working the process."

The stories Elizabeth heard from Darla and Nicole and the teenage girls in the project engendered a sense of authenticity, empowerment, and connection—all of which the social science literature has demonstrated as key to successful youth development. Elizabeth has felt honored to be able to work on this essay, in the hopes of inspiring other social scientists and practitioners who work with youth to consider the incredible potential of dance to promote transformative experiences and social justice. As Nicole explained to Elizabeth when reflecting on her work with the young women:

> It is a very moving and powerful experience to see young artists embrace and express their vulnerable and human selves through the medium of dance. To be part of a project that celebrates thoughtful and authentic art making processes and that encourages people to connect with themselves and their communities has given me and continues to give me my sense of purpose.

Community dance possesses transformative possibilities. As one JUSTICE Project high school student communicated, "dance is a freeing art that benefits all who encounter it. Everybody is a dancing body, and movement can encompass so many kinds of art and human expression that [dance] is invaluable tool."

NOTE

1. Nicole did not live in Austin, where the high school was located so she was only able to work with the students periodically. She participated in eight sessions, rehearsals, etc.

REFERENCES

Durham-DeCesaro, G., & Sharp, E.A. (2013). Immersion in the muddy waters of a collaboration between a social scientist and a choreographer. *The International Journal of Social, Political and Community Agendas in the Arts*, 7, 57–66.

DeCesaro-Durham, G., & Sharp, E. A. (2014). Almost drowning: Data as a troubling anchor in a dance/social science collaboration. *International Journal of Qualitative Methods*, 13, 411–421.

Evans, A., Riley, S., & Shankar, A. (2010). Technologies of sexiness: Theorizing women's engagement in the sexualization of culture. *Feminism & Psychology*, 20, 114–131.

Fitzgerald, M. (2008). Community dance: Dance Arizona Repertory Theatre as a vehicle for cultural emancipation. In N. Jackson and T. Shapiro-Phim (Eds.), *Dance, human rights and social justice: Dignity in motion*, pages 256–269. Lanham, MD: Scarecrow Press.

Johnson, D., & Wesley, N. (2013). The JUSTICE Project: The ideology of social shifting through physical engagement, collaboration and authentic performance. *ATINER's Conference Paper Series*. Retrieved from http://www.atiner.gr/papers/ART2013-0447.pdf.

Kant, M. (2008). Practical imperative: German dance, dancers and Nazi politics. In N. Jackson and T. Shapiro-Phim (Eds.), *Dance, human rights and social justice: Dignity in motion*, pages 5–19. Lanham, MD: Scarecrow Press.

McRobbie, A. (2009). *The Aftermath of Feminism: Gender, Culture and Social Change*. Thousand Oaks, CA: Sage.

Ringrose, J., Harvey, L. Gill, R., & Livingstone, S. (2013). Teen girls, sexual double standards and "sexting": Gendered value in digital image exchange. *Feminist Theory*, 14, 305–323.

Sharp, E.A., & Durham-DeCesaro. (accepted). Modeling innovative methodological practices in a dance/family studies transdisciplinary project. *Journal of Family Theory & Review*.

Sharp, E. A., & Durham-DeCesaro, G. (2013). What does rejection have to do with it? Toward an innovative, kinesthetic analysis of qualitative data. *Forum Qualitative Sozialforschung / Forum: Qualitative Social Research*, 14(2), Art. 4, http://nbn-resolving.de/urn:nbn:de:0114-fqs130245.

Sharp, E. A, & Weaver, S. (2015). Feeling like feminist frauds: Theorizing feminist accountability in feminist family research in a neoliberal, post-feminist context. *Journal of Family Theory and Review*, 7(3), 299–320.

Tolman, D. (2012). Female adolescents, sexual empowerment and desire: A missing discourse of gender inequity. *Sex Roles*, 66, 746–757.

Zeldin, S., Christens, B., & Powers, J. (2013). The psychology and practice of youth-adult partnership: Bridging generations for youth development and community change. *American Journal of Community Psychology*, 51, 385–397.

Using Hip Hop Culture and Code Switching as a Way to Connect, Engage and Empower Youth

JESSE SILVA, STELLA SILVA
and JOSHUA QUINN

The means to create communal change for and with marginalized and underrepresented youth are inherently ingrained in the creation, legacy, and perpetuity of Hip Hop. A close examination of the conditions in which Hip Hop and its culture were established provides a framework for understanding how code switching can be used to connect, educate, and empower youth. Essentially, Hip Hop culture and vernacular can be used to translate formal English language and bureaucracy associated with college transition, academic success, and civic engagement to promote youth to live productive lives. More specifically, code switching becomes a viable tool and strategy for enabling youth to understand and engage their social realities and educational opportunities. Hip Hop culture is rooted in themes of diversity, persistence, creativity, community, innovation, authenticity, empowerment, and transformation. When these themes are harnessed and maintained by institutionalized supported programs created by Hip Hop professionals and advocates, safe spaces are created for underrepresented, oppressed and/ or marginalized youth to learn and exchange ideas which promote living productively.

Hip Hop and Its Background

Hip Hop and Its Social, Economic, Political and Racialized Environment

Hip Hop has a tremendous influence on and around the world (Abe, 2006). It was formed as a result of the destruction and displacement of the economic and physical environment of working class families living in ethnic neighborhoods in the Bronx, New York (Petchauer, 2015; Travis, 2012). Through these conditions, black and Puerto Rican youth utilized Hip Hop as a form of expression and response to their social status and condition. This unrest impacted the identity formation and social status of youth living in these communities. The youthful response manifested into forms and elements of deejaying, emceeing, break dancing and graffiti that have helped to expand and influence various genres including music, dress and language (Chang, 2006; Rose, 2008). Hip Hop music and culture engaged and used code switching within a broader definition that moved beyond language, and included the physical, ideational, and symbolic (Omoniyi, 2005; Travis, 2011). In doing so, marginalized youth communities, especially those early trailblazers of Hip Hop culture, were vital in establishing Hip Hop as part of American and international youth and popular culture (Abe, 2006; Travis & Bowman, 2011). Hip Hop music and culture became generally accessible and available at unprecedented levels through technology and social media over time (Rose, 2008; Travis, 2012). Hip Hop captures and presents a style of code switching that is a ubiquitous and transcultural experience and lends itself to youth from disadvantaged and underrepresented communities to communicate within and beyond.

The current consumer of Hip Hop music cannot be limited to a stereotype, but rather are from all races, ethnicities, genders, ages, and locations (Rose, 2008). Rap music is integrated into the essence of pop-culture and is created from environments of injustice and oppression as much as environments of wealth and prosperity (Travis & Bowman, 2011). Hip Hop music is a multi-billion-dollar industry in the U.S. and is widely accessible and affordable with many themes centering around group level realities (Travis & Bowman, 2012). Hip Hop as a global phenomenon transcends the acceptance of music genres, and has become a transnational cultural product with predispositions towards globalization (Liadi & Omobowali, 2011). In such case, Hip Hop culture demonstrates a great potential to create a system of solidarity that crosses all borders and collectively unites youth in a common language or vernacular that is accessed through code switching.

From its inception, Hip Hop culture has provided youth with an innovative medium for expressing and understanding authenticity. The notion of "keepin' it real" and narratives of "realness" stem from Hip Hop culture's innate ability to articulate and depict self and their social conditions. Pennycook (2005) suggests that "keepin' it real" represents the conjoining of the fluidity of art, politics, representation, performance, and individual accountability that mirrors all aspects of youth experience. In other words, "keepin' it real" is both the articulation and the youth's lived reality.

This symbiotic process is unique to Hip Hop culture because it allows youth to be authentic in describing self and their community. Telling it as it is or "keepin' it real" can mean recognizing and creatively vocalizing the social ills of poverty, the decaying of urban communities to one's personal attempt to protect dignity, the commodification of rap by mainstream culture, or the existential act of selling one's soul to the evils of capitalism or assimilation (Pennycook, 2007). Just as importantly, authenticity and being "true to oneself" is an important part of Hip Hop because it allows Hip Hop culture to be translated universally to different places and languages (Low, 2011). Code switching in Hip Hop culture provides youth with the opportunity to process, reflect, translate and communicate internally and externally about self and society.

Hip Hop as a Culturally Diverse and Creative Discourse

Hip Hop's early and formative years depict how Hip Hop culture created a type of code switching that lends itself to discourse because of its cultural diversity. During the early days of Hip Hop, other cultures made significant contributions in its development (McFarland, 2009). These include Jamaican music, dance, and oral tradition; Asian martial arts and philosophy; Italian gangster fantasy; Japanese technology; Chicano dress and style; Islamic faith; Euro-American capitalist ideology; and Puerto Rican dance and music (McFarland, 2009). Code switching brings together multiple languages from different parts of the world and local cultures (Omoniyi, 2005). As a result, Hip Hop instituted its own creative language, discourse, and type of code switching that uses terms and phrases understood by and within various cultures.

Code switching is the co-presence of patterns from two or more languages in a stretch of discourse. It reaches beyond an immediate physical context of its use to include a broader definition that includes individual and group narratives (Omoniyi, 2005). Omoniyi (2005) suggests that within an expanded framework of interpretation, linguistic code switching can accommodate other signifying codes, such as age, gender, religion, nationality, talk, music, walk, dress, dance, and costume. In Hip Hop, code switching is utilized as much more than a stylistic language tool—code switching becomes a way for youth to create solidarity, engage in common understanding, and connect through culturally relevant pedagogy. Code switching within the Hip Hop community possesses this ability because Hip Hop is comprised of the experience of culturally diverse and marginalized communities.

Hip Hop as Communal Culture

Much of Hip Hop's foundation is based in community. In general, early Hip Hop facilitated an avenue for youth identity formation and expression as well as an opportunity to construct meaning that interacts with the social realities within a youth's environment. The formation of such talents and formalized mediums of expressions are largely attributed to the creation of safe spaces in which expression and language can thrive. Just as importantly, these elements are the best representation and concrete manifestation of Hip Hop's ability to create new and long-lasting forms of expression generated from communal effort and into popular culture.

This in essence allows youth to create and access their "voice" in a "brave space." This space consistently provides youth with the opportunity to define, recreate, and establish narrative through "voice" and "resistance" (Arao & Clemens, 2013). In doing so, providing safe and brave spaces for youth to feel comfortable allows them to be their true selves. Safe spaces are social justice spaces in that they express and validate diversified truths (Arao & Clemens, 2013). As a result, these spaces allow youth and members of the Hip Hop culture to use language from Hip Hop that includes code switching. Youth can interpret social cues about who they are and their worth in a variety of ways including messages that they hear through Hip Hop music. Just as importantly, the popularity of Hip Hop generates the possibility for youth to communicate more than narratives of self.

Additionally, brave and safe spaces that are integrated with Hip Hop music promote positive moods, ease negative tension, and provide an opportunity to reminisce about past experiences as well as opportunities to develop strategies for overcoming future obstacles (Miranda & Claes, 2009; Travis, 2010). When youth have a strong sense of cultural pride and awareness, they are able to construct a healthy self-concept that assists them in acts of agency and resistance against negative psychological forces in their environment (Hall, 2007). This awareness can instill in youth the notion that their communities' success is interconnected with their families' success, which is also related to their own individual success (Dimitriadis, 2015). In essence, Hip Hop provides an appealing and popular discourse for youth to engage, connect and learn in a community and in order to form their value systems.

Hip Hop as an Empowerment Agent and a Transformative Genre

Though the climate of Hip Hop may have changed since the 1970s, Hip Hop still maintains characteristics of oppression and innovation that can be used to establish "voice" (Travis, 2012). Voice, in the form of Hip Hop vernacular, conveys feelings and authenticity. This self-expression creates "voice" for so many disenfranchised and marginalized youth and can supersede time and socio-economic structure (Travis, 2012). In general, Hip Hop music enables youth to feel valued, validated and free to express themselves (Travis, 2012). Due to the use of code switching in Hip Hop music, youth have found this type of music to provide them with a sense of value, validation, and even as a resource toward resistance (Delgado & Staples, 2008; Travis, 2012). Hip Hop culture, music, and code switching assist in the establishment of "voice" and convey to youth that they are connected to a larger community that has also experienced oppression.

Music, in general, is a very powerful tool of engagement. It can change one's mood, promote a positive mood, as well as reduce a negative mood (Miranda & Claes, 2009). This type of interaction with music in general provides both adults and youth coping skills acquired through their engagement with music (Travis, 2012). As a coping mechanism, music is rich with messages about life experiences, and messages about how to prioritize strategies for overcoming life obstacles. Hip Hop encourages "pushing the envelope" and feeds into the adventurous nature of youth. In this same sense, the underlying tone of rebellion and resistance that is part of so much rap music and Hip Hop culture entices young people across cultures to engage in this genre of music (Liadi & Omobawali, 2011). Hip hop culture, music in particular, serves as an agent of empowerment for youth to develop a sense of worth, connect with issues within their community, and participate in pro-social behavior that may improve their communal life experiences. Just as importantly, it teaches youth how to persist and engage the conditions limiting their success.

Hip Hop grounded in social justice gives youth a common language, experience and avenue for engaging in sensitive topics. In particular, Hip Hop allows for exposure to topics that may be considered taboo in regular discourse or in educational settings where sensitive or controversial topics need an attractive format. Abe (2009) suggests that Hip Hop can be used in the school curriculum as a unique conceptual tool for students to examine social issues such as race, class, gender and oppression. With this newfound ability, youth can address educational inequities by increasing their awareness of systemic disparities through Hip Hop culture. This awareness emphasizes the value of empowerment among all and assists youth in identifying with others as they develop their skill level and become aware of societal or institutional components of their problems (Gutierrez, 1995; Freire, 1990). Hip Hop can be used as a potent weapon in the fight to keep youth engaged with education and social justice (Abe, 2009). As a culture, it contains coping mechanisms for identity, culture and lyrics that may be instrumental in capturing principles of social justice and activism (Delgado & Staples, 2008; Flores Gonzales, 2006).

Hip Hop culture also increases personal, interpersonal or political power so individually each person can take action to improve their own life situation (Gutierrez, 1990). Youth experience empowerment that can be reciprocated at the individual level and assist the collective community to feel empowered (Travis, 2012). Put simply, individual and community empowerment is interrelated and reinforcing. As a result, Hip Hop's strength comes from empowering individuals through community mobilization and social action (Travis, 2011; Flores & Gonzalez, 2006; Travis, 2012). This can result in feelings of empowerment which serve as a powerful tool for marginalized individuals and communities facing social inequalities. Furthermore, Hip Hop transforms youth from active listener to social justice advocate in their lives and community.

Hip Hop Culture, Outreach Program and Code Switching

Hip Hop scholarship should not be limited by critical frameworks because Hip Hop has moved far beyond expectations that early academics had for it (Dimitriadis, 2015). In doing so, Hip Hop demonstrates a strong capacity to improve the lives of youth, but requires a quantifiable track record to legitimize its ability. Hence, more analysis and measurement of the use of Hip Hop in outreach programs should be used as it impacts education, prevention, intervention and social change strategies at both the individual and community levels (Travis, 2012). The outreach program highlighted in this essay provides a tangible representation for creating and documenting successful Hip Hop–based educational and entertaining outreach programs.

Youth served in Texas State's outreach program interacted with Hip Hop culture through "edutainment." Edutainment is the convergence of the concept of education and entertainment and was used to introduce information concerning secondary and post-secondary education in a manner that is engaging and allows youth opportunities to feel connected, empowered and incorporates code switching. Hip Hop culture was used as intervention strategies and valuable tool of empowerment. Edutainment is embraced by college age youth from Texas State University (Texas State) who engage in outreach to San Marcos youth community through the Texas State Hip Hop Congress, a registered student organization.

Hip Hop Congress

The Texas State Hip Hop Congress (HHC) is a community service-based organization that strives to unite cultures through the art of Hip Hop by encouraging creativity, cultural expression, and social activism. The Texas State chapter of Hip Hop Congress was charted in fall of 2004 at Texas State University by Dr. Sherri Benn, assistant vice president for student affairs and director of the Office of Student Diversity & Inclusion, and five young students, Ray "Ray C Cordero, Ernst "Young Mischiff" Bernard, Jefferey "JP" Plummer, Vincent "V-Nice" Milson, and Dustin "D–Ray" Ray. Since 2004, HHC has created original and innovative signature programs and initiatives at Texas State including the *A Texas STATEment: Volume I, II & III* (CD Mixtapes), Bobcat Preview Diversity Presentation, Congress Kidz, the Annual Hip Hop TRiO X-Change, and The Epidemic: Hip Hop Freestyle Battle & Showcase. These programs are sponsored by the Office of Student Diversity & Inclusion (SDI) at Texas State University. Most importantly, the majority of the creation, coordination, implementation and assessment of these programs are facilitated by HHC student leaders and members under the mentorship and guidance of SDI staff and HHC advisors.

The Texas State Hip Hop Congress is chartered through the Hip Hop Congress, a 501©3 non-profit corporation and an international organization. The Hip Hop Congress (2015) provides the Hip Hop generation and the post–Hip Hop generation with the tools, resources and opportunities to make social, economic and political change on a local, regional and national level. Hip Hop Congress is the product of a merger of artists, students, music and community and comes into fruition in the form of chapters in universities, high schools and communities. Hip Hop Congress chapters produce or sponsor over 200 events a year including Awareness Weeks, a week of different events focusing on Hip Hop culture (panels, speeches, emcee/b-boy/DJ exhibition/battle, awareness festivals, and screenings).

Hip Hop TRiO X-Change

The Hip Hop TRiO X-Change (HHX) establishes a common ground where students learn the importance of education through the culture of Hip Hop. This outreach program connects, engages and empowers marginalized youth in and around Austin and San Marcos, Texas, to complete secondary and pursue post-secondary education. The program was created in 2005 by Jesse Silva as an undergraduate senior internship project under the supervision of Dr. Sherri Benn and in the Office of Student Diversity & Inclusion. HHX continues to grow annually with the collaborative support of SDI, the TRiO Programs, and the Texas State Hip Hop Congress.

In previous years, TRiO students received presentations on college life, culture shock, and financial literacy and budgeting, and attended a panel discussion by Texas State student leaders on the importance of using family and friends as a support system and to ensure collegiate success in and out of the classroom. The three session topics were selected specifically for TRiO pre-college students because the workshops encourage participants to complete their secondary education process and then continue on to college.

HHC members and presenters incorporate rap, poetry and skits centered on their day-to-day collegiate experiences as underrepresented students and students who are underrepresented or who identify as first-generation students, students of color, women, LGBTQIA persons, undocumented students, religious minorities, and Hip Hop heads. Students in junior high and high school love Hip Hop music and culture. By incorporating Hip Hop and working with Texas State student leaders to vocalize their collegiate experiences, college is presented as attainable, important and a realistic goal for middle and high school students from disadvantaged backgrounds. The Hip Hop TRiO X-Change concludes with the Rally of the Delegates, a Hip Hop showcase where a DJ mixes and Texas State students rap, perform poetry or spoken word, and breakdance.

The target population for the HHX is youth who reside in and around Austin and San Marcos, Texas and are enrolled in a precollege TRiO Program. The TRiO Programs are funded through the U.S. Department of Education, housed out of Texas State University and include Educational Talent Search, Rural Talent Search and Upward Bound programs. San Marcos is a community that is approximately 45 miles south of the state capital of Austin and approximately 40 miles north of San Antonio. It is home to approximately 54,076 residents and encompasses approximately 38 square miles. San Marcos is populated by a high number of families designated as "low-income individual" (as defined by the Department of Education) or individuals whose family's taxable income for the preceding year did not exceed 150 percent of the poverty level. Fifty-two percent of families in San Marcos are living below the poverty level compared to the national average of 15.7 percent. In addition, over half of the approximate 2,193 out of the 4,333 students participate in the free and reduced lunch program.

Methodology

To examine and demonstrate how code switching was performed as part of HHX, a combination of ethnography self-reflections, content analysis of language used in workshop descriptions and findings from a master's applied research project were used and interwoven. Triangulation of these methods provide a more clear understanding of how code switching is effective on a university campus. Ethnography self-reflection of language used in the development and implementation of the outreach program is conducted by Jesse Silva, creator of the annual Hip Hop TRiO X-Change and, now, assistant director of SDI. Previous research has shown that a self-reflective approach is beneficial and essential in the study of popular culture to ensure that the cultural phenomenon can be examined and understood within a global context (Dimitriadis, 2015).

There is much to learn from *"Don't Forget the Hip-Hop!" Recruiting Economically Disadvantaged Minority Students in Higher Education: An Assessment of Postsecondary Programs at Texas State University* (Cordero, 2008). This master's applied research project is unique because it was completed by Ray Cordero, Texas State Hip Hop Congress co-founder, now grant coordinator for Upward Bound at Texas State University. Additionally, Cordero's (2008) research project sought "to empirically test the effects that hip-hop music and culture can have on marketing a university, promoting enrollment, and creating interest in high school students—particularly economically disadvantaged minorities" (p. 52). This research provided SDI with findings that validated strategies using Hip Hop in existing and new programs and initiatives. Silva's implementation of the HHX for over ten years, Cordero's (2008) applied research project and Dr. Sherri Benn's vision, institutional support and resources and leadership in starting and sustaining HHC were key instruments in institutionalizing and legitimizing student-led Hip Hop programs and initiatives like the HHX that support and assist marginalized youth.

A content analysis was conducted by examining workshop titles and paired descriptions of 49 of 50 workshops that were developed and implemented over the span of eleven years as part of the HHX (see Chart 1). Workshop titles and descriptions were selected to demonstrate code switching because they show that language used over an extended number of years to connect, engage and empower youth. Secondly, this language was created and used by Texas State students to describe workshops to youth in printed material used in the HHX. Lastly, there is no recorded audio or video, and with written consent, of Texas State students in to demonstrate code switching in action. Very few of the presentations were scripted, and relied heavily on PowerPoint presentations to communicate topics. As a result, personal reflection on the from Silva and Cordero's findings are included to provide more well-rounded analysis. Key workshop titles and descriptions will be highlighted to anecdotally describe the type of language used in the workshops.

Chart 1

A—Empowerment	B—Community	C—Diversity	D—Authenticity
E—Persistence	F—Transformation	G—Creativity	H—Innovation

No.	Title	Description	
1	Street Credibility: Maintaining Respect through a Hip Hop Lifestyle	This workshop will be a discussion of the various methods for gaining and maintaining street credibility through the music one listens to. It will also be a discussion of the harms and benefits of street credibility and the types of respect amongst their peers. This workshop will hopefully teach all the youth to understand how one's lifestyle can affect their decisions and actions in gaining respect.	2005; A, B, D, E, F
2	5 Elements: Break Dancing, Lyricist, Graffiti, DJ, Attire	This workshop incorporates the 5 basic elements of Hip Hop. It will emphasize on the adaptability of each element in business, entertainment, and leadership. Visual art, dance performances, and a lyrical session will be utilized to enhance the learning experience. This workshop will draw attention to the versatility of Hip Hop in one's style and stresses the importance of deciding what to wear when the occasion calls for it.	2005; A, D, G
3	Thugs and Gangstas: A Discussion of the Stigmas Placed on Hip Hop	This workshop serves to openly converse about the various images Hip Hop artist send to today's youth. It will highlight importance of selecting artist with positive messages as role models and how the youth can help to change existing stigmas or perceptions. Also, participants will discuss the importance of changing the content of Hip Hop music.	2005; A, B, C, F, G
4	Film and Hip Hop: Discussion of Movie Excerpts	This workshop will permit participants to explore the dynamics of being influenced by Hip Hop. Also, the workshop will give the participants an opportunity to view films starring Hip Hop artists or centered on Hip Hop. The workshop will hopefully motivate and encourage participants to become multitalented and multitask.	2005; A, C, F, G, H
5	Put Yo Hood Up!: A Discussion about the Media's Role in the East-West Coast Violence	A workshop dedicated to exploring the portrayal of violence in music videos and news coverage. This workshop will highlight several incidences in the history of Hip Hop that ended with violence and death. The principle of this workshop is to teach participants methods for finding solution	2005; A, B, C, E, G, H

No.	Title	Description	
		and venting through music and art. The purpose of this workshop is to provide incentive to create positive forms of interaction with peers through art, media, and Hip Hop.	
6	Desegregation through Music and Film: A Discussion of Unity and Integration	As Texas becomes more diverse, we devote this workshop to discussing the various ways Hip Hop has allowed for a more integrated and multicultural society. This workshop will be a discussion of artist and individual who have been influenced by Hip Hop and have committed themselves to a diverse society. Also, this workshop will permit the participants to describe how Hip Hop has influenced their own lives in meeting individuals of different race, color, or creed.	2005; A, B, C, D, F
7	Why you hatin'?: When Individuals from Different Cultures, Races, or Gender Rap	This workshop is a discussion on the effects of race and culture on an individual representing a Hip Hop lifestyle. By engaging in this discussion, participants will be able to discuss preservation of one's culture, ethnicity, or gender while respecting others.	2005; A, B, C, D, E, F
8	Bling-Bling, But No Books: Spending Rappers Money	This workshop is a discussion of the efforts Hip Hop artists have attempted in assisting and educating the youth. The purpose of this discussion is to promote a positive Hip Hop lifestyle through leadership and awareness. This workshop will raise awareness of the positive and negative consequences of addressing a mass audience. Also, the workshop will discuss the importance of art and activism.	2005; A, B, C, E, H
9	Peace, Not "Peace out": Keeping Peace with Others	This workshop is a discussion about unity and collaboration through Hip Hop. The principle of this forum is to teach the participants Hip Hop is supposed to bring each other together, not create problems or separation. Also, this workshop is a discussion of what statements Hip Hop artists make through their music. The workshop will permit participants to discuss how Hip Hop has allowed them to become more political and the benefits of making a movement in order to be heard.	2005; A, B, D, E, F
10	Hip Hop and Spoken Word: The Rise of the Poet	Callin' all prophets, lyricists, writers and poets! Come get to know more about your art form and the evolution of the poet in	2006; A, B, G, H

No.	Title	Description	
		Hip-Hop Society. In this workshop, we will discuss and present the various aspects of Spoken Word, Poetry Slam, and its connection to Hip-Hop.	
11	Thugs and Gangstas: A Discussion of the Stigmas Placed on Hip-Hop Because of Artist's Violence and the Content of the Music	This workshop will highlight the importance of selecting artists with positive messages as role models and how they can help to change existing stigmas or perceptions.	2006; A, B, C, F
12	The 5 Elements of Hip-Hop	Come krunk ya'll!! This workshops breaking down the elements of Hip-Hop culture as they exist today. The B-Boy, Turntabilism, Emceeing, Beat Box, and Graff Art will all be covered!!!!	2006; C, G
13	Put Yo Hood Up!– A Discussion of Violence, Stereotypes and the Media	A workshop dedicated to exploring the portrayal of violence in music videos and news coverage. This workshop will highlight several incidences in the history of Hip-Hop that ended with violence and death. The principle of the workshop is to teach the participants methods for finding solution and venting through music and art.	2006; A, B, D, F
14	Film and Hip-Hop: Discussion of Movie Excerpts	This workshop will permit participants to explore the dynamics of being influenced by Hip-Hop. Also, the workshop will give the participants an opportunity to view films starring Hip-Hop artists or centered on Hip-Hop. The workshop will hopefully motivate and encourage participants to be multitalented and multitasked.	2006; A, B, C, D, F, G
15	Hip-Hop in Film and Media	As Texas becomes more diverse, we devote this workshop to discussing the various ways Hip-Hop has allowed for a more integrated and multicultural society. This workshop will be a discussion of artists and individuals who have been influenced by Hip-Hop and have committed themselves to the diversity of society. This workshop will also discuss how Hip-Hop can influence individuals to meet persons of different race, color and creed.	2006; A, B, C, D, G
16	Politics: Right or Left Wing Music (featuring Texas State Democrats)	This workshop is a discussion of what statements Hip-Hop artists are making through their music. This workshop will permit the participants to discuss how Hip-Hop has allowed them to become more	2006; A, B, C, F

No.	Title	Description	
		political and the benefits of making a movement in order to be heard.	
17	Peace, Not Peace Out—Keeping Peace with Others	This workshop is a discussion about unity and collaboration through Hip-Hop. The principle of this forum is to teach the participants Hip-Hop is supposed to bring each other together, not create problems or separate.	2006; A, B, C, F, G
18	Back to the Basics: The Hip Hop Movement	We're taking it back to the foundation. Participants will learn the history and evolution of the Hip Hop culture. This workshop is a fact-based presentation that revisits Hip Hop's pilgrimage from its grassroots to the 5 Elements and future direction. The workshop will also highlight how the Hip Hop Congress is influencing educational systems on a local, national, and global scale.	2007; A, B, C
19	Hip Hop, Not Gift Shops: Entertainers and Entrepreneurs	Is Hip Hop for sell? This workshop provides an open forum on popular artists who have demonstrated financial gain without compromising their artistic integrity. Topics discussed will include personal and professional marketing techniques, publications, the implications of commercial Hip Hop, and cultural creativity. This workshop will highlight visionary artists that have demonstrated the capacity to make the leap from entertainer to entrepreneur. Also, presenters will provide students with information pertaining to the Hip Hop Congress Mixtape.	2007; A, D, G, H
20	Workshop for Those Who Don't Know Which Workshop to Go To	You know what you want out of life ... but are confused on how to get it? You are not alone. The emphasis of this workshop is to reinforce assurance about attending college and provide information to students about application processes in State of Texas. Participants are encouraged to share their dilemmas about life after high school, anxiety from leaving home, and personal success stories.	2007; A, B, D, E
21	HIV/AIDS Awareness and Community Mobilization through Hip Hop	What is Hip Hop doing to solve the HIV/AIDS epidemic? Do misogynistic rap lyrics promote sexual misconduct? This workshop will take an in-depth look at the HIV/AIDS epidemic and awareness in the Hip Hop community. Also explored in this workshop will be solutions for the	2007; A, B, E, F, G, H

No.	Title	Description	
		mobilization of the artistic, political, and social community in assisting with the cause. Participants will also learn basic methods for maintaining a healthy lifestyle through self-affirmation, respect, and artistic creativity.	
22	What Is War Really Good For?: A Discussion about the War in Iraq	There's a war going on outside and it isn't getting safer. As America continues to seek resolution for the War in Iraq, this workshop calls on the future politicians and representatives to share their solutions and opinions. In this open forum, participants can express their mind about America's involvement in the war in Iraq. This workshop also explores how Hip Hop is directly connected to soldiers on the battlefield. Participants will be informed on the importance of registering, voting, and remaining informed on political decisions which affect their lives.	2007; A, B, C, D
23	Kinfolk and Them-folks: Healthy Relationships and Partnerships	The emphasis of this workshop is to learn methods for maintaining healthy relationships or partnerships with family, friends, employers, and others during transitional periods of one's life. The types of relationships which will be discussed will include professional, romantic, educational, and familial. Also, participants will be exposed to ways of preserving older relationships while building newer ones during these transitions. Presenters will provide participants with useful knowledge for balancing these relationships with long-term goals.	2007; A, B, C, E
24	Build Ya Street Cred' … Literally: Solutions for Keeping More Money in Your Pockets	Paying for an education is not easy … let Uncle Sam do it. This workshop will explore the benefits and risks of making financial decisions in order to pay for a higher education. Discussion about financial options, debt, and freedom from presenters will provide insight on dilemmas for participants with future plans of attending college. This workshop will also include a discussion about how those decisions can be directly affected as result of replicating popular artists' lifestyles.	2007; A, E, F
25	Knowledge of Self: Strictly for the Gentlemen	Can your character defend Hip Hop? In this workshop be prepared to debate the good, bad, and ugly facades of Hip Hop. Presenters will utilize prominent artists that exemplify	2007; A, B, C, D

No.	Title	Description	
		each dimension in order to demonstrate how facades change after the cameras go off. Also emphasized in this workshop are the implications of imitating such behaviors in one's life. More importantly, this workshop will explore the roles men have as leaders.	
26	Real Talk: Strictly for the Ladies	As the title states.... This workshop is strictly for the ladies! In this workshop, presenters will discuss the correlations between music, misogyny, and materialism. In this male-free environment, participants can share their opinion and experiences about/ with music in various genres. This workshop principally emphasizes the solutions for creating social reform in rap music, preservation of self, and defeating stigmas and stereotypes.	2007; A, B, C, D, E, F, G
27	MySpace and Facebook It: Planning, Marketing, and Public Relations	How many times a day are you on MySpace or Facebook? Personal webpage accounts are currently a multimillion dollar industry. Learn how to use their contents for the planning, marketing, and PR of any group or event. Presenters will also give you the basic do's and don'ts of Internet communication. They'll also provide you with the what's up on layouts, blogging, webpage privacy, hidden dangers of the Internet, and other necessary tools to keep your account fresh and safe.	2008; A, B, D, G
28	The History of Hip Hop: Grand Masters of the Hip Hop Universe	We're taking a trip back to the roots of this Hip Hop movement. From Grand Master Flash to Lupe Fiasco, participants will learn the history and evolution of the Hip Hop culture. This is a strictly fact-based presentation that revisits Hip Hop's pilgrimage from its grassroots to the 5 Elements and future direction. During this presentation, presenters will highlight Hip Hop's influence in academics and economics.	2008; A, B, C, H
29	Culture, Class, and Change: Making an Easy Transition from High School to College	Graduation is around the corner and you're up to doing grown up things. How prepared are you for this challenge? In this workshop you'll learn from real college students how to live the "real" college life. Come prepared to learn about the importance of financial aid, note taking skills, balancing friends and classes, relationships, and fresh college opportunities. Learn how to adapt to this new lifestyle	2008; A, B, C, D, E, F

No.	Title	Description	
		without compromising your individuality, education, and love for music.	
30	ProFRESHionalism: Preserving Your Swagger in a Professional Setting	There is nothing wrong with styling, looking fresh, and looking your best. From the classroom to the board, our presenters are ready to share their ideas on keeping it real and dressing for the part in a professional setting. Presenters will provide you with the tips for selecting appropriate clothes, maintaining a balanced budget, and interviewing. This workshop is NOT about changing you and how you dress … rather we expect participants to demonstrate confidence and comfort in their Air-Ones and Wingtips. Lastly, this workshop will grant you insight on what older folks really mean when they shout, "Pull up your pants!" or "That outfit is too short!"	2009; A, C, D, E, F
31	History of Hip Hop: The 4 Elements	We're talking a trip back to the roots of this Hip Hop movement. Participants will learn the history and evolution of the Hip Hop culture. This is a strictly fact-based presentation that revisits Hip Hop's pilgrimage from its grassroots to the 4 Elements and its future direction. During this presentation, participants will gain a better understanding of the Hip Hop culture.	2009; C, G, H
32	Making an Easy Transition from High School to College: Texas State University Undergraduate Panel Discussion	In this portion of the X-Change, you will hear from current Texas State undergraduate students about their experiences. Each panel member will highlight specific aspects of the undergraduate experience, including the "Freshman 15," dorm life, involvement in student organizations, professors, FAFSA and finances, freedom and responsibilities, internships and applying for graduation.	2009; A, B, E, F
33	Texas State Hip Hop Congress Diversity Presentation	One of Texas State University' most premiere presentations that has been viewed by over 15,000 incoming freshman and transfer students since 2006, the Texas State Hip Hop Congress *Diversity Presentation* is a humorous and thought provoking presentation that focuses on diversity. Participants learn what diversity is, understand the importance of valuing diversity, and become skilled in the various ways of valuing diversity. This presentation incorporates original skits, YouTube video	2010; A, B, C, D

No.	Title	Description	
		clips, and live performances to provide edutainment and get HHC's messages across to participants.	
34	True Scenarios	Let's do work. Now that you aware of the various colors, presenters will provide you with real life scenarios in which you will apply your knowledge of your personality and behavioral type. Through these reenactments will be able to understand why others may have a different perspective and how you may use this understanding to improve relationships. This workshop will also help you identify and demonstrate how to utilize personality types to improve interpersonal communication.	2010; A, B, C, D, E, F, G
35	Texas State Hip Hop Congress Diversity Presentation	One of Texas State University' most premiere presentations that has been viewed by over 15,000 incoming freshman and transfer students since 2006, the Texas State Hip Hop Congress *Diversity Presentation* is a humorous and thought provoking presentation that focuses on diversity. Participants learn what diversity is, understand the importance of valuing diversity, and become skilled in the various ways of valuing diversity. This presentation incorporates original skits, YouTube video clips, and live performances to provide edutainment and get HHC's messages across to participants.	2011; A, B, C, D
36	Hip Hop Pedagogy, Application	Now that you have learned the facts about diversity, we want to hear how you add to the diversity mix. Art is multifaceted; it has the power to heal, transform, and raise awareness about social, political, familial, and education issues. Presenters will provide you with a series of photos. Your challenge is to free-write 16 bars, a poem or spoken word piece about your life in higher education. This is a chance for you to tell and share your story in your own style and manner.	2011; A, C, E, F, G, H
37	Hip Hop Pedagogy, Application	During this portion of the Hip Hop TRiO X-Change, we invite you to perform your piece of art ... but no pressure. We challenge you to step out of your comfort-zone and share your experience with others. After each of you have participated, we'll invite individual	2011; A, B, C, D, E, G, H

No.	Title	Description	
		members to showcase their art pieces at the Rally of the Delegates.	
38	About That Life: Getting Ready for College Life and Culture Shock	In this workshop, we compare and contrast your school with colleges and universities. We also describe how and why life on campus can be challenging. Lastly, we provide strategies for making your future college or university feel like home.	2012; A, B, C, D, E
39	Balling on a Budget: Hip Hop, Financial Aid, and Needs vs. Wants	In this workshop, we provide a brief overview of the types and amounts of financial aid (including grants, scholarships and loans) that you may expect to receive and develop a budget. We end the presentation with a discussion about how music including hip hop may influence your future spending or budgeting.	2012; A, E
40	High School to College	This is a discussion with high school and college students about you should know about getting college-ready	2012; A, B, C, D, E
41	Myths about College, Financial Aid and College Life	HHC provides an interactive workshop about college myths to reduce stress on students coming into college	2013; A, B, C, E
42	About That Life (2): Getting Ready for College Life	This presentation is on student life on a college campus	2013; A, B, C, D, E
43	High School to College Panel	This is a discussion with high school and college students about you should know in order to get ready for college	2013; A, B, C, D, E
44	Diversity Presentation	The Diversity Presentation incorporates original skits, YouTube video clips and live performances to provide "edutainment." Participants learn what diversity is, how history has made diversity complex and challenging, and how diversity is valued at Texas State University.	2014; A, B, C, D
45	Knowledge of Self: Hip Hop Reflection	Participants learned their how to identify and label the identities of self and others. Additionally, this workshop helps participants to become more aware of their and peer's academic and financial goals. Lastly, the workshop will help participants to identify with their peers' goals and concerns.	2014; A, B, C, D, E, F, G, H
46	Keeping It Real: Hip Hop Expression	This workshop will teach participants how to express themselves and improve their ability to work as part of a team. Additionally, the workshop assist	2014; A, B, C, D, E, F, G, H

No.	Title	Description	
		participants to express their concerns and connect with their peers. Lastly, the workshop helps participants how to value their identity as they continue their education.	
47	Activism Yesterday: Young People & Hip Hop	This workshop has four goals. Students will learn what "social justice" and "activism are; learn the history of youth/adolescents in activism; learn examples of how Hip Hop as serves as the voice of the people; and connect education and activism.	2015; A, B, C, D, E, G, H
48	Activism Today: Photography of Social Injustices	This workshop has five goals. Students will learn that people experience injustices; learn how to recognize inequality; learn how people take action to address injustices; develop empathy for co-marginalized groups; and increase confidence in their ability to speak up (modeled after workshop offered by Teaching Tolerance)	2015; A, B, C, D, E, F, G, H
49	Activism Tomorrow: The New Voice of Protests	This workshop has four goals. Students will develop and share a medium of expression in the form of spoken word and rhyme; increase ability to share and express concerns related to their education; connect and build solidarity with peers; and increase confidence in protesting social injustices.	2015; A, B, C, D, E, F, G, H

Examining HHX Workshop Titles and Descriptions

With relations to code switching, the HHX is code switching in action. The HHX serves as a platform for collegiate students to convert language, knowledge, and experience most normally associated with university bureaucracy, processes, and transitions to youth. Additionally, this language also reflected and is associated with issues related to community, identity, skill development, media, and education. It is important to note that although the workshops were focused on a variety of topics, the underlying themes were essentially what was being conveyed as part of the outreach program and through code switching to promote post-secondary education.

Empowerment

Out of the 49 workshop titles and descriptions, 47 of them possessed a theme of empowerment. This was an expected result as the goal of the HHX is to establish a common ground where students learn the importance of education through the culture of Hip Hop. The themes of empowerment were most notable in workshops titles that included *Street Credibility: Maintaining Respect through a Hip Hop Lifestyle, Activism Yesterday: Young People & Hip Hop, Activism Today: Photography of Social Injustices,* and *Workshop for Those Who Don't Know Which Workshop to Go To.*

Community

The HHX provided 40 of 49 workshops that has theme of community. Specifically, the workshop titles that clearly depict the theme of community included *HIV/AIDS Awareness and Community Mobilization through Hip Hop, Put Yo Hood Up! A Discussion about the Media's Role in the East-West Coast Violence, Desegregation through Music and Film: A Discussion of Unity and Integration, Kinfolk and Them-Folks: Healthy Relationships and Partnerships,* and *Peace, Not "Peace Out": Keeping Peace with Others.*

Diversity

Thirty-seven of the 49 HHX workshops had a theme of diversity. The following workshop titles specifically presented a theme on diversity: *Diversity Presentation, Real Talk: Strictly for the Ladies, Why You Hatin'? When Individuals from Different Cultures, Races, or Gender Rap, Put Yo Hood Up! A Discussion of Violence, Stereotypes and the Media,* and *Culture, Class, and Change: Making an Easy Transition from High School to College.*

Authenticity

Additionally, 30 of the 49 workshops possessed a theme of authenticity. The titles that most closely represent the theme of authenticity included *ProFRESHionalism: Preserving your Swagger in a Professional Setting, Keeping It Real: Hip Hop Expression, Knowledge of Self: Hip Hop Reflection,* and *MySpace and Facebook It: Marketing and Public Relations.*

Persistence

Of the 49 HHX workshops facilitated by HHC, 28 workshops included themes of persistence. Workshop titles that were expressly themed as persistence included *Making an Easy Transition from High School to College: Texas State University Undergraduate Panel Discussion, Activism Tomorrow: The New Voice of Protests, Balling on a Budget: Hip Hop, Financial Aid, and Needs vs. Wants, Culture, Class, and Change: Making an Easy Transition from High School to College, About That Life: Getting Ready for College Life and Culture Shock.*

Transformation

Just as importantly, 22 of the HHX workshops had themes of transformation. The theme of transformation were reflected in *True Scenarios, Thugs and Gangstas: A Discussion of the Stigmas Placed on Hip Hop* and *Desegregation through Music and Film: A Discussion of Unity and Integration.*

Creativity

During the tenure of HHX, 22 of the 49 workshops had a theme of creativity. Titles such as *5 Elements: Break Dancing, Lyricist, Graffiti, DJ, Attire* and *Hip Hop, Not Gift Shops: Entertainers and Entrepreneurs* display the theme of creativity.

Innovation

Lastly, out of the 49 workshops, 15 were themed on innovation. Fewer titles provided examples in of code switching as part of their titles—these included *Bling-Bling, But No Books: Spending Rappers Money* and *Activism Tomorrow: The New Voice of Protests.*

General Observations and Reflections

In general, many of the workshop titles incorporated common Hip Hop vernacular, catch-phrases and terminology that were popular during each particular year that the program was implemented. The titles themselves served to entice and grab students' interest on topics being presented and connected them to a larger purpose. Various workshop descriptions used a similar approach in describing the intended outcomes of the specific workshop. By establishing interest, youth were able to associate or relate to the issues being presented. The topics and program were likely treated as presumably more engaging than what youth typically associate as an educational setting. Just as importantly, many of the workshops incorporated Hip Hop performances further amplifying student's interest. After each successful year, students shared their experience with other students and encouraged participation the following year. Code switching served as an appropriate tool to introduce or reinforce concepts, topics and experiences related to empowerment, community, diversity, authenticity, persistence, transformation, creativity and innovation. As a result, these themes, especially because of how they are introduced and by whom, become values and concepts that are exciting and worthy of interest for youth.

Beyond creating initial interest and buy-in, Hip Hop and code switching helped establish credibility of college students as near-peers. In other words, code switching allowed HHC members to connect as Hip Hop heads, collegiate students, someone of diverse backgrounds, and members of similar marginalized communities. Through this connection, HHC members experienced less push back or challenge in opening, facilitating or teaching sensitive topics or conversations. Additionally, using Hip Hop culture and vernacular calmed and reshaped the learning environment. HHX came to represent a credible and safe space, along with it the information being presented. As a result, the presenters themselves were not treated as experts, but rather as fellow fans and creators of Hip Hop with an informed opinion on a particular subject matter. The position as near-peers respects youth as experts in their own reality and challenges them to think more critically about their realities and education. Just as important, code switching in HHX demonstrated that a collegiate student could be savvy in the "streets" and on college campuses. In such case, code-switching presented the opportunity for trust to be quickly established in the near-peer relationship and promote willingness to engage in conversations surrounding these themes and related topics.

A final observation is that the HHX workshop titles and descriptions reinforce the idea that code switching can be used to empower and teach. Based on interactions with youth attending these programs, it is fair to estimate that they possess a firm understanding of each of these themes (empowerment, community, diversity, authenticity, persistence, transformation, creativity, and innovation). HHC members then facilitate the opportunity to expand youths' ability to think more critically about concepts related to the themes. Code switching in programs like HHX assists in this process. Essentially, code switching using Hip Hop vernacular likely allowed students to perceive issues associated with themes as more manageable, in their control and achievable. This, in return, is likely to encourage youth to continue their educational path and improves confidence in future aspirations. Additionally, a primary goal of the workshops, regardless of the topic, is to improve youth's esteem, self-worth, and knowledge of their various identities. In achieving this, youth are likely understand that their experiences are connected to those of other marginalized and oppressed groups. At the same time, HHX attempts to help youth connect their individual and communal experience to that of local, national, regional and global institutions and systems. Code switching using Hip Hop communicates to youth that they have allies and supporters of similar and diverse backgrounds while engaging in their education and in society. Just as importantly, code switching with this kind of purpose trains youth to serve as allies and advocates for other marginalized groups.

Collectively, these workshops were presented in a similar style and fashion as that of the "Hip Hop themed presentation about Texas State University to high school students" conducted by Cordero (2008, p. 53). Cordero's (2008) applied research project showed that "the majority of students surveyed found the PowerPoint presentation they were shown to be attention-grabbing, interesting, better in comparison to other PowerPoint presentations from other Universities, easy to understand and informative" (p. 53) Cordero's (2008) recommendation for incorporating Hip Hop music and culture into curriculum stemmed from strong support of evidence which showed that high school students expressed a mass appeal to the content, design, font and layout of the presentation delivered. HHX, as an outreach program that was developed by college students and that serves youth, seemingly recreates and reinforces Cordero's findings. By allowing college students, who are Hip Hop heads, to create and implement programs that are reflective of youths' preference in interest, comprehension and needs youth are more receptive to information and knowledge. When trained, mentored, and challenged to converse, think and engage more critically on issues and topics related to empowerment, community, diversity, authenticity, persistence, transformation, creativity, and innovation, college students will reproduce and rearticulate themes in their own forms of code switching and that engender benefits younger generations.

The examination of the use of Hip Hop, Hip Hop culture and code switching as a methodology is important in addressing inequities, disparities and issues for youth in Austin and San Marcos, Texas. Youth and communities benefit from educational outreach programs produced by college students and with the support of staff at colleges and universities. Outreach programs like the annual Hip Hop X-Change provide youth with opportunities to establish "voice" in safe and brave spaces. The use of code switching within Hip Hop Culture creates a system of engagement, connection and empowerment for marginalized communities including predominantly Latino and African American youth communities served by these programs. Future programs and initiatives benefit from institutionalizing programs that are based and created from ideas generated by students and professionals who love Hip Hop or understand how it can be harnessed.

REFERENCES

Abe, D. (2009). Hip-hop and the academic canon. *Education, Citizenship and Social Justice, 4*(3), 263–272.
Arao, B., Clemens, K., (2013). *From safe spaces to brave spaces: A new way to frame dialogue around diversity and social justice.* In *The art of effective facilitation.* Stylis.
Chang, J. (2005). *Can't stop, won't stop : A history of the hip-hop generation* (intro. DJ Kool Herc). New York: St. Martin's Press, 2005.
Cordero, R. (Spring 2008). *"Don't forget the Hip-Hop!" Recruiting economically disadvantaged minority students in higher education: An assessment of postsecondary programs at Texas State University.* Master's Thesis, Texas State University.

Delgado, M., & Staples, L. (2008). *Youth-led community organizing: Theory and action.* New York: Oxford University Press.

Dimitriadis, G. (2015). Framing Hip Hop: New methodologies for new times. *Urban Education, 50*(1), 31–51. doi:10.1177/0042085914563185.

Flores-Gonzalez, N., Rodriguez, M., Rodriguez-Muniz, M., (2006). *Beyond resistance! Youth activism and community change: New democratic possibilities for practice and policy for America's youth* New York: Routledge, 2006.

Gutierrez, L. (1995). Understanding the empowerment process: Does consciousness make a difference? *Social Work Research, 19*(4), 229–237.

Friere, P. (1990). *Pedagogy of the oppressed.* New York: Continuum.

Hall, H. R. (2007). Poetic expressions: Students of color express resiliency through metaphors and similes. *Journal of Advanced Academics, 18*(2), 216–244.

Hip Hop Congress. (2015). Website. http://www.hiphopcongress.com/mission.

How young Latinos communicate with friends in the digital age (2010). 2010-07-28.

Liadi, O., F., & Omobowale, A., O.,. (2011), Globalization of Hip Hop Music, multilingualism and hip hop consumption among youths in Nigeria. *International Journal of Sociology and Anthropology, 3*(12), 469–477.

Low, B. E. (2011). *Slam school: Learning through conflict in the hip-hop and spoken word classroom.* Stanford: Stanford University Press, 2011.

McFarland, P. (2008). Chicano hip-hop as interethnic contact zone. *Aztlan: A Journal of Chicano Studies, 33*(1), 173–183.

Miranda, D., & Claes, M. (2009). Music listening, coping, peer affiliation and depression in adolescence. *Psychology of Music, 37*(2), 215–233.

Omoniyi, T. (2005). Toward a re-theorization of code switching. *The Forum,* TESOL.

Pennycook, A. (2007). Language, localization, and the real: Hip-hop and the global spread of authenticity. *Journal of Language, Identity, and Education, 6*(2), 101–115.

Petchauer, E. (2015). Starting with style: Toward a second wave of hip-hop education research and practice. *Urban Education, 50*(1), 78–105. doi:10.1177/0042085914563181.

Rose, T. (2008). *The hip hop wars: What we talk about when we talk about hip hop—why it matters.* New York: BasicCivitas.

Travis, R. J. (2010). What they think: Attributions made by youth workers about youth circumstances and the implications for service-delivery in out-of-school time programs. *Child & Youth Care Forum.*

Travis, R. J. (2013). Rap music and the empowerment of today's youth: Evidence in everyday music listening, music therapy, and commercial rap music. *Child & Adolescent Social Work Journal, 30*(2), 139–167. doi:10.1007/s10560-012-0285-x.

Travis, R., Jr., & Ausbrooks, A. (2012). EMPOWERMENTODAY: A model of positive youth development and academic persistence for male African Americans. *Children & Schools, 34*(3), 186–189. doi:10.1093/cs/cds026.

Travis, R., Jr., & Bowman, S.W. (2011). Negotiating risk and promoting empowerment through rap music: Development of a measure to capture risk and empowerment pathways to change. *Journal of Human Behavior in the Social Environment, 21*(6), 654–678. doi:10.1080/10911359.2011.583507.

Travis, R., Jr., & Deepak, A. (2011). Empowerment in context: Lessons from hip-hop culture for social work practice. *Journal of Ethnic & Cultural Diversity in Social Work, 20*(3), 203–222.

Youth Culture and Its Influence on Children's Sport

SCOTT WESTFALL *and* DANIEL GOULD

Youth culture has been described as the "sum of ways of living adolescents; it refers to the body of norms, values, and practices recognized and shared by members of the adolescent society as appropriate guides to actions" (Rice, 1996, p. 405). Components of youth culture can include the unique beliefs, behaviors, styles, music, and interests of adolescents, as youth often display an inclination for popular fashion, music, sports, and dating. These characteristics are emblematic of youth culture and distinguish it from other age groups (Fasick, 1984). Through youth culture young people are able to develop their own set of values that do not necessarily reject, but clearly distinguish them from adults.

Closely associated with youth culture is the notion of popular culture. While difficult to define, popular culture generally refers to the ideas, attitudes, and images of the masses. Author John Storey (2006) developed several themes to describe popular culture. First, he asserted that popular culture is a synonym for mass culture. It includes the sale of books, CDs, and DVDs, along with attendance at concerts, sporting events, and festivals. These categories help quantify the inclinations and preferences of a large collection of individuals based upon how they devote their time, money, and resources.

Furthermore, Storey asserted that popular culture is different from high culture. Whereas high culture is the result of an individual act of creation, popular culture is mass-produced for the purpose of mass consumption. While this concept of popular culture is largely based in commercialism and consumerism, Storey contended that popular culture originates from the people, and it is never imposed upon them. Moreover, Storey reasoned that within popular culture there is little hegemony, as what is considered to be "popular" frequently fluctuates, thereby causing popular culture to be divided into subcultures, with which mainstream popular culture has only a slight familiarity.

A common theme of contemporary youth culture is young peoples' immersion in technology. During the lifetimes of today's youth, technology arrived and was disseminated at a rapid pace, thereby inundating the modern generation in the digital age. Contemporary youth are the first generation to spend their entire life surrounded by digital technology such as computers, video games, cell phones, and the Internet (Prensky, 2001). A study from Junco and Mastrodicasa (2007) indicated that over 97 percent of college students owned a computer; 94 percent owned a cell phone; and, over 56 percent owned an MP3 player. Furthermore, over 75 percent of respondents reported using some type of instant messaging program and being logged into an instant messaging program (median score of) 35 hours per week. Due to the ubiquity of technology and this singular and abrupt generational engagement, Prensky (2001) dubbed contemporary youth "Digital Natives" (p. 1).

Tapscott (1998) coined the phrase the "Net Generation" to describe youth who grew-up surrounded by digital media. He stated, "Today's kids are so bathed in bits that they think it's all part of the natural landscape. To them, the digital technology is no more intimidating than a VCR or toaster" (p. 1). However, a darker viewpoint suggested that technological gadgets have caused Net Geners to display symptoms that resemble attention deficit disorder, which results in a shallow, distracted generation that lacks the ability to focus (Hallowell, 2006). Moreover, Damon (2008) asserted that today's students are drifting aimlessly and that many of the employers where Millennials work have banned social networks like Facebook because of the time dump and subsequent loss of productivity.

However, characteristics of the Net Generation do not entirely forecast doom and gloom for the future. Tapscott (2008) declared that overall, youth of the Net Generation are "more than alright," asserting that Net Geners are quicker, smarter, and more tolerant of diversity than previous generations. On social fronts, they care about justice and are often engaged in some kind of civic activity in school, work, or their community.

Many of today's youth are considered to be part of Generation Y. Although no precise dates have been given, it is generally accepted that Generation Y, or the Millennial Generation, is comprised of individuals born between the early 1980s and early 2000s. Millennials have been characterized as being sheltered, confident, pressured and achieving (Howe & Strauss, 2000). While the explanations for these portrayals are somewhat unclear, it has been suggested that post–1980 parents decided that children should always feel good about themselves, which led to a society-wide push to increase children's self-esteem. Thus, many school districts across the country implemented programs to enhance youth self-esteem, most of which unintentionally developed a greater sense of self-importance and narcissism within this generation's children (Twenge, 2006). Furthermore, Twenge, Konrath, Foster, Campbell, and Bushman (2008) asserted that Generation Y adolescents are more narcissistic than youth from previous generations. This proclaimed generational shift related to Twenge's (2006) portrayal of "the Entitlement Generation," characterizes them as being disengaged, narcissistic, egotistical, entitled, and self-centered.

Whether it be youth culture, popular culture, or Generation Y, the current youth culture climate has a major influence on both young people and the communities in which they live. In many ways it can be thought of as a double-edged sword. On one hand, it empowers youth to access knowledge, communicate and connect with others, and demonstrate agency like no generation before. At the same time, the contemporary youth climate leads to a number of social problems such as physical inactivity, cyber-bullying, and social isolation. In fact, Steinberg (2011) indicated that contemporary times have created a new childhood where young people take on more adult roles and are characterized by greater cognitive capabilities than adults previously thought they were capable of possessing. They are also receiving mixed messages from the media, such as abstaining from sex, while at the same time, feeling the need to wear provocative, in vogue attire. Current culture not only teaches children and youth to become hedonistic consumers but it changes how they view society, their self-image and their interactions with adults. Corporate media culture, then, inundates young people with information that shapes their preferences, values and themselves. Finally, Steinberg (2011) argues that it is very difficult for parents to control their children's experiences, as they cannot protect them from the information of the world, whether it is good or bad. In fact, many parents struggle with knowing how to interact with their children and the role they should play as a socialization agent for today's digital generation.

One area that has received little attention in writings on youth culture is how contemporary youth and youth culture both influence and are influenced by organized sport. This is important because organized youth sport is one of the most pervasive childhood activities for youth. Organized sport also has been shown to have important consequences on youth development (Gould & Carson, 2008; Gould, Cowburn, & Shields, 2014). A void in the literature exists and the relationship between youth culture and organized youth sport has not been examined.

This review is designed to fill this void in the literature. In this essay we will discuss the role of youth sports in the United States, including its pervasiveness and importance for both youth and society. The relationship between popular youth culture and sport will then be discussed by examining the traditional goals of youth sports, its importance in contemporary society, the benefits and detriments of sport involvement for children and youth, how the sport experience may be shaped by Generation Y youth and their youth culture, and how Generation Y youth may be influenced by contemporary sport involvement. Threats to creating empowering youth sports experiences for young people will be discussed and include sedentary lifestyle concerns, a decrease in publicly funded sports programs which have created a divide in youth sport opportunities based on socioeconomic status, sport specialization, entitlement attitudes on the part of youth, sport-related bullying and hazing practices and the use of social media. Finally, implications for guiding youth sport involvement and programs will be discussed.

The Role of Sport in America

Sports are an important part of youth culture in the United States with over 21 million children and youth between the ages of six to 17 participating in organized sporting activities on a regular basis. Meanwhile, an additional five million children and youth engage in organized sports occasionally (Aspen Institute, 2013). Organized sport also represents the most prevalent out-of-school activity for children and youth (Duffett & Johnson, 2004). Not only is organized sport involvement highly prevalent in the lives of young individuals, but these children and youth are often intensely involved. For years, scholars (e.g., Coleman, 1974; Larson, 2000) have argued that children feel their sport-related actions are important and valued by significant others like parents, peers and members of the general community. For this reason, sport participation is thought to have major effects on young people's physical and psychological development; a position supported in reviews of the literature.

One reason scholars are so interested in youth sports is because participation has been linked to a number of important physical, social, and emotional outcomes. For example, participation in sport is linked to a variety of physical health related benefits such as better nutrition and increased physical activity levels (e.g., Pate, Trost, Levin, & Dowda, 2000; Strong, Malina, Blimkie, Daniels, Dishman, Guten, Hergenroeder, Must, Nixon, Pivarnik, Rowland, Trost, & Trudeau, 2005). However, physical benefits are not the only rewards that children and youth derive from sports participation. A variety of psychosocial outcomes like enhanced self-esteem, the acquisition of social interaction and teamwork skills, the formation of positive relationships as well as enhanced confidence, character, pro-social values and positive affect have been associated with sports participation (Gould, Cowburn, & Shields, 2014; Gould & Westfall, 2014). Not all of the outcomes associated with sport participation, however, have been positive. Some scholars (e.g.,

Coakley, 2011) have questioned the positive outcomes associated with sport participation and/or identified negative outcomes associated with participation such as increased stress, burnout, and a loss of motivation (e.g., Gustafsson, Kentta, & Hassmen, 2011; Raedeke, Smith, Kentta, Arce, & de Francisco, 2014). Whether positive or negative, outcomes linked to sport participation are often dependent on factors such as the program context and quality of coaching.

After reviewing the literature in the area, Gould, Carson and Blanton (2013) concluded that: (a) there is a clear relationship between sport participation and social emotional development in young people, although causal links have not been established; (b) coaches who are more effective at fostering social-emotional skills in their athletes have philosophies that place prime importance on the development of these skills; (c) coaches' abilities to develop trusting relationships with athletes are critical for developing social-emotional skills and attributes; (d) creating caring climates that focus on individual development versus social comparison are correlated to the development of social emotional skills in young athletes; and (e) the sport context not only provides opportunities to directly teach life skills but allows young people to test and demonstrate already developing life skills through interactions with their peers and coaches.

One outcome of sport participation that has not been examined until only recently is how participation influences the family. However, several recent studies have begun to examine this area of inquiry. For example, Dorsch, Smith and McDonough (2009) studied child-to-parent socialization in organized youth sport versus the more typically studied parent-to-child socialization. Results of interviews with 26 youth sport parents revealed that their children's youth sport participation influenced these parents interest in sport, their discretionary time usage, financial commitments, their own friendships and emotions. Most interesting were the findings that the sport experience created unique opportunities for parent-child communication and the parent-child relationship. It was also found that parents experienced stronger emotions in the youth sport versus other settings. Thus, the youth sport experience not only has important effects on the child but on their parents and family functioning.

In another study with underserved youth, Riley and Anderson-Butcher (2012) examined the effects of a sport-based youth development summer camp program on youth and their families. These investigators not only found that the camp positively influenced the targeted youth participants, but impacted their parents as well. Specifically, parents worried less because they knew where their children were and felt confident that their children were taking part in a productive activity. These parents also became more health conscious because of their child's participation and were more open to new things. Finally, the parents reported that the camp experience increased communication among family members, increased the child's openness to parent communication, and increased parent-child communication. The youth sport camp experience, then, had important implications for participants' parents.

A final outcome of youth sports focuses on the family finances and, in turn, the effects the sport-related financial commitments families make on young athletes and the parent-child relationship. Youth sports in the U.S. are a big business, a very big business (Hyman, 2012). Although no precise dollar amounts can be given for the youth sports economy, almost all experts agree it is very large. For example, the camp business generates over $15 billion each year with sports camps being a major segment of that market (American Camping Association, 2013). Moreover, over the last 30 years we have seen a government disinvestment in publicly funded youth sport programs which has led to fewer opportunities (especially for economically disadvantaged youth) and the rise of phenomena like "pay to play" in high schools (the practice of charging a participation fee of $100 or $200 for each high school sport played), private coaching, sport clubs, and travel teams. There are no signs these costs are abating.

Youth sports have also become very commercialized with adults making their living as personal performance trainers, sport tour operators, hitting or shooting coaches, or private gym owners. While many of these individuals have good intentions, sport sociologist Jay Coakley (2010) contends that any time adults make their living off of children, there is potential for abuse. For instance, a private gym owner must pay the rent or mortgage so he or she focuses on renting his or her facility space throughout the year, and does not necessarily think about whether it is best for young athletes to have time off from training. Similarly, major media outlets like USA Today or ESPN have national rankings for high school teams or promote All-Star youth sports events, which many experts feel contribute to a focus on winning at the expense of educational and personal development outcomes of youth sports.

Finally, Hyman (2012) contends that today's commercialization of youth sports is so successful because commercial interests and the media are selling hope to parents that their child can earn a college athletic scholarship by developing their athletic skills, or by playing off parental guilt that if they do not do everything possible to help their child develop athletically, they are not a good parent. For example, Coakley (2010) has contended that today's sport parents often unknowingly judge their moral worth as parents based upon their children's sport success.

The financial costs of youth sports are not only a challenge in and of themselves but these costs appear to be influencing the parent-child relationship. In a recent study, for example, Dunn, Dorsch, King and Rothlisberger (2014) found that the more parents invested financially in their child's sport experience the more stress young athletes experienced relative to performing well. The financial costs and commercialization of contemporary youth sport, then, are certainly an issue that plays a prominent role in today's youth sports culture.

Popular Youth Culture and Traditional Youth Sports

Goals for Youth Sports Involvement

There are many goals that the American public, whether it be parents, coaches or young athletes themselves, have for children's involvement in organized sports. These range from having fun and improved health and fitness to the development of social emotional skills and values (USADA, 2011). For example, surveys and interviews with young athletes have repeatedly shown that youth have multiple motives for sport involvement including having fun, improving their skills, staying in shape, experiencing the excitement of competition, to be with and meet new friends, and for winning or success (Ewing & Seefeldt, 1996; 2002). Moreover, most young athletes are motivated by more than one of these factors. Winning and success, while cited as a reason for involvement, is typically not cited as the most important motive. Underlying these more descriptive reasons for participation are more deep-seated motives like feeling competent, experiencing feelings of relatedness and sensing some autonomy by having choices and control over involvement (Weiss & Ambrose, 2008). Thus, young athletes who perceive themselves to be competent are more likely to be involved in youth sports while children who do not feel competent tend to discontinue involvement. Similarly, children are more likely to be motivated when they have friends involved in their activities and when they feel they have some control over their involvement.

Given the multiple motives and goals for youth sports involvement, debates in the youth sports arena often center around which goals to emphasize. That is, what emphasis should be placed on winning, personal development, friendship and fun and physical development? Or how are these multiple objectives balanced? It is common to read media reports of winning being emphasized over other goals like affiliation and personal development. Likewise, local clubs are often accused of allocating more resources such as funds, superior equipment and better practice times to travel versus house teams.

What is ironic about these debates is that these objectives are often seen as being mutually exclusive when in fact most models of athlete development feel that all these objectives need to be met if children and youth are to develop as athletes and ultimately lead active lifestyles. For example, many sport organizations have adopted long-term athlete development models that depict the ideal progression of children progressing through stages of development over time with various goals for participation changing in emphasis over time (Aspen Institute, 2013). Understanding these stages of athlete development is critical to understanding contemporary youth sports.

Stages of Long-Term Athlete Development

Stages of long-term athlete developed have been developed based upon studies like the ones conducted by Bloom (1985), Côté (1999) and Durand-Bush and Salmela (2002). In these studies the careers of elite athletes were retrospectively analyzed looking at how they started sport, developed over time, and then became elite competitors. According to these studies, there are stages that an individual needs in order to progress from child athlete to world class or Olympic level performer. These include: (a) the sampling; (b) the specializing; (c) the investment; and (d) maintenance states. Each of these will be briefly described below.

The sampling stage involves the early years of sport involvement where a child has many opportunities for participation, receives positive coach and family encouragement/support, learns fundamental motor skills, develops a love of sport and physical activity, and participates with little emphasis placed on performance and competitive results. In the *specializing stage* (around 14 years of age) the young athlete participates in fewer sports, family commitment and support increases, the young person experiences increased success, has more specialized coaching, and a greater focus on sport specific skills. Winning is more important but is still not the primary goal emphasized. The *investment stage* (around age 18) is where the athlete engages in more intense and high quality competitive training, orchestrated by an expert coach while receiving continued but different types of family support. It is within this stage that he or she pursues excellence and winning and losing take on more important roles. The final stage is the *maintenance stage* and for most sports, typically occurs in the adult years and is characterized by an elite performance focus and efforts to deal with the many demands of becoming and maintaining world-class performance success.

Understandably, only a small number of talented and highly motivated individuals will progress through all four stages and become elite athletes. However, in the early years of involvement, all children, whether they are highly talented or more modest in ability, need similar sport experiences—experiences that stress multiple sport participation, focus on fun and fundamental skills, provide time to meet affiliation needs and develop physical literacy skills. It is felt that if children have good experiences in the early sampling and investment stages they develop the skills and motivation to pursue recreational sports or healthy physically active life styles and, if they have the talent and interest, can pursue more elite levels of sport participation.

Threats to Long-Term Athlete Development and Youth Sport Goals: The Professionalization of Youth Sports

While youth sports can have a number of beneficial effects on young people, they have also been shown to have negative outcomes in some circumstances. Most experts feel the key to ensuring the benefits of youth sports outweigh the detriments is to focus on creating caring climates, multiple goals of sports and provide coaches with trainings that enable them to facilitate the fulfillment of these objectives. Focusing on winning, rankings, intense year-round training and elite performance in the early years of participation is seen as counterproductive, not only in terms of enhancing holistic child development but relative to athletic talent development. There is growing concern, however, that youth sports are becoming increasingly professionalized with more and more children specializing in single sports and engaging in year round training and intense competitions at early ages (Farrey, 2008; Gould, 2009).

There are efforts to try to curb the professionalization of youth sports. In addition to books and articles being written on the topic (e.g., Gould & Carson, 2004; Farrey, 2008), the Aspen Institute (2013) has conferred panels of experts and is holding national events in an effort to bring attention to the negative consequences of the professionalization of youth sports. Similarly, the U.S. Anti-Doping Agency has initiated a True Sport campaign designed to create a culture change in youth sports to reduce the overemphasis on winning, along with the moral transgressions that often accompany this win at all costs mentality. Jim Thompson (1995) and his Positive Coaching Alliance has trained over one million coaches, emphasizing the importance of not only taking a positive approach to coaching, but emphasizing the importance of coaches focusing on the personal development of athletes, as well as competitive success. Finally, the National Federation of State High School Associations and its state affiliates like the Michigan High School Athletic Association have repeatedly emphasized the importance of multisport participation and the educational goals of school sport beyond winning and losing (Roberts, 2014).

With this general context as a backdrop, specific "hot topic" issues associated with contemporary youth sports will be addressed. These include:

physical inactivity on the part of youth; the socioeconomic youth sports divide; entitlement attitudes on the part of youth; sport specialization and year round training; cheating and moral transgressions; national championships and social media.

Hot Topics in Contemporary Youth Sports

Youth Physical Inactivity Patterns

The rise of physical inactivity and obesity in children and youth has become a major health concern in the United States. Recent statistics, for example, reveal that only one-quarter of U.S. children and youth (ages 6–15) meet the Physical Activity Guidelines for Americans, which recommends at least 60 minutes of moderate-to-vigorous physical activity per day (National Physical Activity Plan Alliance, 2014). Furthermore, as recently as 2011–2012 nearly one-third of youth were shown to either be overweight or obese (Ogden, Carroll, Kit, & Flegal 2014). These findings are often highest for children who come from communities of low socioeconomic status. For example, minority girls often exhibit the lowest levels of physical activity and highest overweight/obesity levels. Explanations for these increases are varied and include poor nutrition, having inactive parents, increased screen time, and a lack of access to facilities (Kumanyika, 2008; Anderson & Butcher, 2006; Clarke, O'Malley, Johnston, & Schulenberg, 2009).

Many feel that youth sports participation is an essential element in combating the physical inactivity and obesity crisis because of the number of these programs that exist throughout the country and because of the inherent physical nature of the sport activities and emphasis on good health that is often associated with them. However, we argue that the more youth sports become professionalized with a focus on athletic performance and success, travel teams and specialization, the less likely sports will serve as a vehicle for overweight and inactive children—the very youth who need it the most. In fact, recent statistics reveal that while still involving a high percentage of children, traditional team sport participation in the U.S. has declined in recent years (Aspen Institute, 2013). Moreover, because the vast majority of youth sports coaches in the United States receive little or no formal training to coach, it is unlikely that they will be prepared to work with children who are less capable and motivated to participate.

The question needs to be asked, then: "what role should youth sports play in combatting the physical inactivity and obesity crisis in children and youth?" In particular, should youth sports programs focus more on creating welcoming and nurturing environments for less skilled and physically inactive children than be geared for the more athletically talented and gifted ones? Can both audiences be served? Do coaches need to be educated as to how best motivate less motivated and skilled children? Should the government play a more active role in providing greater access to sports venues, especially for the underserved? It is essential that these questions be addressed.

The Socioeconomic Status Youth Sports Divide

There is a socioeconomic divide in contemporary youth sports, often creating youth sports "haves versus have-nots." That is, middle and upper middle class children typically live in communities where they have greater access to gyms, pools and athletic fields. Their parents often have the financial ability to purchase sports equipment, pay to access programs, and hire coaches and trainers. In contrast, low socioeconomic status children are the "have-nots" of youth sports. They live in communities with far fewer facilities, have less access to programs, and their parents often cannot afford the costs associated with participation. Not only is it the initial levels of sport involvement where these inequities occur, but as youth sports become increasingly specialized and characterized by early specialization, travel teams and year round training (which are all associated with increased financial obligations), underserved youth are less likely to be involved or will be put at competitive disadvantages. They simply have less access and fewer opportunities.

Cheating and Moral Transgressions

The American public expects that children and youth will develop a number of positive attributes and morals from youth sports participation (USADA, 2011). Chief among these is the development of good character assets like honesty and integrity. However, not a month seems to go by without some reference to cheating or moral transgressions occurring in youth sports. So a key question is whether sports builds character or characters?

Fortunately, researchers have been studying moral behavior in youth sport coaches and athletes for a number of years and have discovered a number of important principles that help answer this question. For example, studies have shown that young people do not automatically develop positive morals and prosocial behaviors from merely participating in youth sports. In fact, the research suggests that the more experience one has in sport, the more likely they exhibit lower levels of moral thinking (Shields & Bredemeier, 2007). This does not suggest, however, that sport participation always results in lower levels of moral functioning. Investigators have established that the moral actions of young people in sport are influenced by a variety of factors including whether a task (focused on self-improvement) versus ego (focused on beating others) climate is created by coaches and parents (Kavussanu & Ntoumanis, 2003); the values and behaviors of peers involved support immoral behavior (Shields, LaVoi, Bredemeier, & Power, 2007); and individuals own characteristics (Long, Pantaleon, Bruant, & d'Arripe-Longueville, 2006). Game reasoning or "bracketed morality," where young athletes feel that certain moral behaviors like fighting are accepted in sport but not in real life (Shields & Bredemeier, 2001) and moral disengagement where athletes often find ways to self-justify moral transgressions (Kavussanu, 2008) have often been identified. Lastly, studies have shown that when intentionally designed, sport can facilitate character and prosocial behavior in young people (Weinberg & Gould, 2015). It is clear, then, that sport can both build character and facilitate moral behavior or foster immoral actions depending on the sport context.

In an interesting and insightful book, *True Competition*, Shields and Bredemeier (2009) have suggested that one key factor in determining how sport affects the moral development of young people is how competition is defined. Too often sport does not achieve its moral potential because competition, or what these authors label as false or decompetition, occurs. Decompetition happens when significant others in sport define competition as a battle or war, where young athletes are taught that winning counts at most any cost, one's opponent is an enemy and should be viewed as such, rules are to be, at best, tolerated and worked around, and officials are opponents that get in the way. In contrast, true competition involves a partnership with one's opponent and respect for him or her, the pursuit of personal excellence along with one's competitor, love of the game, and a view that officials are facilitators of the game, not enemies to be worked around. Thus, Shields and Bredemeier (2009) make a strong case that when true competition contexts are created, character development is more likely to occur in young athletes. True competition also leads to greater enjoyment and more likely fosters excellence in young people. Decompetition, however, is socially destructive, leads to less enjoyment, lower morality and does not foster excellence.

In addition to creating an environment characterized by true competition, the research on moral development in sport suggests that a number of strategies can be implemented to foster moral development and prosocial behavior and attitudes through sport (Weinberg & Gould, 2015). These include (a) specifically defining what good moral behavior does and does not involve; (b) reinforcing positive moral behavior while penalizing inappropriate of amoral behavior; (c) modeling appropriate behavior; (d) taking the time to explain to the young athlete why moral actions are appropriate or inappropriate; (e) having athletes discuss why actions are moral versus amoral (versus just telling them); (f) engineering environments where athletes must make moral choices; (g) fostering cooperation and teaching principles of cooperation; (h) creating task-oriented environments that focus on self-improvement more than competitive outcomes; and (i) allowing young people to have the power to make choices.

Bullying and Hazing

A topic that is related to character and moral development in young athletes is bullying and hazing. Bullying and hazing in sport have received considerable attention in the last decade due to increased media coverage along with the heightened efforts to eradicate these practices from youth sports altogether. Bullying has been characterized as a systematic harassment of weaker individuals using means such as humiliation and torment (Lines, 2008). Within the context of youth sport, bullying can come from parents, players, and even coaches. Sport bullying can include verbal taunts, name-calling, put-downs, threats and intimidation. Socially, it can involve ostracism from a group, ganging-up on an individual or group teasing. Meanwhile, bullying can also occur in physical forms such as hitting, kicking and/or damaging personal property. In recent times, cyber bullying has transpired through technological devices such as computers, cell phones, social media, and other forms of online communication (Government of Alberta, 2005). While bullying has been historically viewed as being most prominent in public schools, and being part of adolescent behavior since at least the eighteenth century (Dunning & Sheard, 2005), it is certainly not only limited to youth sports; recently bullying was reported as existing as high up as the NFL's Miami Dolphins (Shpigel, 2014).

Hazing is defined as "any activity expected of someone joining a group that humiliates, degrades, abuses or endangers, regardless of the person's willingness to participate" (Hoover, 1999, p. 8). While hazing has historically been thought of in the context of American fraternities and sororities, recent reports have shown that hazing is prevalent in youth sports and poses significant dangers to the recipients of the hazing, physically and psychologically (Waldron & Kowalski, 2009). Examples of these risky behaviors include, players being forced to consume large amounts of food and/or alcohol, players being mocked, ridiculed, physically beaten, stripped naked, and even sexually assaulted.

While bullying and hazing are dark areas of youth sports, there have been increased efforts in recent years to solve these problems. Crow and Phillips (2004) have developed anti-bullying and anti-hazing policies to help rid sport teams and clubs of this type of behavior. Their recommendations include:

1. Defining bullying and hazing for everybody associated with the program.
2. Listing the punishments for both of these behaviors.
3. Knowing how to respond to these behaviors and how to report offenders.
4. Implementing alternative ways for players to "initiate" or bond with new athletes.

Alternative methods of team building activities can include ropes and challenge courses, community service projects, programs where older players mentor younger players, scavenger hunts, outdoor recreation, sightseeing tours, and shared meals (Johnson & Miller, 2004). Moreover, Waldron (2012) has challenged coaches to conduct anti-hazing workshops and has outlined a five-step approach to empower athletes to prevent hazing:

1. Notice the hazing event.
2. Interpret the hazing behaviors as a problem.
3. Feel responsible for the solution.
4. Acquire or have the skills to react.
5. Intervene to prevent the hazing from happening.

Bullying and hazing in youth sports have existed under the guise of team traditions, rites of passage, and harmless fun for decades. Through the implementation of anti-hazing and anti-bullying programs, combined with committed coaches and properly educated youth, stakeholders in the youth sport community are optimistic that these harmful practices will soon become a thing of the past.

Dependence and Entitlement Attitudes

While seldom addressed in the research, interviews and surveys with coaches have suggested young athletes today are often characterized by over dependency on their parents, the need for constant feedback, and, in some cases, entitled attitudes (Martin, Ewing & Oregon, 2014). This is not unexpected as many Generation Y youth were raised with parents constantly involved in their activities, were often given trophies for everything they have done, and were often told how special they were. Hence, the youth sports world, especially at the more intense levels, can be very difficult for young people and their parents. This is one reason why there is such an emphasis on sport parent education today. It also suggests that sport may play a valuable role in helping young people learn independence, that rewards must be earned and are not always available and that their needs must at times be sacrificed for the larger team good. Coaches, however, may need educational assistance in learning how to do this in such a way that does not force young athletes out of their sport but instead helps them learn important life lessons.

Early Sport Specialization and Intense Year-Round Training

Over the last few decades there has been increased attention given to sport specialization, specifically the concerns that year-round training, especially at early ages, can be detrimental to youth, physically, psychologically, and socially. Sport specialization is characterized by year-round training in a single sport at the exclusion of other sport or non-sport activities (Wiersma, 2000), and is often associated with more intensive levels of training and competition. Many coaches, parents, and student-athletes see specialization at a young age as a requirement to achieve mastery and eventually obtain a college scholarship (Gould, 2010). There are, however, some unrealistic perceptions of scholarships as only 2 percent of male and 2.2 percent of female high school sport participants received athletic scholarships (full or partial) in 1999–2000 (Malina, 2010). Additionally, it has been argued that sport diversification during the initial and early years of athletic involvement leads to a greater range of fundamental motor skill development, the ability to try different sports, and, in so doing, determine which one is a best fit for a child, and protect against burnout and motivation losses.

Proponents of sport specialization have cited the work of Anders Ericsson (1996) positing that ten years or 10,000 hours of consistent practice is necessary to develop expertise. Other reasons for sport specialization include access to better coaches/skill instruction (Gould, 2010) and transforming an athlete's body to be more conducive to that particular sport, (e.g., figure skaters developing a leaner torso, so the long axis of the body can spin faster) (Mattson, 2010). However, there are many studies showing that sport specialization can yield detrimental effects.

Physical detriments of early sport specialization are seen through overuse injuries. Overuse injuries usually happen over time with the daily repetitive movements of sport-specific skills. When these movements are practiced again and again, the repetitions tend to strengthen certain parts of the body at the expense of others (Swanson, 2005). Common overuse injuries include Osgood-Schlatters' disease, osteochondrosis (Baker, 2003), Sinding-Larsen-Johansson syndrome and Sever's disease (Callender, 2010). More gender-specifically are the increased number of anterior cruciate ligament tears seen in adolescent females (Outerbridge & Micheli, 1996). Studies have shown that due to young people starting sport participation at a younger age, training year-round, and now competing at specialized levels, that upwards of 50 percent of pediatric sports injuries are caused by overuse (Koutures, 2001; Callender, 2010).

The harms of youth sport specialization are not entirely physical. Psychological detriments of early specialization and year-round training can include emotional stress, loss of motivation, and ultimately burnout (Gould, 2010). The roots of burnout are linked to the organization of high performance sport and the athlete feeling a lack of control over his or her life (Coakley, 1992). Burnout develops over time and is associated with the athlete's perception that they cannot meet the physical or psychological demands placed upon them (Malina, 2010). Burnout can cause a drop in performance, mental fatigue, lack of focus and desire, and even depression (Myers, 1995). Negative social outcomes associated with youth sport specialization include narrowing of a social group, social isolation, and even loss of one's childhood. In a qualitative study with burned-out youth tennis players, Gould, Tuffey, Udry, & Loehr (1997) interviewed a female participant who stated, "I completely had no social life whatsoever. I wouldn't do anything except tennis and study" (p. 264).

In the end, most experts contend that sport specialization is needed if someone is to become an elite athlete. However, most athlete talent development models suggest that this does not occur until later in an athlete's career (ages 14–16 in most sports). So the issue is not really sport specialization but early sport specialization and year-round training at young ages.

The negative outcomes associated with early sport specialization and year-round training has been assessed by the International Society of Sport Psychology (ISSP). It has published a position on sport specialization (Cote, Lidor, & Hockfort, 2009). This position is based on existing research on the topic and advances seven postulates:

1. Early diversification (sampling a number of different sports) does not hinder elite sport participation.

2. Sampling is linked to a longer sport career and sport involvement.

3. Sampling allows participation in a range of contexts that most favorably affects positive youth development (PYD).

4. High amounts of deliberate play during the sampling years builds intrinsic motivation.

5. High amounts of deliberate play during the sampling years builds a wider range of motor and cognitive experiences that children can ultimately bring to their sport of preferred interest.

6. No sooner than age 13 should a child specialize in any sport.

7. Around age 16 adolescents have developed the proper physical, cognitive, social, emotional, and motor skills needed to focus their efforts into a specialized training for one sport.

National Championships and Rankings

Another area of concern in children's sports focuses on the advisability of national champions like the Little League World series or the suitability of national rankings for young athletes. Proponents argue that these events provide wonderful opportunities for young people to travel and experience success, while critics suggest that these practices place undue stress and pressure on youth competitors. Unfortunately, studies examining the desirability of such practices do not exist. However, indirect evidence suggests that the more importance placed on athletic performance, the more young people experience stress and burnout (Gould & Dieffenbach, 2003). Moreover, a study by the Women's Tennis Association revealed that by instituting an age eligibility rule that prevents players under 16 years of age from taking part in a full schedule of competitive professional tournaments was correlated to longer careers, less injuries and less stress (Otis, Crespo, Flygare, Johnston, Keber, Lloyd-Koklin, Loehr, Martin, Pluim, Quinn, Rotert, Storia, & Terry, 2006).

Social Media and Youth Athletics

Social media is on the rise and has shown no signs of declining anytime soon. Social media vehicles such as Twitter, Facebook and Instagram have become a new sensation in the digital and communication world. Given the decline of traditional forms of media, online media has become more important and has given sport organizations the opportunities to make news while also managing their online messages (Hume, 2014). Social media has been heralded as being an innovation emblematic of the democratic nature of the web, as one can now publish without the barriers of the publishers of the pre-digital age. However, it has also been argued that social media can provide a means for almost anyone to broadcast positive or negative content to the masses without going through the (previous) gatekeeping functions of journalists and trained members of the media (Farrington, Hall, Kilvington, Price, & Saeed, 2014; Hutchins, 2011).

Social media has given sport organizations the ability to expand their reach to new markets and fan bases that were once previously difficult to engage. Meanwhile, individual players are able to have instant access to their fan base to showcase themselves without traditional media outlets (Hume, 2014). Social media tools such as Twitter and Instagram have often been lauded as a means for players to reach out to fans and develop closeness between them and their supporters (Farrington et al., 2014). Another advantage can be for smaller teams or clubs who previously did not have access to, or had difficulties maintaining a team website. Many of these small teams have found it easier and more cost-effective to create a team Facebook page that can be easily updated (Hume, 2014).

However, some people are using the force of social media to abuse players and other fans. While social media offers people the freedom of expression and the ability to communicate with others, it also comes with a flow of content that some might find unpleasant or even harmful. Its platform for free discussion often connects individuals with their critics, menaces, and those out to verbally abuse them (Farrington et al., 2014). Moreover, social media is often a fertile ground for "trolling"—the act of making repeated inflammatory and offensive comments. However, some of the most extreme cases of verbal abuse happen by overzealous fans making sports stars targets for abuse through mass publication of racist views and stereotypes (Farrington et al., 2014). In some rare cases crazed fans have even made death threats.

One bad decision can often lead to a lifetime of regret. An example of social media backfiring was seen through the disgrace of Australian Olympic swimmers, Nick D'Arcy and Kenrick Monk. These Olympians took a controversial photo while holding high-powered firearms, which was quickly circulated and deemed inappropriate by the Australian Olympic Committee. Although this photo was taken in a foreign country's sporting goods store with no harm intended, the rapid dissemination of this photo and the embarrassment of Australia was enough to scar their images, ultimately leading to their early exit from the 2012 Olympic Games. While many college coaches outwardly bemoan the advent of social media, some sport organizations such as the NBA have made league policies that no players may "tweet" up to 45 minutes before or after games. Moreover, the NFL has had to continuously remind players that they are not allowed to "tweet" during games (Read & Koch, 2009; Battista, 2009).

The rapid arrival of social media has left many people in sports scratching their heads as to whether it is a positive innovation or not. On one hand, teams and players are able to better reach their fans, and smaller teams who have traditionally been unable to connect with their stakeholders now have improved communication with them. However, on the other hand, the large platform of social media often brings out people's emotions that can sometimes be filled with negative and harmful messages. One thing to keep in mind is there is no cancel button on social media; once it's been sent it's out there forever. Nationally syndicated sports radio host Jim Rome often states, "Treat Twitter like a loaded gun." Yet, despite these repeated warnings and people's negative experiences with social media, almost no one within sport wants to hit the "off switch" and curtail their right to freedom of expression (Farrington, Hall, & Kilvington, 2014).

Finally, most of social media discussion has focused on high performance college and professional athletes. However, we know young athletes are involved in and affected by social media and numerous problems can arise (e.g., teasing, cyber-bullying, hazing). Constant media attention can also place young athletes under intense pressure by setting expectations and providing constant evaluation.

Youth Sports and Popular Culture: The New Youth Sports

As we have seen in this essay, fueled by unprecedented technological developments, changes in family structure, commercialization of all aspects of life and an information revolution, a new period of childhood and adolescence is being experienced today. These changes in young people are providing both tremendous opportunities and challenges for those interested in providing optimal sport experiences for youth. In fact, the Australian government (Hajkowicz, Cook, Wihelmseder, & Boughen, 2013) and the Aspen Institute (2013) in the U.S. have published reports that focus on how current cultural and technological changes affect contemporary sport and how sport must adjust to keep abreast of these changes.

In a report titled *The Future of Australian Sport: Megatrends Shaping the Sports Sector Over Coming Decades*, Hajkowicz et al. (2013) identified a number of major trends that would influence sport over the coming decades. Some of these included the rise of non-organized physical activity and the decline of traditional youth sports as individuals today are more likely to run on their own and or take a trip to the gym than engage in traditional youth sports. Interestingly, this trend is not confined to Australia as a recent survey revealed that traditional youth sport participation has started to decline in the U.S. (Aspen Institute, 2013). While some traditional sports are declining in popularity extreme sports like those represented in the X games are on the increase. It is suggested that these might be more attractive to youth, not only because of the risk involved, but because they are less structured, allow young people more decision making relative to their participation, let them be more creative, and are not dominated by adults. A third identified trend is that sport as a vehicle for health and personal growth (e.g., developing life skills like goal setting, empathy) is increasing. A more diversified and inclusive youth sports is also evolving so youth coaches are more likely to have children and youth involved from all sorts of backgrounds and physical capabilities. Finally, the social media is influencing sports both in the way youth sports are initiated, administered and consumed but also as a competing activity taking children's interest away from traditional physical activity.

There are a number of important questions and challenges that these mega trends raise. First, if we believe that youth sports participation is beneficial for children, how do we counteract potential declines in involvement by better catering to youth who are unfit and perhaps overweight? How will we make youth sports more inclusive for children with special needs? Attracting more children, and children from varying backgrounds to sport will certainly involve restructuring programs, being clear about priorities relative to talent development and mass participation, and emphasize coach training (e.g., teaching coaches how to work with less motivated and talented youth). In addition, what can be learned from extreme sports like the X games that are growing in popularity and applied to more traditional youth sports (e.g., the need to allow youth to make more decisions about their involvement, allow children to explore and be more creative, employment of nontraditional uniforming, lessening of zero sum competitive structures that eliminate youth). Third, how can youth sports be used to better develop healthy young people and enhance their personal growth? For example, should high schools be asked to accommodate all children who would like to play by offering multiple basketball teams versus cutting the less gifted youth who are not good enough for the varsity or junior varsity teams? In addition, should coaches and sports administrators be held accountable on metrics beyond winning and losing such as personal growth variables like participation rates, improvements in school attendance, and gains in self-esteem? Finally, how should the youth sports world positively embrace technology and social media? Possibilities might include allowing youth to track performance improvements on their cell phones, providing technique podcasts and/or facilitating team cohesion via social media connections. At the same time using the sport experience to teach more traditional values and attributes that digital natives may need like delaying gratification, working physically hard, and interacting with others are sport values. Lastly, should we protect youth from their own or others misuse of social media (e.g., teach our athletes about cyber bullying, about what sportspersonship involves in a digital world, how sexual predators use social media to exploit young people like themselves)?

For several years the Aspen Institute has brought leading experts and key figures in the youth sports world together to discuss ways to combat many of the challenges that are occurring in American youth sports today. In their recent Project Play report, The Aspen Institute (2013) recommended eight steps to improve youth sports in the USA. These included:

1. *Asking youth what they want from youth sports.* Focus on young people's motives for participation, not what adults consciously or unconsciously desire. For example, the electronic gaming industry gives children what they want—e.g., action, freedom to try new things, competition without exclusion. Youth sport programs would do well to better listen to youth and provide programs that better meet these needs.

2. *Reintroduce free play.* Because of concerns over safety, sandlot or unsupervised free play has been primarily eliminated in American youth sports. However, this does not mean that children do not need free play or that it is impossible to provide. For instance, coaches could do more by just letting youth play versus constantly instructing them. Recreational organizations could also do more to create safe places for children to play with each other in non-adult directed but supervised settings like open gym.

3. *Encourage sport sampling.* Having children sample multiple sports, especially at younger ages, has a number of benefits and is recommended by most youth sports experts. More initiatives are needed that expose children to the range of sports available (e.g., fencing, water polo) and programs need to be set up so multiple sport participation is possible (e.g., a 12-year-old is not forced to select between travel soccer and swimming).

4. *Revitalize town leagues.* To help control for the rising costs of sport participation and to help combat the obesity epidemic, Project Play recommends that town leagues be revitalized. The trend toward travel teams must be re-examined and strategies need to be revised in order to offer affordable programs for all children, not just those who are talented or financially well-off.

5. *Think small by developing small play spaces in urban areas.* There are not enough places for children to participate, especially low-income children. Hence, there is a need to find and develop numerous small places to play versus focusing resources on large youth sports complex.

6. *Design for development by scaling equipment, fields and games to sizes that are developmentally appropriate for children.*

7. *Educate all coaches.* The youth sports research literature clearly shows that quality coaching leads to quality youth sports experiences (Smoll & Smith, 2001). It is not enough to be a well-intended but untrained volunteer. Trained youth sport coaches have been shown to make a major difference on youth outcomes. Therefore, it is critical that America increases standards relative to the education and training of youth coaches.

8. *Emphasize injury prevention and safety.* While sports can have highly positive effects on young people there are inherent risks when individuals engage in physical activity, especially when safety training has not taken place. All those involved should have basic safety training. It should also be noted that such safety training not only needs to focus on physical issues such as concussion prevention but protecting young people from sexual abusers as was brought to light with the Jerry Sandusky sexual predatory practices that occurred at the Pennsylvania State University.

Conclusions

This review has shown that youth sports are an important part of contemporary youth culture. At the same time, contemporary youth culture has important influences on the structure of contemporary youth sports. The key is to understand and maintain the positive elements of contemporary youth sports, while at the same time adapting youth sports to meet the needs of a very new and ever changing generation of young people. It is hoped that this essay can help meet these needs.

REFERENCES

Anderson, P.M., & Butcher, K.F. (2006). Childhood obesity: trends and potential causes. *The Future of Children, 16*, 19–45.

American Camping Association. (2013). *ACA Facts and Trends*. Retrieved from http://www.acacamps.org/media/aca-facts-trends.

Aspen Institute (2013). Project play: Reimagining youth sports in America. "Early positive experiences: What is age-appropriate?" Roundtable summary. Retrieved from http://www.aspeninstitute.org/sites/default/files/content/upload/What_is_Age_Appropriate_Summary_Report.pdf.

Baker, J. (2003). Early specialization in youth sport: A requirement for adult expertise? *High Ability Studies, 14*(1), 85–94.

Battista, J. (2009). The NFL has identified the enemy and it is Twitter. *New York Times*, August 4.

Bloom, B. S. (1985). *Developing talent in young people*. New York: Ballantine.

Callender, S.S. (2010). The early specialization of youth in sports. *Athletic Training & Sports Health Care, 2*(6), 255–257.

Clarke, P., O'Malley, P., Johnston, L., & Schulenberg, J. (2009). Social disparities in BMI trajectories across adulthood by gender, race/ethnicity and lifetime socioeconomic position: 1986–2004. *International Journal of Epidemiology, 38*, 499–509.

Coakley, J. (1992). Burnout among adolescent athletes: A personal failure or social problem? *Sociology of Sport Journal, 9*(1). 271–285.

Coakley, J. (2010). The "logic" of specialization: Using children for adult purposes. *Journal of Physical Education, Recreation & Dance, 81*(8), 16–25.

Coakley, J. (2011). Youth sports: What counts as "positive development?" *Journal of Sport & Social Issues, 35*, 306–324.

Coleman, J.S. (1974). *Youth: Transition to adulthood*. Chicago: University of Chicago Press.

Côté, J. (1999). The influence of the family in the development of talent in sport. *The Sport Psychologist, 13*, 395–417.

Côté, J., Lidor, R., & Hackfort, D. (2009). ISSP position stand: To sample or to specialize? Seven postulates about youth sport activities that lead to continued participation and elite performance. *International Journal of Sport and Exercise Psychology, 9*, 7–17.

Crow, R.B., & Phillips, D.R. (2004). Hazing: What the law says. In J. Johnson & M. Holman (Eds.), Making the team: Inside the world of sport initiations and hazing (pp. 19–31). Toronto: Canadian Scholars' Press.

Damon, W. (2008). *The path to purpose: How young people find their calling in life*. New York: Free Press.

Dorsch, T. E., Smith, A. L., & McDonough, M. H. (2009). Parents' perceptions of child-to-parent socialization in organized youth sport. *Journal of Sport and Exercise Psychology, 31*, 444–468.

Duffett, A., & Johnson, J. (2004). *All work and no play? Listening to what kids and parents really want from out-of-school time.* New York: Public Agenda and the Wallace Foundation.

Dunn, R., Dorsch, T. E., King, M., Rothlisberger, K. (2014). Understanding and enhancing the involvement of parents, families, and coaches in youth sport: Parents' sporting experiences and their involvement in youth sport. *Journal of Sport & Exercise Psychology, 36*, S6-S8.

Dunning E., & Sheard, K. (2005). *Barbarians, gentlemen and players: A sociological study of the development of rugby football* (2nd ed.). London: Routledge.

Durand-Bush, N., & Salmela, J. H. (2002). The development and maintenance of expert athletic performance: Perceptions of World and Olympic champions. *Journal of Applied Sport Psychology, 14*(3), 154–171.

Ericsson, K.A. (1996). *The road to excellence: The acquisition of expert performance in the arts and sciences, sports and games.* Mahwah, NJ: Erlbaum.

Ewing, M.E., & Seefeldt, V. (1996). Patterns of sport participation and attrition in American agency-sponsored sports. In F.L. Smoll & R.E. Smith (Eds.), *Children and youth in sport: A biopsychosocial perspective* (pp. 31–45). Madison: Brown & Benchmark.

Ewing, M.E., & Seefeldt, V. (2002). Patterns of participation in American agency-sponsored sports. In F.L. Smoll & R.E. Smith (Eds.), *Children and youth in sport: A biopsychosocial perspective* (pp. 39–56) (2nd ed.). Dubuque: Kendall/Hunt.

Farrey, T. (2008). *Game on: The All-American race to make champions of our children.* New York: ESPN Books.

Farrington, N., Hall, L., Kilvington, D. Price, J., & Saeed, A. (2014). *Sport, racism and social media.* Routledge Research in Sport, Culture and Society. New York: Routledge.

Fasick, F. (1984). Parents, peers, youth culture and autonomy in adolescence. *Adolescence, 19*(73), 143–157.

Gould, D. (2009). The professionalization of youth sports: It's time to act! *Clinical Journal of Sports Medicine, 19*, 81–82.

Gould, D., & Dieffenbach, K. (2003). Psychological issues in youth sports: Competitive anxiety, over training and burnout. In R. M. Malina and M. A. Clark (Eds.), *Youth sports: Perspectives for a new century (pp. 149–170).* Monterey, CA: Coaches Choice.

Gould, D., Tuffey, S., Udry., E., Loehr, J. (1997). Burnout in competitive junior tennis players: III. Individual differences in the burnout experience. *The Sport Psychologist, 11*(1), 257–276.

Gould, D. (2010). Early sport specialization: A psychological perspective. *Journal of Physical Education, Recreation & Dance, 81*(8), 33–37.

Gould, D. & Carson, S. (2004). Myths surrounding the role of youth sports in developing Olympic champions. *Youth Studies Australia, 23*(1),19–26.

Gould, D., & Carson, S. (2008). Personal development through sport. In H. Hebestreit & O. Bar-Or (Eds.), *The Encyclopedia of Sports Medicine - The Young Athlete* (pp. 287–301). Oxford: Blackwell Science.

Gould, D., Carson, S., & Blanton, J. (2013). Coaching life skills. In P. Protrac, W. Gilbert, & J. Denison (Eds.), *Routledge handbook of sports coaching* (pp. 259–270). London: Routledge.

Gould, D., Cowburn, I., & Shields, A. (2014). *"Sports for all"—A summary of the evidence of psychological and social outcomes of participation.* Elevate Health Series 15(3). Presidents Council on Fitness, Sports and Nutrition Science Board, Rockville, MD.

Gould, D., & Westfall, S. (2014). Promoting life skills in children and youth: Applications to sport contexts. In A. Rui Gomes, R. Resende, & A. Albuquerque (Eds.), *Positive human functioning from a multidimensional perspective. Vol. 2: Promoting healthy lifestyles* (pp. 53–77). New York: Nova.

Government of Alberta (2005). *Bullying prevention in sports.* Retrieved from http://bullyfreealberta.ca/pdf/sports_fs.pdf.

Gustafsson, H., Kentta, G., & Hassmen, P. (2011). Athlete burnout: An integrated model and future research directions. *International Review of Sport & Exercise Psychology, 4*(1), 3–24.

Hajkowicz, S. A., Cook, H., Wihelmseder, L., & Boughen, N. (2013). *The future of Australian Sport: Megatrends shaping the sports sector over coming decades.* A consultancy report for the Australian Sports Commission. CSIRO, Australia.

Hallowell, E. (2006). *Crazy Busy: Overstretched, overbooked about to snap.* New York: Ballantine.

Hoover, N.C. (1999). National survey: Initiation rites and athletics for NCAA sports teams. Retrieved from http://www.alfred.edu/sports_hazing/docs/hazing.pdf.

Howe, N., & Strauss, W. (2000). *Millennials rising: The next great generation.* New York: Vintage.

Hume, C. (2014). *Social media and sport.* Australian Clearinghouse for Sport. Retrieved from https://secure.ausport.gov.au/clearinghouse/knowledge_base/organised_sport/sports_administration_and_management/social_media_and_sport.

Hutchins, B. (2011). The acceleration of media sport culture. *Information, Communication & Society 14*(2), 237–257.

Hyman, M. (2012). *The most expensive game in town: The rising cost of youth sports and the tool on today's families.* Boston: Beacon Press.

Johnson, J., & Miller, P. (2004). Changing the initiation ceremony. In J. Johnson & M. Holman (Eds.), *Making the team: Inside the world of sport initiations and hazing* (pp. 19–31). Toronto: Canadian Scholars' Press.

Junco, R., & Mastrodicasa, J. (2007). *Connecting to the net.generation: What higher education professionals need to know about today's students.* Washington, D.C: NASPA.

Kavussanu, M. (2008). Moral behavior in sport: A critical review of the literature. *International Review of Sport and Exercise Psychology, 1,* 124–138.

Kavussanu, M., & Ntoumanis, N. (2003). Participation in sport and moral functioning: Does ego orientation mediate the relationship? *Journal of Sport and Exercise Psychology, 25,* 501–518.

Koutures, C.G. (2001). An overview of overuse injuries. *Contemporary Pediatrics* (Nov.). Downloaded from www.healthcaresouth.com.

Kumanyika, S. (2008). Environmental influences on childhood obesity: Ethnic and cultural influences in context. *Psychology and Behavior, 94,* 61–70.

Larson, R.W. (2000). Toward a psychology of positive youth development. *American Psychologist, 55,* 170–183.

Lines, D. (2008). *The bullies: Understanding bullies and bullying.* London: Kingsley.

Long, T., Pantaleon, N., Bruant, G., & d'Arripe-Longueville, F. (2006). A qualitative study of moral reasoning of young athletes. *The Sport Psychologist, 20,* 330–347.

Malina, R.M., (2010). Early sport specialization: Roots, effectiveness, risks. *Current Sports Medicine Reports*, ACSM, *9*(6), 364–371.

Martin, E.M., Ewing, M.E., & Oregon, E. (2014). Coaches' views of the characteristics of today's college athletes. Symposium. American Alliance for Health, Physical Education, Recreation and Dance, St. Louis.

Mattson, J.M., Richards, J., (2010). Early specialization in youth sport: A biomechanical perspective. *Journal of Physical Education, Recreation & Dance, 81*(8), 26–28, 39.

Myers, D.G. (1995). *Psychology.* New York: Worth.

National Physical Activity Plan Alliance. (2014). The 2014 United States Report Card on Physical Activity for Children and Youth. Retrieved from http://www.physicalactivityplan.org/reportcard/NationalReportCard_longform_final%20for%20web.pdf.

Ogden, C.L., Carroll, M.D., Kit, B.K., Flegal, K.M. (2014). Prevalence of childhood and adult obesity in the United States, 2011–2012. *The Journal of the American Medical Associated, 311*(8), 806–814.

Otis, C.L., Crespo, M., Flygare, C.T., Johnston, P., Keber, A., Lloyd-Koklin, Loehr, J., Martin, K., Pluim, B.M., Quinn, A., Rotert, P., Storia, K., & Terry, P.S. (2006). The Sony Ericsson WTA tour 10 year eligibility and professional development review. *British Journal of Sports Medicine, 40,* 464–468.

Outerbridge, A.R., & Micheli, L.J. (1996). Adolescent sports medicine: Changing patterns of injury in the young athlete. *Sports Medicine and Arthroscopy Review, 13*(1), 93–98.

Pate, R. R., Trost, S. G., Levin, S., & Dowda, M. (2000). Sports participation and health-related behaviors among US youth. *Archives of Pediatrics and Adolescent Medicine, 154*(9), 904–911.

Positive Coaching Alliance: Better athletes. Better people. Retrieved from http://www.positivecoach.org.

Prensky, M. (2001). Digital natives, digital immigrants. *On the Horizon. MCB University Press, 9*(5), 1–6.

Raedeke, T. D. Smith, A. L., Kentta, G., Arce, C., & de Francisco, D. (2014). Burnout in sport: From theory to practice. In A. Rui Gomes, R. Resende, & A. Albuquerque (Eds.), *Positive human functioning from a multidimensional perspective. Vol. 1: Promoting stress adaptation* (pp. 113–141). Hauppague, NY: Nova.

Read, B., & Koch, D. (2009). Twitter revolution strikes sporting establishment. *The Australian*, August 22, 2009.

Rice, F. (1996). *The adolescent. Development, relationships and culture* (7th ed.) Boston: Allyn & Bacon.

Riley, S., & Anderson-Butcher, D. (2012). Participation in a summer sport-based youth development program for disadvantaged youth: Getting the parent perspective. *Children and Youth Services Review, 34*(7), 1367–1377.

Roberts, J. (2014). The fun factor. From the Director blog. Michigan High School Athletic Association. Retrieved from http://www.mhsaa.com/news/blogfromthedirector/articletype/articleview/articleid/3326/the-fun-factor.aspx.

Shields, D.L.L., & Bredemeier, B.J.L. (2001). Moral development and behavior in sport. In R. Singer, H. Hausenblas, & C. Janelle (Eds.), *Handbook of sport psychology* (2nd ed., pp. 585–603). New York: Wiley.

Shields, D.L., & Bredemeier, B.J.L. (2007). Advances in sport morality research. In G. Tenenbaum and R.C. Eklund (Eds.), *Handbook of sport psychology* (pp. 662–684). Hoboken, NJ: John Wiley & Sons.

Shields, D. L., & Bredemeier, B.J.L. (2009). *True competition.* Champaign, IL: Human Kinetics.

Shields, D.L., LaVoi, N.M., Bredemeier, B.J.L., & Power, F.C. (2007). Predictors of poor sportspersonship in youth sports: Personal attitudes and social influences. *Journal of Sport and Exercise Psychology, 29,* 747–763.

Shpigel, B. (2014). A classic case of bullying on the Dolphins, report finds. *New York Times,* February 14.

Smoll, F.L., & Smith, R.E. (2001). Conducting sport psychology training programs for coaches: Cognitive-behavioral principles and techniques. In J.M. Williams (Ed.), *Applied sport psychology: Personal growth to peak performance* (4th ed., pp. 378–400). Mountain View, CA: Mayfield.

Stenberg, S. R. (2011). Kinderculture: *The corporate construction of childhood* (3rd ed.). Boulder, CO: Westview Press.

Storey, J. (2006). *Cultural theory and popular culture: An introduction* (4th ed.) Athens: University of Georgia Press.

Strong, W. B., Malina, R. M., Blimkie, C. J. R., Daniels, S. R., Dishman, R. K., Guten, B., Hergenroeder, A. C., Must, A., Nixon, P. A., Pivarnik, J., Rowland, J., Trost, S., & Trudeau, F. (2005). Evidence-based physical activity for school-age youth. *Journal of Pediatrics, 146*(6), 732–737.

Swanson, J. (2005). A new youth epidemic? *Rehab Management, 18*(6), 20–24.

Tapscott, D. (1998). *Growing up digital: The rise of the net generation.* New York: McGraw-Hill.

Tapscott, D. (2008). *Grown up digital: How the Net generation is changing your world.* New York: McGraw-Hill.

Thompson, J. (1995). Positive coaching: Building character and self-esteem through sports. Portola Valley, CA: Warde.

True Sport: A movement powered by the U.S. Anti-Doping Agency (USADA). Retrieved from http://truesport.org.

Twenge, J., Konrath, S., Foster, J.D., Campbell, W.K., & Bushman, B.J. (2008). Further evidence of an increase in narcissism among college students. *Journal of Personality, 76*(4), 919–928.

Twenge, J. (2006). Generation me: *Why today's young Americans are more confident, assertive, entitled – and more miserable than ever before.* New York: Free Press.

USADA (2011). What sport means in America: A study of sport's role in society. *Journal of Coaching Education, 4*(1), 2–27.

Waldron, J. (2012). A social norms approach to hazing prevention workshops. *Journal of Sport Psychology in Action, 3,* 12–20.

Waldron, J.J., & Kowalski, C.L. (2009). Crossing the line: Rites of passage, team aspects and the ambiguity of hazing. *Research Quarterly for Sport and Exercise, 80,* 291–302.

Weinberg, R.S., & Gould, D. (2015). *Foundations of sport and exercise psychology* (6th ed.). Champaign, IL: Human Kinetics.

Weiss, M. R., & Ambrose, A. J. (2008). Motivational orientations and sport behavior. In T. Horn (Ed.). *Advances in sport psychology* (3rd ed.) (pp. 115–154). Champaign, IL: Human Kinetics.

Wiersma, L.D. (2000). Risks and benefits of youth sport specialization: Perspectives and recommendations. *Pediatric Exercise Science, 12*(1), 13–22.

The Use of Popular Culture Research in Deconstructing Stereotypes and Developing Identities

Perspectives of American Youth in Amsterdam's Coffeehouses and Red Light District

MARTHA MONTERO-SIEBURTH

The word "Amsterdam" is often associated with open sex and promiscuity, as found in the Red Light District where sex workers are scantily clad appearing in red light windows to attract spectators and coffeehouses in all corners of the city promote the sale of marijuana. It is the illicitness of these two practices that often attracts tourists and youth to visit Amsterdam and to vividly experience it in person. These assumptions—often characterized as generally accepted stereotypes—have been on the one hand, primarily fostered by the media's advertisement of Amsterdam from abroad, and on the other hand, by the promotional marketing of these practices as Amsterdam culture. Further conflagrating such stereotypes, Brants (1998) states, "The practice of not prosecuting certain offences, yet not officially legalizing them" which she says "is not merely a matter of the police turning a blind eye" (p. 624). In fact, such strategies conducted at the local level may inadvertently be part of the government's design. This gedogen or practice of "pragmatic tolerance," explains Buruma (2007), makes the legal use of tolerance effective in promoting policies towards drugs, prostitution, and even euthanasia in the Netherlands.

Each year, Amsterdam attracts close to 12.7 million tourists and two million visit coffeehouses (Gowling, 2014). The "debauchery" of the Red Light District and coffeehouses becomes part of the required tour for most tourists. In fact, Iamsterdam.com is the central website of the cities branding campaign conducted by Amsterdam Partners, a "public private partnership" consisting of actors from tourism, hospitality industry and commercial organizations (Kavaratkis & Ashworth, 2007, p. 23). Tours of the Red Light District in several languages are daily offered as part of the exposure to the "seamy side" of Amsterdam. Throughout the city, the scent of marijuana hangs in the air and both of these practices are included along with notable museums, architectural sites and canals as must-see sites.

The question of how one penetrates such stereotypes to arrive at a more objective and descriptive sense of what goes on in the Amsterdam's Red Light District or in coffeehouses presents a challenge. What better way is there to deconstruct these stereotypes than to use Amsterdam as a study site and explore it fully in its uniqueness through teams of students engaged in such realities and analyzing face to face factual information. In that vein, this essay presents the author's reflections about having taught a course entitled "Ethnic Diversity and Popular Culture" during 8 semesters (2008–2012) for the International School at the University of Amsterdam to diverse bachelor level students, particularly American students, carrying many of these stereotypes in their heads.

Popular Culture Research

The Ethnic Diversity and Popular Culture course, launched in 2008, had three foci: (a) a theoretical component, (b) a practical and applied component consisting of fieldwork in Amsterdam, and (c) a reflective component about the meanings derived from popular culture explorations.   Students   were asked to unpack such theories and deconstruct their meaning in an attempt to understand Storey's (2006) statement about "popular culture is often conceived as an empty conceptual category because it can be filled in a variety of ways, depending on its use" (p. 1). Thus, students not only needed to understand what popular culture is about, but what it meant, especially in the way it is manifested and represented, and how it relates to issues of ethnicity and culture.

Students were also required to identify an aspect of popular culture they considered reflected ethnic diversity. They were to collect data, describe, and interpret any of the manifestations of popular culture they identified through the use of participant observation, shadowing, in depth interviews, and focus groups. This was to be done by observing, while taking notes, thinking about these issues in relation to theory, and recording them for future representation—a demanding and time-consuming practice.

Notwithstanding, the hardest obstacle for these youth was to learn how not to judge the people or the data they collected through labeling or ideas that would immediately lead to singular interpretations, such as "Dutch people, or sex workers are...." Many of the students had not been exposed to deconstructing their way of thinking about language use, or active listening of what people think say, and do—that is, identify and describe words and meanings of respondents before interpreting these. The notion of identifying, describing, and only after having sufficient data, interpreting" became one of the class's mantras.

From its initial intake in 2008 of 18–20 students during each semester a year, the course grew to 22–25 students by 2010, and rising numbers of foreign students at the International School of the University of Amsterdam in 2011, compelled the administrators to offer the course twice a year. The course was offered until 2012 when due to program changes, the International School at the University of Amsterdam closed down.

Methodology

As student papers were collected at the end of each semester, they were categorized by themes. Represented among these papers were topics which primarily included Amsterdam's coffeehouses, the Red Light District, graffiti, food markets, tokos,[1] book and clothes markets, vintage shops, museum experiences, street players and vendors among other topics.[2] Of all of the papers in any class, one to three were normally written on coffeehouses by equal numbers of males and females, resulting in eight to 15 papers over the eight semesters. Of those interested in sex workers, one to two were written by females, which resulted in eight to 16 papers over the eight semesters.

A total of 12 papers on these two practices were selected by the author based on the saliency of the coffeehouses or sex workers in the student's minds, the issues students concurred or differed on, and the behavioral and attitudinal changes reflected. Of interest were those papers that could provide a vision of student interest, motivation, and reflection about the research process and more importantly, their inner growth and development of identity. These papers were cross-checked with the reports, documentation and research that exist about these practices in the Netherlands.

Six focused on coffeehouses and were written during semesters in 2010 and 2011, and six dealt with sex workers and were written during 2009, 2010, 2011, and 2012. Content analysis was conducted and from such analysis, the themes that emerged became the basis for the discussion of students' identification, deconstruction and subsequent reflections of stereotypes.

Background

Gedogen

Using Schuyt's definition as the accepted meaning of tolerance in the Netherlands, Buruma (2007) explains it as "a legal way of deferring negative reactions to things we don't approve of" (p. 74). Not only does tolerance apply to freedom of conscience but also to putting up with or living in the vicinity of others. Originally, tolerance meant accepting those who were persecuted for religious issues, but has evolved to include cultural differences and legal policies applying to practices and acts that otherwise might be met with disapproval such as prostitution, drugs, and euthanasia. This "regulated tolerance … involves self-regulation, enforced if necessary through administrative rules, but always with the criminal law as a threat in the background" (Brants, 1998, p. 624). Buruma acknowledges that "in the Netherlands, tolerance is no secret: written rules indicate when the official must look the other way" (p. 87). *Gedogen*, on the other hand, refers to the "practice of discriminatory enforcement," of what is considered "a regulatory system of organized toleration and targeted repression" (Uitermark, 2004, p. 511) and explains the ways in which both of these practices of Dutch life are accepted.

In coffeehouses and Red Light Districts in the Netherlands, although there are general laws regulating drugs and prostitution, both the public and the authorities tend to look the other way when it comes to enforcement. Thus, while cannabis is considered officially an illicit drug, it has been decriminalized as long as it is made available to clients only through a network of coffeehouses serving the retail market, a kind of blurred legal line whose intent is to keep sales cannabis off the streets and back alleys.

Cannabis

As early as The Hague Opium Act of 1919, a legal determination and identification of destructive drugs and recreational soft drugs was made. The import and export of cannabis was added to the act in 1928, and by 1953 the possession, manufacture and sale became offences (Korf, Wouters, and Benschop, 2011). During and after the cultural revolution of the 1960s and the arrival of hippies, particularly in Amsterdam, normal cafes whose owners dealt with marijuana as a side business became transformed into "coffeehouses" and cannabis became statutorily decriminalized by the Opium Act of 1976. According to Uitermark (2004), the passage of this law has made it possible to regard the topic of a drug policy as a non-issue among the Dutch public and official tolerance of the coffeehouses began in the 1980s.

Coffeehouses which comply with the following restrictions and whose owners maintain these laws, can sell their recreational marijuana to customers and remain open: no more than a maximum of five grams can be sold to each customer, no advertising, no sale of alcohol, no hard drugs, no nuisances, no selling to minors under 18 and no large stocks of more than 500 grams at any time (Buruma, 2007).

Notably, the use of cannabis is not significantly higher in the Netherlands than other European countries (Buruma, 2007). Close to 50 percent of youth have tried or used marijuana (Luscombe, 2008) and according to ter Bog et. al (2006), seasoned users pass on what they know and stimulate and initiate youth to smoke, conveying a normative use of cannabis. In fact, ter Bog et al.'s (2006) study of over 816 students sampled in 31 countries, shows a higher prevalence of cannabis use occurs in wealthier countries and is found in a subculture of young mostly males compared to female teens and adults. Among such youth, those from Eastern and Southern Europe are less reserved about using marijuana than other substances, and cannabis is more commonly used than tobacco, but half less than alcohol.

The number of coffeehouses however has been decreasing due to conservative government policies and local level licensing decisions. Korf, Wouters, and Benschop (2011) indicate that while in the 1980s there were 1500 coffeehouses throughout the Netherlands, by 1999, they had decreased to 846. In 2002, Buruma (2007) noted "there were 782 officially tolerated coffee shops, of which 51 percent were located in cities with over 200,000 inhabitants," yet "in 78 percent of all Dutch municipalities, coffee shops are not tolerated" (p. 91). By 2009, less than 666 coffeehouses were open and most were located in Amsterdam (Korf, Wouters, & Benschop, 2011). Currently, close to 200-plus coffeehouses are functioning in Amsterdam.

While the reductions in coffeehouses were meant to keep the attractions of Amsterdam thriving, such decreases Uitermark (2004) explains have resulted in adverse consequences. Evident is the illicit growth of marijuana which has risen to keep up with the demand, rise of alternate distribution channels, higher prices and the substitution of neighborhood coffeehouses, frequented by community members with large commercial businesses. Wholesale supplies of marijuana to coffeeshops along the border towns have created a concern for authorities in neighboring Germany and Belgium

Counteracting this in 2012, the government introduced a proposal for mandatory club memberships or "weed pass" for coffeeshop clients, over 18 years of age. However the *"wietpas"* in the border provinces was abolished by November 19, 2012, and coffeehouse data destroyed since such a practice was deemed to have infringed on an individual's civil rights by having data collected on *who* and *where* marijuana was smoked (Korf, Wouters, & Benschop, 2011).

In keeping Amsterdam tourist-friendly, maintaining a semi-legal status for coffeehouses, has not been without repercussions. Coffeehouses in Amsterdam near schools and school playgrounds need to close during school hours. Attic home grown marijuana has also led to a rise in supply shop sales. However, this type of criminality stands in sharp contrast to the organized crime of rising mafia rings, which even though well-controlled by the police, keeps growing (Buruma, 2007).

Prostitution

The other manifestation of popular culture widely studied by students in Amsterdam was prostitution. The concept of *gedogen* here cannot be separated from the historical development of prostitution in Amsterdam. As Sabat (2012) recounts prostitution was viewed as a necessary part of life, on the one hand, and on the other hand, as an immoral image of the city. Confining prostitution to one section of the city, De Wallen, one of the oldest and largest areas, the Red Light District gained prominence. Because Dutch wealth came from the sea through trade, most notably the Dutch East India Company, these areas of the city became "sailor friendly." Sailors' wives maintained brothels, taverns and boardinghouses (Caterrel, 1998).

Despite the immorality attached to prostitution, men from many different social and economic backgrounds including patricians frequented prostitutes thereby ending the associative divide between high and low cultures and maintaining the viability of prostitution (Catterall, 1998). Prostitution contributed to the city's growing economy by providing jobs. Dance halls became a major attraction and families visited the Red Light District as a fashionable area (Catterel, 1998).[3] Prostitution went through several changes into the 19th century. During the French occupation of the Netherlands, Napoleon Bonaparte created what Brants (1998) calls the regulationist view of prostitution, whereby "prostitution is accepted as a social fact and strictly regulated by law in order to protect not prostitutes, but the public from any adverse effects" (p. 622).

By the beginning of the 20th century, the abolitionist view prevailed where "the prostitute [is seen] not as a criminal, but as the victim of criminal exploitation" (Brants, 1998, p.622). Groups backed by feminists, socialists and the church, argued that the mandatory health examinations were yet another aspect of what they believed was a degrading profession. Brants indicates that it was in fact not "until the end of the sixties … one of the safest parts of town. Many ordinary people lived there and were on good terms with their somewhat unusual neighbors, on whom they could rely to keep the nuisance of it all to a minimum. The police patrolled on foot, and they too enjoyed the amicable relationship with all concerned. The girls were rough perhaps, but kindhearted and together they formed a complex and protective social network" (Brants, 1998, p. 626). The "heterogeneity of the Red Light District in the 1960s meant the red light windows did not make the neighborhood but were part of it" (Sabat, 2012, p. 161).

However, as drugs and particularly heroin came into the Red Light District this romanticized aura of prostitution, changed from a "normal" neighborhood to a commercialized sex industry of sex shops, live porn shows, cinemas, and sex clubs. Starting in the eighties the Red Light District had a criminal backing of drug-trafficking, human-trafficking and money laundering which enabled these organized crime members to buy legitimate businesses in the area and gain monopolizing control (Brants, 1998). Dutch prostitutes moved onto the sex clubs and escort services attracting more elite clientele, and gradually were replaced by immigrants, many from the Third World, former Dutch colonies in the West Indies and after 1989 former East-bloc countries (Brants, 1998). The Tampep International Foundation "estimates that 70–75% of the prostitutes in De Wallen are not Dutch citizens but migrant foreign nationals" (Brussa, 2009, p. 16). Moreover, much of the control of brothels and red light windows has shifted hands from older Dutch prostitutes to foreign pimps (Sabat, 2012).

Prostitution currently has given way to the legalization perspective where "prostitution is seen as regular labor, governed by market forces," and is part of the Dutch tolerance (Brants, 1998, p. 622).Within this legal framework, prostitution became recognized as just another job, where prostitutes have rights and benefits under the law like any other independent professional. Pro-prostitution coalitions have been able to change the label of "prostitute" to that of sex worker as a more legitimate term against the stigma of "prostitute" (Sabat, 2012). Thus by 2000, the Dutch attitude of tolerance and *gedogen* enabled prostitution to be legalized and the Red Light District to exist and flourish the way it has for years.

Notwithstanding, criminality has penetrated the coffeehouses and the Red Light District in a variety of ways. The sale of illicit drugs has grown despite its control within coffeehouses. Inequalities within the sex industry, promulgated by illegal sex-trade, have targeted migrant and ethnic minorities making them vulnerable victims within this legalized practice.

Amsterdam authorities are attempting to introduce regulations against human trafficking in the prostitution industry by raising the legal age from 18 to 21, preventing long working hours, obligating operators to have business plans that include how they will prevent abuse and insure good working conditions and greater security. Yet business as usual will continue as restrictions for visitors in Amsterdam will not be imposed. The mayor of Amsterdam, Eberhard van der Laan, recently said: "Amsterdam will always have a Red Light District and it sure will remain world famous. But it also will be normal and more caring of each other." Furthermore, the Red Light District "has become a symbol of Dutch progressive tolerance, a place with no legislative or social boundaries, a 'place where anything goes'" (Sabat, 2012, p. 159).

Identifying and Confronting Stereotypes: Coffeehouses

Of the 12 student papers, the six on coffeehouses were written by four males and two females, whereas the six papers on sex workers and the Red Light District were all by females. While a myriad of stereotypes with pre-judgments or categorizations attributed by one group of members to another, and with positive or negative evaluations related to attitudes, were evident, a few were particularly salient. The stereotypes most represented were those commonly expressed by friends or teachers from the U.S. but also those expressed about Americans by Dutch persons in Amsterdam and finally, the stereotypes students had.

Starting with the coffeehouses as one of the target of analysis, it is clear that students had to first identify the following stereotypes in order to confront these. These represented herein have been clustered from all of the papers and appear to be the most common.

1. Coffeehouses are all about smoking marijuana, getting high, and being totally free and the city of Amsterdam represents all of that.

Several of the students who worked on this topic explained initially how much they were teased by friends, colleagues and even their instructors back home about their reasons for wanting to study in Amsterdam:

As Dorothy reports:

> Even when people used to ask me where I was studying abroad I was apprehensive with stating Amsterdam, because of the negative connotations it receives from my community at home. Through interviewing, observing, and actually living in Amsterdam, my whole thought process transformed.

Keith felt head on what his leaving California and coming to Amsterdam meant, especially from his closest friends.

> Everywhere I went I could not escape the stigma that I was this protected Californian going to Amsterdam to finally be free and smoke a lot of marijuana—even my closest friends tell me I am trying to escape the real world to smoke myself out for a semester, and this is simply not true. I chose to study in Amsterdam for this exact reason, … to be open to all the pragmatic laws the Dutch inherit … learn why they institute such laws and where the misconceptions occur between the Dutch and the rest of the world who choose to judge their way of life.

This was also confirmed by Sonny when he explains some of the escalation taking place:

In the months leading up to the beginning of my study abroad experience I encountered the same exchange between myself and friends, family, and acquaintances. Someone would ask me where I was studying abroad and I would—with a wry smirk—reply simply, "Amsterdam." Upon my response I would usually receive a smirk in return, or perhaps a chuckle, followed by a sarcastic, "I'm sure you'll be doing plenty of studying there. I hear the coffee is good."

Unexpectedly, his own advisor upon hearing he was planning to study in Amsterdam let him know that:

he was concerned about how potential employers and law school admissions representatives would view such an "academic" excursion. When he finally signed the requisite forms granting me permission to go abroad, he handed them back to me saying, "As long as you're over there you might as well bring something good back" — of course was said with a sarcastic tone and another wry smirk.

Finally once in Amsterdam, Sonny sees his own peers falling prey to the stereotypes they had come with about coffeehouses:

I didn't end up visiting a coffeeshop until my fourth day in Amsterdam. Most of the students on my program made pit stops on the first day—even before getting their key to their dorm rooms. Perhaps after months of sarcastic comments and wry smirks my appetite for coffeeshops had been satiated.

Several students wrote about how other reasons also supported the existence of these stereotypes. Peter acknowledged that on the one hand, the film industry, media and music added to the stereotypes with films such as *Deuce Bigelow* or *European Gigolo* or even *Ocean's 12*, *High Times Magazine*, and Snoop Dog and Bob Marley emphasizing Amsterdam's coffee houses. But at the same time, the yearly November celebration of the "Cannabis Cup" a global competition in Amsterdam's Melkweg Club also added to this global image. He argued that the dance club cultures of Amsterdam, also contributed to the stereotype by having different hours. Coffeehouses closed at 1:00 p.m. while clubs were open from 12 to 4 a.m. and in such clubs youth consumed different kinds of drugs than marijuana, which he considered a downer.

2. Smoking of marijuana is without limits in the Netherlands.

This stereotype and all of the underlying assumptions was interestingly accepted by most of the male student writers as a trade mark of Dutch culture. Coffeehouses, according to Troy, are viewed as "an extremely prevalent stereotype of the Netherlands, with Dutch identity being made up of clogs, tulips, and marijuana."

Peter noted that over the semester his peers actually believed Dutch people would be heavy smokers in coffeehouses, yet upon examination of his Dutch interviewees, he found out they considered coffeehouses existed due to their having become legalized and being able to make money off of drug tourism. In fact, when he accompanied Ramon to some of the neighborhood coffeehouses, he found mostly Dutch males with a few females smoking marijuana after work. The females reported that the coffeehouses were also places were young people came to relax and enjoy the marijuana fudge cookies which seemed to be as great as an attraction as weed.

3. *Marijuana smoking spoils youth and leads to criminality.*

In addressing this stereotype, Patrick read Mulder's (2004) guidebook, *Misunderstanding the Netherlands*, and found out that soft drugs are consumed by young people between the ages of 20 and 24, and that 38 percent smoke joints in Amsterdam compared to 17 percent in the rest of the country. Patrick deduced that smoking marijuana is more an issue that a young person is interested in and not that one of nationality, of being Dutch or American.

Using statistics in class, Patrick showed his classmates that in terms of criminality that the Netherlands does not have the levels of criminality reported for other European countries or compared to numbers in the U.S. since coffeehouses are strictly regulated. He stated:

> Another very interesting consequence of the tolerant Dutch view towards cannabis is the arrest rates within particular European Union countries. By tolerating recreational cannabis use the Dutch police enforcement aren't worried about busting recreational users with small amounts of marijuana on them. Instead Dutch police officers are much more concerned with the large scale drug traffickers in their country. An interesting statistic helps illustrate this point, "between 1995 and 1998 the police took 120,000 kilos of cannabis and 5,000 kilos of cocaine to be destroyed, which resulted in no more than 43 arrests per 100,00 inhabitants. In the same period Germany collected 21,000 kilos of cannabis and 200 kilos of cocaine, but they managed to arrest no fewer than 250 of every 100,000 inhabitants" [Mulder, 2004].

Patrick acknowledged how much of the confusion arises from the assumption that the material production of marijuana is equivalent to the smoking of a joint and relaxing in a coffeehouse culture. So for him, he argued vehemently that illegality has somehow become conflagrated under the umbrella of coffeehouse culture, but in fact, much more than weed makes up the coffeehouses—smoking paraphernalia, cookies, drinks, etc., and that needed to be noted.

4. *Coffeehouses exist only as money making premises set up to attract tourists.*

Peter identified coffeehouses as places for relaxation, with weed often hidden out of sight, but with music tracks, food items, board games, booths, lounge chairs, billiards, massage chairs, and access in some places to the Discovery channel being the attractions from his interviews with clients and managers at three coffeehouses. Most of the papers written by males and the two females reiterated that not only tourists but Dutch people use coffeehouses as places where they meet and are able to relax, but they frequent such coffeehouses as meeting places within a neighborhood, where people go to socialize, contribute monies to support buying of the local football team uniforms.

These youth based their interpretations on objective data derived from multiple sources, not only the owners, managers and clients, but their own classmates who frequented the coffeeshops. Thus their portrayal of the atmosphere of coffeehouses, the environment and particularly social aspects as gezellig (cozy, warm, inviting) was characterized by most as a reality they felt comfortable with.

Joe interviewed barmen who had worked in coffeehouses, and noted from their statements, that rowdiness and fighting in the bars during the week was frequent and the bartenders had to usually break up the fights, yet in contrast, coffeehouse clients did not engage in such behaviors. He told the class how Jan who worked as a bartender and coffeehouse salesman, considered alcohol was more of a violent drug than marijuana.

Yet as cozy as coffeehouses might be, Jerry also noticed that they also represented a space for silence, as anti-social behavior. He remarked:

> While alcohol is commonly viewed as a social lubricant—capable of facilitating interaction between strangers—cannabis doesn't necessarily have the same effect. Indeed, while the BB could be viewed as a meeting space—and thus social in many regards—there were many aspects of the establishment and the activity of smoking that could be viewed as *asocial*. Groups of customers rarely interacted with each other. Additionally, interactions *within* groups of customers were at time limited. Long periods of silence were common within groups.

He compared this to another student paper he had read which also mentioned silence. Jerry remarked that Teresa

> also observed such silences at the JJ Coffeeshop—she writes: "At both coffeeshops, silence has a special social meaning that differentiates the coffeeshops from other social spaces. Unlike other places, silence at coffeeshops does not imply a pejorative meaning, when done while smoking. When smoking, silence means enjoying the joint, the cannabis, and also means appreciating it inside the body. For that reason, interactions are characterized for being constantly interrupted by socially allowed intervals of silence."

Identifying and Confronting Stereotypes: Red Light District

For the experiences among sex workers and the Red Light District, the prevalent stereotypes that the female students identified were as follows.

1. Prostitution is being profited upon by Amsterdamers and covers up illegal sex trade happenings.
As Dorothy points out:

Amsterdam has been described by people who have never been as a "place to smoke weed" or a "place to have sex with a hooker." Take one simple step into any souvenir shop and you'll witness these phrases on t-shirts, pens and coffee mugs. To most people that is all they know about the lovely place. Having lived in Amsterdam myself for almost six months, I have come to know it as much more than that. Prostitution is a part of the city, and for the sex workers, a part of normal daily life.

Elise though Amsterdam initially would be a "diverse, free spirited, fun place," and after spending six weeks collecting data about sex workers, confirmed, "The Red Light district embodied all of that." She drew a parallel between the people who visited Amsterdam just to party and think nothing of it and those who had a chance to live there for the semester. Her fun and frilly notions turned to the meaning of gezillig— of warmth and coziness. During that time, she became comfortable with seeing the Red Light District and sex workers being part of Dutch culture and as she stated, appreciated the opportunity to see another part of life that is often considered taboo.

2. *The Wallen, or Red Light District, exists as a zone for promiscuous sex and outright sexual degradation.*

Judith explains how she first felt when she walked through the Red Light District:

While walking through there I certainly felt somewhat uncomfortable as I watched these women being gawked at like animals in a zoo. However, I also felt extremely naive about the industry and acknowledged the fact that I could not take this at face value. Coming from America there is so much stigma surrounding sex and prostitution that I wanted to know more about Dutch society and how the Red Light District and these women in the windows came to be.

Later as she connected theory to practice, she explains,

the sole fact that the Red Light District reeks issues about sex, female power, and/or the subordination of women places it in the context of popular culture because those issues are always part of contemporary discussion. However, what is most interesting about the Red Light District in relation to popular culture is its pure existence as a cultural product.

Betsy on the other hand had direct contact with one of the ex-sex workers at the Prostitute Center in the Red Light District and through her interviews, began to see the connections of the sex industry tied in to popular culture:

Amsterdam's Red Light District is used as a spectacle to attract people while empowering the sex workers by making it a safe, regulated, choice. All of this contributes to the liberal and alternative spirit of Amsterdam, giving the city its unique flair making it unparalleled to any other city in the world. With regards to popular culture and mass media as a whole, we can see that Amsterdam is capitalizing on society's obsession with sex. Women are constantly sexualized in advertisements, magazines, films and other types of media around the world. Not only is Amsterdam capitalizing on this idea to bring visitors, but the women who work in the Red Light District are as well.

Yet she did not concur that such a spectacle was part of Dutch culture:

> While the Red Light District is a part of Amsterdam's culture in the sense that it attracts visitors and adds to the relaxed nature, it is not seen to be attributed to a Dutch culture.

Elizabeth on the other hand wondered how Dutch youth also felt about sex workers and whether they had any issues with its morality. When she interviewed several Dutch youth, she was amazed to find out that they basically told her the following:

> The Dutch are very cool with prostitution as long as it's not too close to them. Yup. Yup. Yup, they're very tolerant, but it should not be your daughter, the neighbor, or the one that works part time in the daycare center, for instance. "Eek there's a prostitute watching my children." Like, she could be the best but ah, there is still a lot of prejudice.

3. Sex workers are totally dehumanized and are victims acting against their will.

This was a stereotype that Judith accepted and she regarded sex workers as victims not only of the economic system but more importantly of patriarchy. As a feminist she was startled to find that there was in some cases, sex workers who talked about their own vision of themselves as feminists or even empowered women:

> Mariam, the ex-sex worker I interviewed expressed feelings of confidence, being in control, having a thrill and even having little respect for the clients—all feelings which are not generally a part of the typical discourse surrounding sex work.

Judith connected her ideas to Chancer's (1993) theory that "for some sex workers, narcissistic enjoyment can emanate from seeing desire in someone's eyes, knowing the dependency admitted by this attentiveness (however transient and fleeting), and making him pay and in fact 'getting paid' from a sense of controlling the interaction and/or in giving him, and at moments oneself, pleasure" (p. 163). She noted in her paper:

> In an interview conducted by Michel Martin on National Public Radio (2007), Xaviera (Hollander) says that she feels more respect as a prostitute than just a girl about town, "because I was the one setting the rules"

Judith considered this flip side of the victim and bully syndrome and she began to test her ideas by collecting the comments of onlookers as they walked the streets of the Red Light District viewing the sex workers in the red lighted window rooms. From many of the males she picked up negative and judgmental comments of the sex workers and from some of the females walking, she overheard them state how "wrong" is was to have a church in the middle of the Red Light District, attributing the "right" morals in their opinion with the church, and the "wrong" with prostitution. She also recognized some of the young men's nervousness as they were taunted by their peers and pressured to show their "manhood by approaching a sex worker":

A male stated "I'm going to hell for this" before he entered into a window. With regards to culture, the tourists using the windows, or seeing the area for the first time are mostly shocked. They only see the negative because that is what they were raised in their own culture to see.

In essence, she gathered evidence of the nervous laughter to the giggles and expressions of machos objectifying women, but such contrasts helped her to understand the very fortitude of the women working in the red windows. As Aalbers (2005) points out: "Although it may be assumed that men in a red light district are the ones watching and prostitutes the ones being watched, the socially and spatially specific rules of a red-light district may turn things upside down: 'Big Sister' is watching you!" (p. 61).

Discussion on the Process of Deconstruction of Stereotypes and Self-Reflection

The analysis of paper and the themes derived based on the popular culture research of these youth indicates how much popular culture was a vehicle by which students were able to question stereotypes about coffeehouses and the role of sex workers. The questions they raised in class, the detailed field notes they submitted for review and the literature inquiries they conducted beyond their readings of Dutch and hard to find readings provided a balanced and sophisticated analysis of their theory building. Dutch students helped them with the translations of Dutch texts and vice versa American students helped decode some of the readings and idiomatic expressions of English. Since they worked in pairs, comparisons and contrasts were constantly being made.

In their papers was evidence of how they spent time inside coffeehouses, logging several hours of fieldwork each day, observing and engaging in informal conversations and interviewing workers, clients, shop owners, sex workers, former madams, and their own peers. Peter reminded the class, how he biked past three coffeehouses and noticed tourists with marijuana logos, went to festivals and rallies, and picked up flyers, photographs and readings along the way. He placed us sensorially on his bike, and as he biked along the canals, shared how he took in the smells of the coffeehouse marijuana that spilled into the streets. Betsy recalled how she now knew several of the sex workers in the area from having walked to class and how she stopped at times to talk with her coffee in hand and her heavy rug sack. As she and others commented, the Red Light District after a while was a natural extension of Amsterdam they got to know.

For the youth who wrote about coffeehouses, they discovered how

Americans frequented coffeehouses through word of mouth and how such information had already been relayed before they even arrived in Amsterdam. The pre-preparation however was nothing compared to the realities they encountered in Amsterdam's coffeehouses, of social mixing, quiet times, and even silence.

It took time for many to begin to deconstruct their pre-conceived stereotypes, and through the reading of government reports comparing the U.S. and Dutch policies in terms of homicide rates, criminality, drug use, and prostitution, they would wonder why and how the U.S. had higher rates than the Netherlands in most of these issues. They were amazed to know that having a toy gun if you are over twelve years of age in the Netherlands can lead to criminal prosecution (Buruna, 2007) and asked about the U.S. gun control policies and why there were so many guns in the U.S.

They could then explore in depth why Amsterdam's attraction of the Red Light District and prevalence of weed friendly coffeehouses was due to the decriminalization of marijuana and its legislative stance on prostitution. Yet they did not paint a rosy picture of what they learned but understood the complexities of capitalism, globalization, and international markets intertwined with coffeehouses and the Red Light District as they checked Amsterdam's tourist websites, and found that these internationally known coffeehouses draw close to two million drug tourists per year, that tourism in Amsterdam has swelled and the per night bed use has rocketed.

These youth's revelations expressed how they met the stereotypes they had heads from: (a) those they heard from friends back home before even arriving in Amsterdam, to (b) those they heard about from Dutch persons about Americans, to (c) their own stereotypes stemming from their backgrounds and cultures. They also used policy analysis, in raising and questioning what they read, not only in terms of what they were learning in Amsterdam, but also what they felt their colleagues and Americans could learn back home.

As Albert commented:

> An interesting question that arises after analyzing both the Dutch and American drug policy towards marijuana is could a Dutch *gedogen* stance work in the U.S.? The initial response from an idealist would most likely be yes the Dutch *gedogen* stance on marijuana would indeed work in America. A pessimist would respond the contrary saying that, no, the Dutch have a very unique policy that only works within their country. I myself find my view right in the middle of the idealist and pessimist. I think that it would be great if America could adopt such a progressive stance on marijuana, but it seems too out of reach at the moment. The first reason that comes to mind is the difference in population size of the two countries. The United States' population is almost 20 times the size of the Netherlands'. It would be much harder to regulate recreational marijuana use in coffeeshops in a country with a population of over 300 million inhabitants

Conclusion

For many of the students of the popular culture class, aside from the academic learning of theory and research, the human dimensions of their interactions with classmates from different backgrounds, nationalities, and languages proved to be worth-while learning. Seeing how three or four languages could be spoken, how code switching could smoothly take place, prompted some to consider learning languages, including Dutch, but knowing that they could rely on each other and build cadres within the pairs they worked in, allowed them to also see their own development of ideas and identities take place. Andrew epitomized this by saying, "There was no language barrier ... working with international students ... was extremely beneficial."

As to their own learning about themselves, being able to speak about a topic with people from different cultures, without judgments being made or morality questioned, was something they had not experienced or explored before. Learning about another culture from a different perspective than their own and doing this together as they explored Amsterdam seemed to foster genuine care and concern.

Their final paper reflections revealed how their own identities once confronted, began to filter information differently, how they changed their language, attitudes and stances regarding the policies and practices that exist in the Netherlands, and what can be learned from these. Many no longer referred to prostitutes, but sex workers and the females in the group shed the notion of victimization for deeper nuanced behaviors of power, identity and control. They identified with and share their own feminism and felt a kindred spirit of sorts in understanding women who could talk about their own empowerment.

Sonny expressed that having learned about the laws on cannabis and understanding coffeehouses as social spaces, gave him a sense of what they are and what their role is within Dutch society. He recognized coffeeshops in the Netherlands are able to create a safe haven for recreational marijuana smokers to smoke freely and safely away from the pressures of hard drugs and successfully create barriers between the soft drug of marijuana from very harmful hard drugs such as cocaine and heroin

Such understanding of the laws and regulations, as well as the philosophical foundations of those laws, became an integral part to understanding the bigger picture of how these establishments (coffeehouses and the Red Light District sex workers) operate in Dutch society and culture. He acknowledged that harm reduction also creates lifestyle pluralism within a society since it allows for those who are addicted to drugs to not be alienated from society. Though drug use may be stigmatized to a certain extent, it is viewed by the government as a health problem and not a criminal problem. Thus, drug addicts aren't pushed to the periphery of society but are accepted and given help to try to minimize the damage they could do to themselves and others. Likewise sex workers have professionalized their work and notwithstanding are demanding their rights.

Maxwell perhaps summarizes one of the mayor lessons from the course:

> This project has taught me lessons in literature as well as life that I will take with me throughout the rest of my being. Through working with a partner in this project I learned how to work with someone who is not from where I am. It was an interesting experience getting to know my partner and considering her different viewpoints than mine. It also helped me learn cooperation skills as well as skills for interacting with different types of people. I had to come out of my shell and be more open to meeting and interviewing people who English wasn't their first language.

Yet Gary's statement leaves us rethinking our views about Amsterdam seen through his eyes:

> Amsterdam is a beautiful, deep-rooted city. Stepping out of the few blocks that make up the District and major shopping areas, an American sees Europe at its most striking as well as most serene. Biking the beautiful canals like Prinsengracht and Herengracht, the windows of scantily clad women disappear, and the real Amsterdam shows its face. An elderly couple sits on the corner, sipping red wine and watching the boats pass. A group of young, hip twenty-somethings dine at a canalside café. A father speeds by on his bike, one child in the front basket, one holding his shoulders on the back.

Andy completes the realization of the ethnographic journey they as a group undertook as he says:

> Many Americans seem to think the Dutch are a strange people, some even saying they are rude and marijuana-addicted. The marijuana obsession is of course false, in fact, the majority of the coffeeshops are marketed towards tourists. In terms of their "rudeness," this is clearly just a cultural divide. The forwardness of the Dutch is perhaps their greatest quality. American culture seems to rely on niceties and false promises, whereas in an interaction between Dutch people, nothing will be said that is not meant. So I will speak as the Dutch do now, freely and without regret: Come to Amsterdam, toss away your stereotypes, and enjoy one of the finest cities in the world.

NOTES

1. Tokos refer to take out shops which have freshly cooked Indonesian food and which are found throughout all of the major cities in the Netherlands.

2. Some students were able to interview several Holocaust victims and their connection to Judaism tracing the experiences of their own families in the U. S. with those of some of the Jewish elders they met through an expert researcher of Judaism in the Netherlands.

3. Lotte van de Pol's book on Het Amsterdams hoerdom: *Prostitutie in de zeventiende en achttiende eeuw* (2006) cited by Catteral (1998) describes the expansion of dance halls as a social popular event during the late seventeenth century.

REFERENCES

Aalbers, M. A. (2005). Big sister is watching you! Gender Interaction and the Unwritten Rules of the Amsterdam Red-Light District. *The Journal of Sex Research*, 42(1), 54–62.

Brants, C. (1998). The fine art of regulation tolerance: Prostitution in Amsterdam. *Journal of Law and Society, 25*(4), 621–635.

Brussa, L. (2009). Sex workers in Europe: A mapping of prostituting in 25 European countries. Tampep International Foundation.

Buruma, Y. (2007). Dutch tolerance: On drugs, prostitution and euthanasia. *Crime and Justice, 35*(1), 73–113.

Catteral, D. (1998). Review of Het Amsterdams hoerdom: Rostitutie in de zeventiende en achitiende eeuw by Lotte van de Pol. Amsterdam: Wereldbibliotheek, 1996. *The Sixteenth Century Journal, 29*(4), 1240–1242.

Chancer, L. S. (1993). Prostitution, Feminist Theory and Ambiguity. *Social Text, 37*, 143–171.

Gans, H. (1999) The popular culture-high culture distinction still relevant? In *Popular Culture and High Culture: An Analysis and Evaluation of Taste* (2nd ed.) New York: Basic Books.

Gowling, A. (2014). The Netherlands had record numbers of tourists in 2013.

Kavaratzis, M., & Ashworth, G. M. (2007). Partners in coffeeshops, canals and commerce: Marketing the city of Amsterdam. *Cities, 4*(1),16–25.

Korf, D., M. Wouters, & A. Benschop (2011). The return of the underground retail cannabis market? Attitudes of Dutch coffeeshop owners and cannabis users to the proposed "cannabis ID" and the consequences they expect. *Bonger International Bulletin.*

Luscombe, B. (2008, July 7). Why grass is green. *Times*, 59–60.

"Marijuana is in, tobacco is out under Netherlands' smoking ban." *Dutch Amsterdam.nl* Retrieved from http://www.dutchamsterdam.nl/324-amsterdam-cofeeshops-smoking-ban.

Mulder, A. (2004, May/June). Why the Dutch don't use drugs. *De Gids*, pp. 74–76.

Nijman, J. (1999). Cultural globalization and the identity of place: The reconstruction of Amsterdam. *Cultural Geographie, 6*(2), 146–162.

Ritzer, G. (2008). The McDonalization of Society. New York: Pine Forge Press.

Sabat, M. (2012). From red light to black light: Spatial transformation and global effects in Amsterdam's red light district. *City, 16*(1–2), 158–171.

Shuyt, K. (2001). Tolerantie en democratie. In D. Fokkema and F. Grijzenhound (Eds.), *Rekenschap 1650-2000.* The Hague: SDU.

Strinati, D. (2004). An introduction to theories of popular culture (2nd ed.). London: Routledge.

Storey, H. (2003). Cultural studies and the study of popular culture (2nd ed.). Athens: University of Georgia Press.

Ter Bog T., Schmid, H., Saoirese, Gahainn, N, Anastasios, F. and Vollebergh, W. (2006). Economic and cultural correlates of cannabis use among mid-adolescents in 31 countries. *Addiction, 101*(2), 241–251.

Uitermark, J. (2004). The origins and future of the Dutch approach towards drugs. *Journal of Drug Issues, 34*(3), 511–532.

van de Walle, R., Picavet, C., van Berlo, W., & Verhoeff. A. (2015). Young Dutch people's experiences of trading sex: A qualitative study. *The Journal of Sex Research, 49*(6), 547–557.

Van Stratten, S. (2000). De Wallentjes als themapark voor volwassenen. *Rooilijn, 33*, 438–443.

Zuckerise, G. M. (2012). Governmentality in Amsterdam's red light district, *City, 16*(1–2), 146–157.

Re-Fashioning the Agriculture

No-gal *(Farming Gals) and Positive Youth Development in Japan*

Mariko Izumi *and* Naomi Kagawa

Dresses, hairstyles, accessories, and makeup have been the staples of youth. Just as punk fashion was a statement against commercial youth fashion in the past (Furlong & Cartmel, 2007), belly-baring T-shirts inspired by Britney Spears, sagging pants like hip-hop artists, or large ear gauges and disks are not just a mere sign of consumer culture but an active ownership of identity. These practices are what Foucault (1988) calls "technologies of the self," the practices or operation that a person engages on her own self or body for the purposes of transforming herself into a fulfilled, wise, disciplined, and productive individual. Imitating celebrity fashion and altering one's outer appearance, for example, are some of the most visible ways youth produce and satisfy their subjective well-being. Despite its seeming superficiality, fashion is one of the important sites where youth negotiate and unfold their relationship to the social, cultural, and political environment that surrounds them.

The scholars and practitioners in youth development may not see obsession with fashion as desirable or worthy for fostering among youth. At worst, they might see youth's fashion obsession problematic, destructing their attention away from academic performance and the "real" world. At best, they may recognize fashion as an important part of the youth's culture and identity, but not the "substantive" or "appropriate" site of positive youth development (PYD). Such concerns reflect anxiety about the historical phenomenon which Ferudi (2004) identified as the instability of modern self. In this historical-cultural context, "we have all become increasingly narcissistic—preoccupied with personal growth and the development of an authentic self. We pursue our biographical projects through consumerism in an often quick-fix instrumental way that prevents us from growing and developing in a rich and deep manner" (Cieslik & Simpson, 2012, p.18). Particularly in the context of youth studies, strong investment in fashion may appear as counterintuitive to the development of "more outward looking social and political perspectives and activities" among youth (Cieslik & Simpson, 2012, p.18).

The *no-gal* (or "farm gals" as translated into English) subculture in Japan, however, provides an interesting case study that challenges the general anxiety about the role of fashion in youth development. These Japanese "gals," whose subculture identity revolves around anime-inspired makeup, bleached hair and flamboyant outfits, connected their obsession with fashion and trends with agriculture, the "uncool" industry, that has been struggling to attract the younger generation. This essay examines the *no-gal* subculture in order to explore the processes of identity development among the Japanese youth. In particular, we pay attention to Shiho Fujita, the icon and the initiator of the *No-gal* Project, by analyzing her blog posts and publications. By applying the theory of positive youth development (e.g., Lerner et al., 2005), this essay will illustrate how Fujita's *No-gal* Project engages in positive youth development and creates an empowering social environment that offers a space for youth to imagine their impact on society.

Although popular culture has not been seen as a site of positive youth development, it offers a unique way to extend the existing studies of PYD. Many of the practices and studies in the field have been situated within structured institutional contexts, such as classrooms, after-school programs, and intervention services. However, as Cieslik and Simpson (2012) note, "the increasing significance of social media through the Internet and diverse patterns of consumerism have all encouraged a more fluid, creative and autonomous youth which throws up patterns of cultural identification and sociability that defy easy class-based classification" (p. xvi). The multi-directional development of the youth's identity requires us to be also multidimensional in our pursuit of positive youth development, extending beyond the structured institutional context. Cieslik and Simpson (2012) call for "situate[ing] young people's lives in their wider social and historical context" (Lerner et al., 2005, p.11). Taking youth's participation in subculture offers a concrete way to make visible the milieu as seen and experienced by the youth (from their perspective). Such an approach "can promote the importance of youth research by documenting how the changing experiences of youth also have in turn significant implications for other parts of society" (Lerner et al., 2005, p.12).

Our preliminary exploration of the popular culture as a site of positive youth development is situated in this trend to see youth as "assets" that emphasizes the strength and reliance of youth. Dismissing young people's obsession with fashion as superficial and shallow would limit us to the "traditional deficit model" of youth that tend to treat them as "lacking" maturity, knowledge, skills, etc. Sukarieh and Tannock (2011) write, "The problem of youth today is that ... wide spread acceptance of deficit models of youth can 'become self-fulfilling prophecies'" (p. 680). The shift in conceptualizing youth from deficit to asset benefit young people provides a positive environment for youth, particularly in schools and after-school programs where the positive idea of youth will be reflected and practiced. But, if a symbolic environment is not immediately available, where can youth turn to develop their positive self-image and identity? According to Bird and Markle (2012), "subjective well-being (SWB) has been a factor that consistently predicts positive school outcomes" and has strong potential for positively impacting young people's sense of fulfillment in life beyond academic settings (pp. 61–62). If so, in what ways can fashion, as a source of youth's subjective-well beings, be the platform for positive development of their individual identity and the society as a whole? The *no-gal* phenomenon in Japan offers an interesting phenomenon to explore the role of popular culture in the positive development of youth. At the intersection of popular culture and positive youth development, this preliminary study illustrates the emergence of entrepreneurship as a new ethos (or model) of positive youth development that allows the youth to claim ownership of their identity and society as their community.

Gal Subculture

Gyaru, a Japanese transliteration of English word "gal(s)," is a subculture that has been animating Japan's youth culture over the last several decades (Kawamura, 2012; Nanba, 2007). It revolves around the idea of fashion, trend, lifestyle, body and self-transformation, characterized by the use of flamboyant outfits, colored hair, and anime-inspired makeup to mark their subcultural identity. Originated in the 1970s, the gal subculture developed around female adults and college students, who saw themselves as "those who don't care if their guy is from money or a good family; they go for trendy looks, clothing, behavior, and are cheerful" (Nanba, 2006, p.102). As one website puts it, "they were party girls" (Marx, 2012). When the subculture that originally developed around adult females was taken up by youth, the subculture became a center of social fascination and criticism simultaneously. In the mid–1990s, middle and high school girls (13 to 18 years old) began adopting the gal fashion into their school uniform. They modified their school uniform by shortening the pleated skirt, bleaching or coloring their hair from black to light brown, wearing leg-warmers like "loose-socks" and platform shoes. *Ko-gals*, small or child-like gals, were born out of the fusion of school uniform and gal fashion.

One of the main reasons why gal culture became a target of social criticism is the sexualization of the youth embodied by the *ko-gals*. They were often criticized by mainstream media as being "impertinent, vulgar or indecent, egocentric, lacking manners, absurd or devoid of common sense, garish, and without perseverance" (Miller, 2004a, p. 236). Particularly, Katsushi Kuronuma's 1998 exposé, *Enjo Kosai* (compensated or subsidized dating) helped fuel the critical scrutiny of the *ko-gal* subculture. It chronicled how middle and high-school girls are making "pocket money" during the after-school hours by sexually engaging middle-age men and helped problematize the highly sexualized style of self-image *ko-gal* fashion promotes among Japanese youth. As Miller (2004b) points out, "The importance of *ko-gal* phenomenon lies not in numbers, for there has never been a large percentage of the teenage population who followed the style, but in how *ko-gals* symbolize the ongoing redefinition of women in late capitalism" (p. 226). In a similar manner, gals who dress in Gothic /Lolita fashion have been criticized for feeding the heterosexual male fantasies and infantalization of femininity (Gagné, 2008; Derek, 2005). Gals who frequent tanning salons and bleach their hair to very light brown were called *ganguro-gal* (black faced gals) and were often ridiculed by mainstream media for their tackiness and shallowness (Kinsella, 2005).

The hyped media scrutiny of the gal subculture reflects the social and cultural anxiety about gals' transgression of established mainstream norms and boundaries. Miller (2004b) wrote, "New youth fashion offer a wider conception of gendered identity than in the past.... The extreme *ko-gal*-style *yamanba* most blatantly flouted female beauty norms of the past, deliberately rejecting ideas about daintiness and sweetness. They created a type of female campiness usually associated with drag queens, calling into question the presumed naturalness of femininity" (p. 84). Indeed, the emergence of *gyaru-o* (gal man) and their feminine appearance and investment in skin care products exemplifies the transgressive power of gal subculture (Saladin, 2011). In addition to challenging the mainstream gender norms, gal subcultures challenge the racial boundaries, wearing blue color contact lenses, colored or bleached brown hair, and curled hair like Western antique dolls. Miller (2004b) observes:

> Japanese fashion innovations are not the surface emulation of many specific foreign trend, but are based on a selection of items from different eras, places and cultures. This practice is sometimes called *mukokuseki* [lacking nationality]. The *mukokuseki* aesthetic of statelessness deliberately invokes images from somewhere or some historical time—Vietnamese peasant trousers, Native American fringe and beads, 1960s paisleys—yet combines or juxtaposes these with Converse running shoes or Japanese geta, baseball caps or Rastafarian knit berets. The end result is a total ensemble that represents no specific place, time, or ethnicity [p. 84].

Just as many subcultures do, gal subculture performs the act of rebellion against the established mainstream norms that seek to govern the identities of the youth, prescribing they are and who they ought to be. Japanese sociologist Koji Nanba (2006) observes, "while the *ko-gal* craze in the '90s appears to be an exorbitant [physical] change among only limited number of youth, it acutely indicates the change in value system among [Japanese] youth in general" (p. 116).

Cieslik and Simpson (2013) call for "situate[ing] young people's lives in their wider social and historical context" (p. 11), in order to explore and document "how the changing experiences of youth also have in turn significant implications for other parts of society" (p. 12). Despite severe social criticisms, gal subculture came to be recognized as Japan important cultural asset. Japanese government's economic initiative, Cool Japan, promotes and exports Japanese popular culture. Along with video games and animations, Cool Japan includes gal subculture as a part of the "creative industry" that marks Japan as a unique epicenter of popular youth culture (Ministry of Economy, Trade, and Industry, Japan, 2014). In 2009, Japan Broadcasting Corporation (NHK), the only public broadcaster in Japan, aired a program *Gals* and traced the role gal subcultures play in "saving" Japan's declining economy. As NHK's documentary exemplifies, the youth's impact on society is getting recognized. The strength of gal subculture is its ability to diversify socio-cultural norms that youth often find confining and constraining. By offering a broad range of styles readily available to anyone willing to create or buy them, gal subculture opens up a new, more "egalitarian" space where the youth negotiates their relationship with the society and, in turn, change the society (Miller, 2004b).

No-Gal *and Gal Revolution*

Shiho Fujita is an iconic figure in the gal subculture. Having worked as a gal fashion model, Fujita initiated Gal Revolution in 2005 by establishing her own business marketing company at the age of 19. Popular mainstream media often treats her initiative as a label to describe familiar gal subculture by labeling her as "gal shacho" (gal president or CEO). Fujita established the company as a challenge against the adult's society that looked down on her as a gal. Her mission was to prove to the society that "there are things that can be done *because* one is a gal, rather than gals can *also* do things" in society (Fujita, 2009). In her first blog in 2005, Fujita reports that she has been recruited by a large entertainment firm and writes as follows:

> If I work for the firm, it's a big company led by proper president, and I will have a manager, and everyone around me will take care of my work even if I don't go out and find

206 The Young Are Making Their World

jobs for myself.... But!! Nothing will change! Entering into the world the adults have created, doing the job they give me.

If I make my dream come true through the company I created myself, then it means society recognized me. If a gal becomes successful with her company she created from scratch, I can change the adults' perception of gals, and there may be more gals who will be encouraged to do what they want to do with confidence, and then, I think it might be a social contribution.

Interestingly, Fujita's Gal Revolution initiative is not only geared toward changing the adults' perception of gals, but also changing the young gals' perception about their own selves. In contrast to the society's attitude toward gals, Fujita points out that gal-ness or identity as a gal is an attained identity, rather than an innate to an individual. Whoever wears gal's fashion, typically very short skirts or pants, darker and shiny makeup with very long false eyelashes, and speaks a unique language with special accents, are given the name, gal. As Fujita (2006) explains in her online biography, "it is the outer society that labels them gal, and there are no gals who actively call themselves a gal."

In the context where "gal" predominantly points to negative meanings, Fujita's Gal Revolution is an initiative for claiming ownership of the very labels youth receive from society at large. Going beyond the pursuit of her own dream of becoming a part of the music industry and having her own live shows, Fujita embarked *No-gal* Project in 2009. With several other active female "gal" fashion models, the project sought to revolutionize the image of farming and agriculture in Japan. What makes Fujita and her *No-gal* Project unique from other gal subcultures and interesting for the scholars and practitioners of positive youth development is its connection to social issues. The *no-gals* transform fashion and subcultural identity as a medium to reconnect the youth to society and social issues.

Agriculture has been an "uncool" industry for many of the Japanese youth. A survey conducted among college students in Japan shows that the youth's general attitudes toward agriculture are "hard" "heavy (physical) labor" and "difficult to manage" (Yauchi, 2012; Life Media Research Bank, 2010; National Agriculture and Food Research Organization, 1995). As an industry, it has been struggling to attract Japanese youth, and the population engaged in agriculture has been steadily declining in Japan (The Japan Forum, 2011). In fact, as the Japanese Ministry of Agriculture, Forestry, and Fisheries has reported, agriculture has not been an option in the minds of youth when they think about their future work and employment (Ministry of Agriculture, Forestry, and Fishery, 2014), and the Ministry has been trying to promote agriculture as youth's future option. Local governments have been trying to appeal to the youth's interests in subculture by creating their own local mascots (Sasaki, Inoue, Kosonoi, & Watanabe, 2014).

Going beyond the realm of fashion and trends, *no-gals* take up this "uncool" industry. Naniwa discerns that gals are animating a new sociological phenomenon in the postwar Japanese society, in which they are transforming into new entrepreneurs by starting their own businesses and serving as the agents of new social networks (Hasebe, Yasue, & Hitakuchi, 2011). *No-gals* represent such trend, turning agriculture into an object of public attention and desire through their fashion-driven subcultural identity. In the following, six characteristics (6Cs) of PYD are used to illustrate how *no-gals* promote positive youth development, changing the youth's self-perception and their position in the society.

Six Characteristics (6 Cs) of Positive Youth Development

Character

The key factor of Fujita's PYD is "character." According to Lerner et al. (2005), the "character" of PYD refers to one's respect for societal and cultural rules, possession of standards for correct behaviors, a sense of right and wrong, and integrity. All of these elements of "characters" have been treated to be conceptually aligned with one another. The expected result of PYD related to "character" is the youth's respect for social and cultural rules and eventually adjust him/herself to fit-in to society by following the rules (e.g., a youth learns to accept the societal rule that we help each other, and s/he becomes to be able to help others). However, as discussed earlier, this transitional or assimilation model of youth development tends to see youth in terms of "deficit"—lacking understandings, respects, knowledge, etc., to successfully enter into society. Such a view diminishes youth's agency, their ability to act and engage in society and feel that they *are* a part of the society.

From the perspective of schema theory, individuals have role schema, which is the theoretical cognitive module that contains information about a group of individuals that are classified by their ethnical background, occupation, age, and other social categories (Taylor & Crocker ,1981). This makes individuals assume that others have certain personalities solely based on the social groups that they belong. This assumption is often wrong, and it could lead to prejudice. Another theory that can apply here is Implicit Personality Theory (Cronback, 1955). It suggests that individuals tend to assume and fill in unknown information about others by using what is already known to them. Regarding the *no-gal* phenomenon, individual spectator may not know anything about a gal's personality, but one tends to assume that the gal is lazy, incapable, and so on. Such naming represents a social action of identifying this youth group as a social "problem."

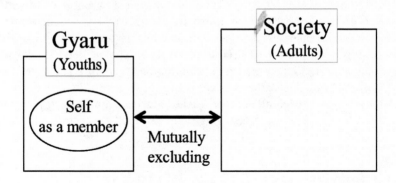

Figure 1. Stage 1: Exclusion Model (Before to the Early Stage of the Gal-Revolution).

Understanding youth and their perspective through rebellious and transgressive subcultures is not the same as celebrating or promoting disrespect toward the established social cultural norms. Rather, the *no-gal* phenomenon suggests that the interpretation of the element, "respect for societal and cultural rules," can be more diverse and complicated than commonly acknowledged. Fujita's path as a young "gal" to successful entrepreneur over the last decade exemplifies how rebellion is an act to dislocate physical appearance from the role schema the society uses for making judgment about the "worth" of the gal youth.

In her autobiographies, Fujita retells how she became a "gal." She did not intend to become gal, but was simply dressing in the way she enjoyed herself. Then, people around her began calling her a "gal." With that social label came the negative treatment as an "incapable" person. She recounts a number of episodes about being mistreated, being suspected as a thief, and being ridiculed openly at her work that "there are no jobs gals can do." These repetitive and consistent negative experiences led Fujita to develop a sense of rivalry against the society, especially against adults (see Fig. 1). Fujita did not see herself being accepted or understood in the society. For her, society existed outside of her self-concept, and the society was something that she had to fight against.

Interestingly, in this context of rivalry, Fujita found gal fashion as an armor that gives her self-assurance and strength to act with confidence. Rather than yielding to the social norms imposed upon herself, Fujita demonstrated resilience. As Chen et al. (2012) have remarked, resilience is one of the characteristics that contribute to the successful process of engaging in psychological challenges during the youth's identity formation. They explain that "resilient youths effectively seek resources and supports from their surroundings that nourish and scaffold identity formations. Through social interactions within their cultural contexts, they start to understand more about themselves and their relationship" (p. 762). Indeed, Fujita turned further to the gal subculture, finding similar youth who care about the fashion and share negative experiences about being gals. One reader of Fujita's blog left the following message in the comment column: "I have been cheered up by your comments so many times. I have been moved by you. I feel that who I am now would not exist without you. I sincerely admire you as a human being." Another person commented, "I was in my first year of high school when I started follow your blog. I sympathized with you about prejudice against gals. I believe that gal-revolution has started to spread out throughout the society. Please continue being who you are, which I love."

Armed with fashion, Fujita initiated the Gal Revolution, which later led her to embark on the *No-gal* Project. While adults may not listen to a gal seriously, they may become interested in talking with her if she is a CEO of a company. Out of her strong desire to change the public opinions about gals, Fujita collaborated with the Japanese retail company Edison and designed denim shorts for farm workers. Wearing a bright pink T-shirt and cute blue denim overalls, long brown hair tied back in a ponytail and perfect makeup, the mismatch of the gal against the rural scene of rice farming field spurred media attention. Fujita labeled herself as a corporate executive to offset the negative attitude toward her identity as a gal. She insists on her unwillingness to give up her gal identity, and this resilience made her successfully function

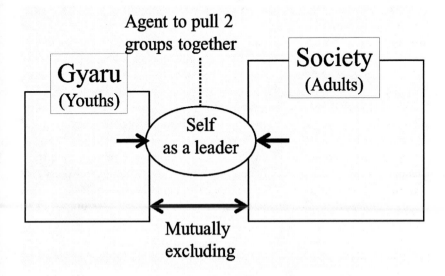

Figure 2. Stage 2: Bridge Model (Mid Stage of the Gal-Revolution).

as an agent to bridge the two social groups: the gal youth group and adult society (Figure 2).

In order for Fujita, a young gal, to prove to society that gals are capable, she needed to become a person whom the adults in the society would admire. As she continues on with her Gal Revolution through the *No-gal* Project, Fujita's identity changed from a mere member in the subculture to the leader of the entire group of gals. She came to see that the Gal Revolution is not only about achieving her own dreams but also about enabling the entire community of gals to have better lives in the Japanese society. In her 2009 autobiography, she describes how the Gal Revolution had enabled her to realize about her own prejudices against adults, just as much as the adults judged her and her gal fashion. This was an important realization for her that the exclusion was not one-way from adults in society against her being gal but, in fact, it was two-way between these two parties. The Gal Revolution brought her the opportunities to learn the self-involved way of thinking. In other words, she learned to think about a solution to problem by assuming that she is a part of the problem as well.

As a leader or a cultural icon who represents the gal subculture and explores the place of gals in the disapproving adult society, Fujita actively engages in social issues, such as HIV and environment. One of the main areas is agriculture, and issues associated with it such as food safety and sustainable farming. In 2009, Fujita and her fellow *no-gals* hosted an event in Ogata, Niigata Prefecture, in which youths participated in rice planning in the field along with 30 *no-gals*. With their colorful gal fashion and bleached brown hair, they "colored" the rice farming field, attracting strong attention from the media. When they harvested the rice they farmed, they marketed them as "gal rice" in Tokyo. The *no-gal*'s physical appearance and active engagement in the industry that has been unpopular particularly among youth has sparked a sense of energy and agency among the youth. For instance, consider the following comments left on Fujita's blog: "Your actions for the last four years have been impressive. Thanks to you, I found what I really want to do, and I have been studying hard for it." Another person writes, "I want to grow to become gal who can do something big." As these comments suggest, Fujita's *No-gal* Project provided a concrete social arena where youths can concretely imagine their agency. These comments usually do not tell us concretely which industry and work area these youths imagines their place to be. However, these comments tell us that *no-gals* helped create social aspiration among the young readers. As Japanese scholars Hasebe et al. (2011) examined, the impression of *No-gal* Project on university students. They found that female undergraduates perceive this project as more positive and impressive compared to male students or graduate students. This result suggests that individuals who perceived more similarities in demography are more likely to be influenced by the *no-gals*.

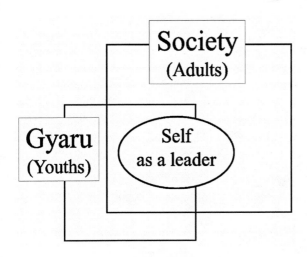

Figure 3. Stage 3: Co-Existing Model (Toward the End of the Gal-Revolution).

The co-existing model depicts the relationship among the youth group, gals, and the adult society. An important part of this model is that gals are not assimilated into society. Fujita has been trying to maintain gal's characteristics and use these characteristics to empower the youth belonging to the social group. As Fujita repeatedly emphasizes in her autobiographies, it is easy to give up on being a gal just to get a job, but that does not solve the problem. Through her *No-gal* Project, Fujita exemplifies that gals can earn unique and irreplaceable positions in society.

Balsano (2005) notes that "civic engagement represents an important vehicle in promoting positive development among youth" (p. 188). The effectiveness of civic engagement for PYD is not confined to the U.S. McBribe, Johnson, Olate and O'Hara (2011) have shown how youth volunteer service experiences impact the development of self-worth among youth in Latin America and the Caribbean. Most of the civic engagement initiatives for positive youth development have been done through educational institutions. Interestingly, the *No-gal* Project shows the impact of civic engagement promoted through the entrepreneurship grounded in subcultures. As studies conducted in Japan show, people who experienced agricultural work demonstrate higher tendency to engage in agriculture in general (Ito et al., 2012). Hasebe et al. (2011) surveyed college students who participated in the aforementioned *no-gal* event in Ogata, Niigata, supports this result. They observed that participating in the *no-gal* events gave some of the students an opportunity to consider agriculture as a possible area of their future employment.

Connection

Fashion first. One's devotion to fashion drives the social network of gals. The gal subculture privileges specific areas in Tokyo, such as Shibuya, which serve as the important source of fashion trends. It is the place for gals to connect with other gals, spending hours discussing fashion, and exchanging neg-ative experiences of being mistreated. This connection with others animates the subculture and individual gals' everyday lives. It is no surprise, then, that Fujita chose Shibuya as the place to leave an office to start her own business marketing company to promote gals as an asset to the society. Her investment in her company, in turn, prompts her to care about the Shibuya as a "my area," and she began cleaning the area surrounding her office building every Monday. This weekly ritual prompted her to invest herself in the issues of environment and ecology, and eventually starting eco-projects. As Fujita tries to bring gals into the ecology related projects, she came to develop a per-spective that her important role is to connect the youth and the society, who are separated by the perceived difference in values and respects for established norms of conducts.

The use of social media contributed to the positive youth development we can see in Fujita's trajectory as the "gal president" as well as her role as a role model for the Japanese youth. As Pew Research Center (2010) reports, each generation has its own "personality," distinct characteristics that guide its way of conducting life and developing their sense of self-worth. The Center identified "confident, self-expressive, liberal, upbeat and open to change" as the defining characteristics of the Millennials. It indicates that the Millennium generation sees themselves distinct from previous generations in terms of their use of technology, particularly the mobile devices such as cell phone.

Like American Millennials, the youth in Japan share similar character-istics with regard to their relationship to the technology, particularly with regard to cell phones and social networking sites. One survey data identifies the mobile technologies, such as cell phone and iPod, are central to the subcultures where Japanese youth identifies themselves (Tachibana, 2008). The same survey identified the youth's willingness to spend money on materials and services that help them "polish" oneself—on consumer goods by designers brand, cosmetics, etc. It is interesting to note here that a cell phone, a key item in the youth subculture, is also identified as an item for self-improvement. Through the mobile device, the subculture and self-improvement are seen as synonymous.

One of the ways the media technology contributes to youth's sense of self-improvement is the sense of connectivity with others. According to the census data collected by the Cabinet Office of Japanese Government, the con-temporary Japanese considers having friendship or fellowship with others as a distinct indicator of their feeling of happiness. Based on this census data, Furuichi (2011) argues that the contemporary Japanese youth seek the pres-ence of fellow beings. In the context in which there is no single "youth culture" to which everyone belongs, youth access Facebook and Mixi, a Japanese ver-sion of Facebook, in search of the companions or fellow beings. This tendency to seek out for the "fellows" is driving the youth toward desiring what's often dubbed as "small village society" (Kawata, 2013). A survey conducted by Japan Nikkei Newspaper in 2012, one of the leading newspapers in Japan, the Japanese youth between the ages of 20 and 30 idealizes/dreams of living in rural region.

As Cieslik and Simpson (2013) rightly point out, "the increasing significance of social media through the Internet and diverse patterns of consumerism have all encouraged a more fluid, creative and autonomous youth which throws up patterns of cultural identification and sociability that defy easy class-based classification" (p. 16). The media technology and social networking sites offer a space for gals like Fujita to seek a place where they can experience the presence of the other gals and develop a sense of solidarity. For instance, Fujita treats her blog as her public journal, recording what she did to achieve her dreams, sharing the emotions and feelings she had about specific encounters, sharing her opinions about social issues such as ecology and food safety. Each entry of her blog-journal receives a large number of comments, many of which express a sense of relief that they are not alone and felt empowered by Fujita.

Palmer's (2013) study shows that new media technology provides a platform where the youth, such as LGBT youth, to experience the sense of inclusion. Similarly, technology offers a sense of access and connection for the youth in rural area. Christie and Lauzon (2014) document a unique potential for PYD with the fusion of technology with the after school program. Individually, it offers youth in rural areas access to a larger peer community outside of their region and gives them a sense of inclusion. Communally, for areas that struggle with youth retention, this technological access offers a potential for reducing the desire to leave the community.

New technologies have strong potential for promoting the PYD (Bears, 2006, 2010). One of the important reasons is because new media technology enables youth to be the content producer, rather than mere recipients of information (Davine et al., 2014). Commenting, uploading images, sharing information and videos, the youths become a participant and producer of a community at the same time. As Bers (2010) puts it, youth are "embarking on personal and community journeys that engage them in many facets of development" as they participate in the social networking sites via their cell phones (p. 2). The use of blogs and Mixi site, as well as Twitter and other social media outlets, Fujita provides opportunities for youth to "construct their sense of identity as having agency toward promoting changes in their own selves and society" (Bers, 2010, p. 2). Survey data from Japan Broadcasting Corporation (NHK) show that the contemporary Japanese youth indicate high desire for making social contribution (Honkawa, 2013). Fujita's use of social media outlets connects youth across gender, age, and geographical boundaries as a community. At the same time, she connects these youth to society by using her fashion as the solution to the social problems, such as declining popularity of agriculture. Through her fashionable appearance, Fujita and *no-gals* make agriculture fashionable. By foregrounding the gal fashion, *no-gals* promote youth's social agency as "contributions and capabilities of the young in society are to be recognized, celebrated and supported" (Sukarieh & Tanmokwrites, 2011, p. 678).

Caring and Compassion

As size and number of social networks that Fujita participates expanded, her sense of care and compassion for others evolved from personal to social level. As Fujita pushes her own boundaries to become successful in revolutionalizing how the society sees gals, she became increasingly cognizant about other fellow gals. In her autobiography (2009), she mentions how she was impressed by one businessman who spoke about the importance of thinking about what was needed in society one lives in. In this anecdote, Fujita shows her realization that she has been thinking what we, the gals, want to do but never thought about what others cared about. This comment was memorable for her, as it gave her a tool to see things from different others' perspectives.

Competence

Fujita believes that she is highly competent in the fashion field, and this perception never changed. With her position as the CEO of her company, she cultivated competence in other fields. She reported that she has experienced many moments full of joy when she realized that she has become competent in new areas. For instance, she did not know how to properly phrase her opinions and emotion when communicating with non-gal members. But, she gradually gained the interpersonal communication skill and felt that she became better at explaining what she is trying to achieve and her passion. Fujita (2006) expressed that she can feel her growth every single second of her life. In her process of learning how to run a business, she first learned how to relate to others, especially non-gal population. She accomplished it by developed her rules, such as "when you want to tell something to others, you should meet them and talk by looking into their eyes."

Confidence

Fujita has a relatively positive self-worth to begin with. In her autobiography, she stated that she chose to go to the school which regulations allowed her to stay as who she really was, by criticizing that the typical schools' regulations force youth to obey the teachers and prevent youth from being themselves. Fujita attitude of trying to be herself reflects her self-confidence.

Her choice of being a gal made her suffer from not receiving confirmation from the society about her self-worth. She has constantly received brutally negative messages about her as a gal. However, these negative messages from the society did not affect her self-worth. The psychological separation of her self-identity from the society functioned as a method to protect her self-worth from being hurt. This was because the outer society was not a social group that she perceived she belonged, and thus it was not a social group that she needed to feel accepted to maintain her positive self-worth. As a consequence, she needed to secure her positive self-worth by emphasizing the gal portion of her self-concept and by differentiated herself from the regular, non-gal population.

Throughout the gal-revolution, her positive self-worth remained supported by her perception of belonging to gal. Fujita noted that putting on gal's clothes and makeup empowered her. Those days when she was involved in agriculture as a part of her *No-gal* Project, she confessed that she chose to wake up early, at 4am, to wear makeup, over sleeping one extra hour. Gal's unique makeup is an important and necessary part of gal's identity, which even affects their mood and motivation. Sasayama and Nagamatsu (1999) found that self-esteem is positively associated with wearing makeup. The unique makeup representing gal-ness functions not only as fashion to enjoy but also as a tool to reconfirm their identity as gal and boost their self-esteem.

Fujita tries to maintain her belief that her project is meaningful for gal population. She (2009) reported that she learned the way to psychologically deal with the adults 'criticisms on her project. She decided to interpret the situation of her being criticized that she failed to successfully explain the purpose and the content of the project to these people and that the project itself is worth doing it. The gal project was very important for her, and doubting the value of the project would cause major damage to her self-worth. Thus, she chose to attribute the criticism to her poor communication skill that she can try to improve.

She gained higher confidence by feeling that her true self was admitted not only within gal's network but also by the society. Her confidence can be also observed in her attitude of seeking her own style in her new developing fields, such as business and agriculture, instead of simply following the instructions obtained from experts in these fields.

Contribution

Five months after she came up with the idea of Gal Revolution, and three months after she developed her personal blog, Fujita (2006) was amazed that her passion has been spread out to the world where she does not personally know. In April 2005, her Gal Revolution was ranked in as the top news in a commercial website. Her personal blog was also ranked in as the most accessed. Many blog comments from the followers expressed sympathy and excitement about Fujita's thoughts and actions. Typical comments were "I love you who have been doing what you really want to do," "I am impressed by your idea to start a business," "I am empowered by you," or "You have been the very influential person in me." Moreover, many blog comments show Fujita's influence on younger generations.

Conclusion: Entrepreneurship as a New Direction in Positive Youth Development

This preliminary exploration outlined how Japanese *no-gals* transformed the gal fashion subculture into a positive platform for social engagement and positive youth development. Applying the 6Cs illustrated how Shiho Fujita, the "face" of the *no-gals*, transformed the gal subculture that has been disempowered and discredited by social criticism. According to Sodateage Net (2008), a Japanese non-profit organization dedicated to solving the joblessness among youth, glamour-ness, stylishness, and social values are some of the important criteria for selecting occupations. Close to 40 percent of the youths surveyed identified "glamour-ness" as an important factor for selecting a work, and 70 percent of the participants indicated the social value of the work as an important factor. Out of the same participants, only 4.5 percent identified agriculture's image as "glamorous" and 37.1 percent perceived agriculture as a socially valued area of work. 84.5 percent of the participants did not associate people in agriculture with stylishness in his or her behaviors and choice of hobbies.

No-gals such as Fujita effectively tap into the youth's desire for social recognition by promoting, rather than surrendering, their gal identity grounded in fashion. On the surface, *no-gals*' refusal to play by the society's rule appears to be a simple defiance and disrespect toward social norms. However, Fujita's entrepreneurship allows her and her fellow gals to claim social agency without giving up their subculture as the source of subjective well-being. With their stylish outfits and makeup, *no-gals* made agriculture not only visible to youth but also fashionable. By showing her fight to earn respect from society as a gal on her blogs and social networking sites, Fujita turned gal subculture into a claim about one's way of life. Her *no-gal* Project not only placed agriculture on the map for the youths' future occupation, but also transformed agriculture as a site for the youths to show their commitment and confidence about their beliefs and values, despite the social disapprovals one may receive.

In the face of strong social ridicules against gals, Fujita's Gal Revolution demonstrates resilience and elasticity. Her refusal to surrender gal fashion as the source of her subjective well-being transformed the subculture into a source of social well-being. At the heart of this transformation, we note the entrepreneurship as a new ethos as the catalyst for positive youth development for the new generation. Fujita's entrepreneurship enabled this transformation possible.

Entrepreneurship offers a promising avenue for further exploring alternative ways of engaging youth in positive development. In the context of high school dropout prevention, Osgood (2012) advocates the integration of positive youth development and system approach developed by the field of business management. She writes:

> What if the business planning process from an entrepreneurial systems approach to positive youth development could be leveraged to become an individual learning plan (ILP) for positive youth development in the public education system? What if the network building process that supports entrepreneurial development and growth could be leveraged to foster youth career development and personal growth?... If similar process [of entrepreneurial business planning and networking building practices] could be developed to assist youth with developing a sense of purpose round life goals and objectives, then the value of education would become more relevant in ways that supported personal engagement and career development progress [pp. 116–117].

The result of Osgood's entrepreneurial systems approach confirm its effectiveness for preventing high school dropouts and developing strong sense of self as an entrepreneur—a player in the society. Similarly, Muniz et al. (2014) also write, "we work with young population, given the potential benefits of the early detection of entrepreneurial spirit, which can be of help, for example, in relation to academic and career guidance for students" (p. 546). The case of *no-gals* extends Osgood's experiment and finds the potentials for positive youth development outside of educational institutions. Given the strong tie between land-grant higher education institutions and 4-H, the largest youth development organization in the United States that adapted the PYD, it is not surprising that much of the research on PYD has been done in institutional context of education. While these researches continue to be beneficial, our study adds by extending the existing works to more discursive phenomenon of popular subculture. Since adult-led initiatives does not always produce the same result as the initiatives made by youth themselves.

For example, a former journalist took a similar initiative to make agriculture appealing to youth by coining a term *nogyo-joshi* (agriculture or faming girls). However, the impact of the initiative is no comparison to that of the *no-gals*. *No-gals* were able to restructure the symbolic environment precisely because it protected and promoted what youth identified as important source of their well-beings: fashion. As Fujita demonstrated her entrepreneurship by starting her own business, those gals who follow in her footsteps also demonstrate their symbolic entrepreneurship through their newly acquired sense of agency. According to Muñiz (2014), there are eight personality traits or profiles that characterize enterprising individuals: achieve motivation, risk-taking, autonomy, self-efficiency, stress tolerance, innovativeness, internal locus of control and optimism. The youths who leave comments on Fujita's blogs indicate many of these personality traits, feeling empowered. Many of them envision their improved self as they imagine their impact on the society.

No-gal subculture shows that integration model of development has its own limits, as it will relegate youth who do not conform to the preconceived social norms and standards into the category of "social problems." While garish fashion and showy makeups are hardly recognized as the window into positive development of youth, *no-gals'* defiance and rebellion challenges us to re-think what we, the scholars and practitioners of the positive youth development, consider as "positive" and work *with* the youth, rather than work *on* them. By extending the application of positive youth development theory into discursive popular culture phenomenon, we see entrepreneurship as an important ethos emerging out of youth, demonstrating ownership of their self-image as an agent of social change.

REFERENCES

Arai, Y. (2009). *Gyaru to Gyaru-o no Bunka Jinrui Gaku* [Cultural Anthropology of Gal and male-Gal]. Tokyo: Shintyosya.

Balsano, A. (2005). Youth civic engagement in the United States: Understanding and addressing the impact of social impediments on positive youth and community development. *Applied Developmental Science, 9*, 188–201. Retrieved from www.isfj.net/ronbun_backup/2012/ab04.pdf.

Bers, M. U. (2006). The role of new technologies to foster PYD. *Applied Developmental Science, 10,* pp. 200–219.

Bers, M. U. (2010). Beyond computer literacy: supporting youth's development through technology. *New Directions for Youth Development, 128,* 13–23.

Bird, J. M., & Markle, R. S. (2012). Subjective well-being in school environment: Promoting positive youth development through evidence-based assessment and intervention. *American Journal of Orthopsychiatry, 82,* 61–66.

Chen, J., Lau, C., Tapanya, S. & Cameron, C. A. (2012). Identities as protective processes: socio-ecological perspectives on youth resilience. *Journal of Youth Studies, 15,* 761–779.

Christie, S., & Lauzon, A. (2014). *Journal of Rural and Community Development, 9,* 157–175.

Cieslik, M., & Simpson, D. (2013). *Introduction: Making Sense of Young People Today?* In M. Cieslik & D. Simpson (Eds.), *Key concepts in youth Studies* (pp. ix-xx). Thousand Oaks, CA: Sage.

Cronback, L. J. (1955). Processes affecting scores on understanding of others and assuming "similarity." *Psychological Bulletin, 52,* 177–193.

Derek, R. (2005). Sweet, more than goth: The rhetorical reclamation of the subcultural self. *Popular Communication, 3,* 239–264.

Divine, S. A., Bull, S., Dreisbach, S., & Shlay, J. (2014). Enhancing a teen pregnancy prevention program with text messaging: Engaging minority youth to Develop Top® Plus text. *Journal of Adolescent Health, 54,* 78–83.

Foucault, M. (1988). Technologies of the self: A seminar with Michele Foucault. Amherst: University of Massachusetts Press.

Fujita, S. (2005, January 26). Kaishano jigyo-naiyou & yume [Business and dream]. Retrieved March 3, 2015, from http://blog.livedoor.jp/sifow/archives/2005–01. html.

Fujita, Shiho. (2009). *Gyaru nougyou* [Gal agriculture]. Tokyo: Tyuokouronshinshya.

Furedi, F. (2004). *Therapy culture: Cultivating vulnerability in an uncertain age.* London: Routledge.

Furlong, A., & Cartmel, F. (2007). *Young people and the social change: A new perspective.* Maidenhead: Open University Press.

Gagné, I. (2008). Urban princesses: Performance and "women's language" in Japan's gothic/lolita subculture. *Journal of Linguistic Anthropology, 18,* 130–150.

Hasebe, T., Yasue, H., & Hitakuchi, Y. (2011). Dousedai no kansou o tooshitemita nogyaru katsudou no fuukeironteki hyouka [An evaluation of no-gal project from fukei point of view based on same generation's impression]. *Nogyo Keizai Kenkyu, 49,* 93–98.

Honkawa, Y. (2013). Toukei deta kara yomitoku hataraku hito to kigyou no mirai zou, 7: borantia shikou ha "honmono" ka [Reading future image of working persons and corporations from statistical data, 7: Is the volunteerism "real"?]. Retrieved from http://www.iec.co.jp/data/007.html.

Ito, Y., et al. (2012). Jyakunen-sou no roudou jinkou kakuho ni yoru kokunai nougyou no kasseika [Vitalizing domestic agriculture by securing labor population from young generation]. ISFJ Forum. Retrieved from www.isfj.net/ronbun_backup/2012/ab04.pdf.

The Japan Forum, Hidamari Newsletter. (2011, March). Retrieved from http://www.tjf.or.jp/clicknippon/ja/archive/docs/TB27_J.pdf.

Kawamura, Y. (2012). *Fashioning Japanese subculture.* London: Bloomingsbury Academic.

Kawata, H. (2013, May). Wakamono no kachikan ni tsuiteno chosa [Survey on youth's value system]. Retrieved from http://log-works.com/blog/?p=1129.

Kinsella, S. (2005). Black faces, witches, and racism against girls. In L. Miller and J. Bardsley (Eds.), *Bad Girls of Japan* (pp. 143–158). New York: Palgrave Macmillan.

Lerner, R. M., Lerner, J. V., Almerigi, J., Theokas, C., Phelps, E., Gestsdottir, S. Naudeau, S., Jeličič, H., Alberts, A. E., Ma, L., Smith, L. M., Bobek, D. L., Richman-Raphael, D., Simpson, I., Christiansen, E. D., & von Eye, A. (2005). Positive youth development, participation in community youth development programs, and community contributions of fifth grade adolescents: Findings from the first wave of the 4-H Study of Positive Youth Development. *Journal of Early Adolescence, 25,* 17–71.

Life Media Research Bank (February 25, 2010). Nougyou ni tsuiteno anketo [Survey on agriculture]. Retrieved from http://research.lifemedia.jp/2010/02/100225_nougyou.html.

Mainichi Shinbun (2014, December 18). Nogyo no omoshirosa o tsutae tai: Kisha kara kanryo ni tenjita Sato Kazue san [Wishing to communicate the joy of agriculture: Ms. Kazue Sato who transformed from a journalist to a politician]. Retrieved from http://mainichi.jp/feature/interview/news/20141217mog00m040011000c. html.

Marx, D. W. (2012, February). *The history of the gyaru-Part one*. Retrieved from http://neojaponisme.com/2012/02/28/the-history-of-the-gyaru-part-one/.

McBride, A. M., Johnson, E., Olate, R., & O'Hara, K. (2011). Youth volunteer service as positive youth development in Latin America and the Carribean. *Children and Youth Services Review, 33*, 34–41.

Miller, L. (2004a). Those naughty teenage girls: Japanese kogals, slang, and media assessments. *Journal of Linguistic Anthropology, 14*, 225–247.

Miller, L. (2004b). Youth fashion and changing beautification practices. In G. Matthews & B. White (Eds.), *Japan's changing generations: Are young people creating a new society?* (pp.83–98). New York: Routledge.

Ministry of Agriculture, Forestry, and Fishery. (2014, March 20). Press release. Retrieved from http://www.maff.go.jp/j/press/keiei/zinzai/140320.html.

Ministry of Economy, Trade, and Industry. (2014, December). *Cool Japan initiative*. Retrieved May 17, 2015, from http://www.meti.go.jp/policy/mono_info_service/mono/creative/.

Muñiz, J., Suárez-Álvarez, J., Pedrosa, I., Fonseca-Pedrero, E., & García-Cueto, E. (2014). Enterprising personality profile in youth: Components and assessment. *Psicothema, 26*, 545–553.

Nainby, K. E., Warren, T. J., & Bollinger, C. (2003). Articulating contact in the classroom: Towards a constructive focus in critical pedagogy. *Language and intercultural communication, 3*, pp. 198–212.

Nanba, K. (2006). Sengo yu-su sabukaruchazu o megutte: Kogyaru to urahara-kei (5) [Concerning youth subcultures in the postwar era, vol. 5: "Ko-gal" and "Urahara-kei." *Shakaigakubu Kiyo, 100*, 102–132.

Nanba, K. (2007). *Zoku no keifugaku: yu-su sabukarucha no sengoshi. [Genealogy of tribes: Postwar history of youth subculture]*. Tokyo: Seikyu-sha.

National Agriculture and Food Research Organization. (n.d.). Seinen ni yoru nogyo no imeeji hyouka [Evaluation and image of agriculture by youth]. Retrieved from http://www.naro.affrc.go.jp/project/results/laboratory/narc/1995/narc95-2-215.html.

Nippon Keizai Shinbun (2012, March 30). Hansuu ga "inaka de kurashitai": 500nin chosa (wakamono, chihou he)—teioinsedai no keizaigaku pa-to 4(4) [Half of them want to live in the country: survey of 500 people (youth toward local areas)—Economics of low-temperature generation part 4 (4). Retrieved from http://www.nikkei.com/article/DGXNASFK23032_X20C12A3000000/.

Nissen, L. B. (2011). Community-directed engagement and positive youth development: Developing positive and progressive pathways between youth and their communities in reclaiming futures. *Children and Youth Services Review, 33*, 523–528.

Osgood, D. A. (2012). An entrepreneurial systems approach to positive youth development: a new approach to dropout prevention. *Applied Developmental Science, 16*, 113–121.

Palmer, N. A. (2013). *LGBT youth online and in person: Identity development, social support, and extracurricular and civic participation in a positive youth development framework*. Dissertation. Retrieved from http://search.proquest.com/docview/1419484911.

Pew Research Center (2010, February 24). Millennials: Confident. Connected. Open to change. Retrieved from http://www.pewsocialtrends.org/2010/02/24/millennials-confident-connected-open-to-change/.

Saladin, R. (2011). Gyaruo zasshi ni egakareru jenda [Gender in gyaru-o magazines]. *Journal of Musashi Sociological Society, 13*, 197–229.

Sasaki, Y., Inoue, T., Kosonoi, A., & Watanabe, M. (2014). Nihongata subculture sen-ryaku: "Yaowarasi" wo motchiita nougaku/nougyou kasseika no kokoromi [Japa-nese-style sunculture strategies: An attempt to vitalize agriculture/agricultural study by using "Yaowarai"]. *Nougyou Jyouhou Kenkyu, 23*, 123–131. Retrieved from https://www.jstage.jst.go.jp/article/air/23/2/23_123/_pdf.

Sodate age netto. (2008). Shu-nou jyousa kenkyu jigyo houkokusho [Report on survey research on agricultural employment]. Retrieved from http://www.sodateage.net/delivery/agri_report.pdf.

Surkarieh, M., & Tannock, S. (2011). The positive imperative: a critical look at the "new" youth development movement. *Journal of Youth Studies, 1*, 675–691.

Tachibana, Y. (2008). Gendai Nihon no Wakamono zou [Figure of youth in contem-porary Japan]. Retrieved from http://www.eonet.ne.jp/~yuzo/pdf.wakamonozou.pdf.

Taylor, S. W., & Crocker, J. (1981). Schematic bases of social information processing. In E.T. Higgins, P. Herman, & M. Zanna (Eds.), *Social Cognition: The Ontario Symposium*, 1. Hillsdale, N.J.: Erlbaum.

Tuji, I. (2013). Zasshi ni egakareta "otokorashisa" no henyo: Dansei fashion-shi no naiyou bunseki kara [Trajectory of manliness illustrated in magazines: From content analysis of men's magazines]. *Jinbungakuhou: Shakaigaku, 48*, 27–66.

Debunking Myths
About Adolescents
Discovering Unique Characteristics of the Adolescent Brain

Lori Hoisington *and*
Noah S.L. Crimmins

Popular culture—what *is* it? The term prompts thoughts of adolescents listening to music, shopping for trendy clothes, going to movies, playing sports, interacting on Facebook or otherwise socializing with friends. Adolescents in the U.S. spend much of their leisure time immersed in activities that help them achieve their goals and develop an image—the way they want to be viewed by others. These activities largely contribute to popular culture. But other variables also contribute, like genetic makeup and environmental conditions—the *nature vs. nurture* part of pop culture. At face value, popular culture might seem vague, intangible, and difficult to comprehend. But when analyzed in "pieces" rather than as a single entity, then elements that contribute to popular culture become more apparent. Things like clothing, music, sports and social media contribute to pop culture in obvious ways; youth typically share common interests related to these things that identify them as part of their developmental group. Other factors that contribute to popular culture are less apparent.

One significant contributing factor for pop culture that is often overlooked is brain development. While brain development generally occurs in a predictable fashion across the lifespan, each individual experiences brain maturity at a different age. This means that one individual might achieve maximum cognitive function at age 22 while another individual does not achieve this level of function until age 26. In practical terms, this translates into varying behaviors between individuals, or different responses to similar situations. For example, one adolescent might react with hostility in response to name calling at school while another student opts to turn and walk away instead. Alternatively, one individual might experience extreme pleasure in response to gaming while another experiences the same level of pleasure listening to music. The adolescent's response and behavior largely reflects the path that incoming signal travels as it enters their brain and is an indicator for how their brain in wired. Variations in brain function relate to different patterns of connectivity between brain cells.

Popular culture encompasses brain development and behavior, but it also reflects the intersection of genetic makeup, social interaction, and environmental conditions. Technological advances over the past few decades have made it possible to record brain activity during studies that introduce controlled stimuli and provide social interaction during Magnetic Resonance Imaging (MRI). These studies inform researchers about brain development and function that correlate with other elements that comprise pop culture, like peer interaction (Redcay, Dodell-Feder, Pearrow et al., 2010). For example, a researcher can explore whether the presence of peers affects an adolescent's risk for substance abuse. To determine this, the researcher can record brain activity for the adolescent during a functional MRI (fMRI) exam while messages or pictures about alcohol consumption appear on a monitor positioned in front of the individual. The individual in the scanner can provide a response through a finger pad that indicates whether they think it is okay to consume alcohol under the conditions described. The researcher can then repeat the process while the individual's peers occupy a room adjacent to the scan room. After the scans are complete, brain activity that is recorded without peers nearby is compared to brain activity recorded with the peers in the next room. This information enables the researcher to calculate the increase or decrease in brain activity that occurs in specific areas of the brain when peers are present. Models such as this reveal information about the intersection of brain activity and interpersonal relationships—elements that help to define pop culture. This is just one of many fMRI models that can provide information to help researchers understand the relationship between brain anatomy and function and social interaction. Findings like this can unravel many of the mysteries of the developing adolescent brain and highlight the relationship between brain development and popular culture.

Popular culture embraces adolescents' drive for independence balanced with society's goals to maintain order. Brain development plays a critical role in this balance as the strategies and behaviors adolescents choose to achieve independence and self-identity largely reflect the way their brain is wired. A key question among researchers is *How does brain development contribute to adolescent behavior?* By exploring brain development through the lens of youth development, researchers can begin to understand the relationship between brain development and behavior and further understand why values, mores and norms vary between adolescents and adults. These things contribute to popular culture and often serve as the basis for inaccurate ideas or "myths" about youth behavior. In order to gain a reasonable understanding about popular culture, it is necessary to first consider some of the differences in brain development and function between adolescents and adults, and to further examine some of the common myths about behavioral differences between the two groups. This essay addresses two common myths about adolescent brain development and provides explanations for why they do not accurately reflect what researchers have come to learn about youth.

Myth #1—Adolescence Is Just a Phase

Historically, society has adopted the viewpoint that adolescent behavior reflects a time of "storm and stress" filled with conflict with parents, mood disruptions and risk-taking behavior (Hall, 1904). Such characterization appears to be a reactive response to adolescent behavior and the way adolescents express emotions. Hall argued that tendencies toward these behaviors are universal and biologically based, but also explained that culture influences how adolescents express themselves and experience this developmental stage (p. 318). Hall also argued that the home, school, and religious institutions failed to recognize the conflicted nature of youth in the past and thus, they do not appropriately adapt their institutions to accommodate them. While some scholars in the past refuted the "storm and stress" theory (see Mead, 1928), other scholars like Anna Freud (1946, 1958, 1968, 1969) expanded on Hall's ideas and further explained that storm and stress result from recapitulation of previous experiences in life. Freud viewed the storm and stress period as universal among adolescents and suggested that its absence reflects psychopathology, "to be normal during the adolescent period is by itself abnormal" (1958, p. 267). This myth discards the idea that brain changes that occur during this developmental stage are foundational to achieving complete development in the adult brain.

Arguments that refute the storm and stress myth are founded both in biological and behavioral sciences. During the past 25 years, advances in technology introduced ways to record brain activity in response to predetermined stimuli. For example, functional Magnetic Resonance Imaging (fMRI) can record brain activity that occurs while an individual plays a video game (Mathiak & Weber, 2006) or reads statements on a screen that elicit moral judgment (Moll, Eslinger, & Oliveira-Souza, 2001). fMRI can also show how political viewpoints relate to risk taking. Schreiber, along with a team of researchers from UCSD (2013) conducted an fMRI gambling study using participants with self-reported political affiliation—either democrat or republican. Participants made choices in response to numbers (20, 40 and 80) that flashed on a screen. The numbers reflected a risk of gain vs. loss of money. Pressing the button while the 20 flashed on the screen resulted in a payoff of 20 cents, but pressing the button while the 40 or 80 flashed on the screen resulted in *either* gain or loss of the respective amount. Results from the study showed that brain activity in response to risk-taking for democrats occurred in different areas compared to brain activity in response to risk taking for republicans. Risk taking models for studying brain activity are particularly useful for understanding adolescent behavior because risk taking among adolescents is a common behavior that contributes to the myth that adolescence is "just a stage" that individuals must get through. Studies such as these reflect opportunity to record brain activity in response to visual, auditory and tactile stimulation as well as cognitive processing. These studies primarily focus on cross-sectional (single point in time) behavior, but other longitudinal fMRI studies monitor longer-term brain development in individuals by repeating fMRI scans at regular intervals (Marsh, Gerber & Peterson, 2008; Skup, 2008).

Longitudinal fMRI studies explore how connections between brain cells change over time. These studies have shown that the human brain continues to develop neural pathways involving complex connections in various areas including the prefrontal cortex throughout adolescence and into the early to mid-twenties. Neural connections are somewhat like super-highways that are paved with myelin, a fatty substance that serves as an insulating layer around nerve cells and facilitates faster transmission of neural signal (Johnson, Blum & Giedd, 2009; Steinberg, 2012).

Biological differences between adolescents and adults begin in the smallest unit of the brain—the nerve cell or neuron. Each neuron includes a cell body (the main part of the cell) along with short extensions—dendrites—that receive signal from neighboring neurons and long extensions—axons—that transmit signal to other neurons. Connections between neurons involve exchange of small electrical currents—a process that is facilitated by chemicals, or neurotransmitters. Some neurotransmitters activate exchange of signal and other neurotransmitters inhibit transfer of signal. Each neurotransmitter is specific to certain neural connections (Lodish, Berk, & Zipursky et al., 2000). With approximately six billion neurons in the human brain, there are an infinite number of possible pathways for signal to travel. The ultimate pathway that signal travels in the human brain largely contributes to human behavior.

Neural Connectivity During Adolescence

Around the time of adolescence, the brain undergoes significant structural changes that involve neural connections. One of the most significant changes involves synaptogenesis—a vast overgrowth of nerve cell synapses just prior to puberty (Giedd et al., 2009; Selemon, 2013). This phenomenon is especially significant because it suggests that adolescents at this stage of development have increased potential for change in their response to sensory input—they can change their behavior in response to positive influence and role models and practice more socially-acceptable behavior. This process reflects neuroplasticity—rewiring of the human brain through development of new neural pathways. Researchers have explored this process through studies that involve exercising the brain to achieve a higher level of function (Andianopoulos, 2008; Arden, 2010; Kawashima, 2005; Kawashima, 2008). For example, Kawashima (2008) described how rewiring of the human brain can achieve weight loss, improve memory and stave off the aging process. Neuroplasticity provides channels for behavioral change. In terms of popular culture, neuroplasticity provides the necessary mechanism for adolescents to adopt new values and assume behaviors that conform to new trends and fashions. This process translates into alternative responses to given conditions and situations for adolescents.

While overgrowth of synapses in the adolescent brain establishes the foundation for neuroplasticity, other variables also contribute to this process. A fatty, membranous layer of myelin coats the axons of nerve cells during development and increases the speed of neural transmission up to 100 times (Blakemore & Choudhury, 2006). Interestingly, myelin does not form consistently through all developmental stages. Brain research during the 1960s, 1970s and 1980s revealed differences in myelination between children, adolescents and adults (Huttenlocker, 1979; Huttenlocker, De Courten, Garey & Van Der Loos, 1983, Yakovlev & Lecours, 1967). During normal brain development, myelination in the brain's emotional system occurs before myelination in the prefrontal cortex—the cognitive center where rational thinking and impulse control occurs. Consequently, when sensory signal enters the adolescent brain through vision, hearing, smell, touch or taste, the emotional network of the brain is wired to respond more readily to the input compared to the cognitive center. With faster connections between sensory input and the emotional center, adolescents tend to respond more emotionally to situations compared to adults. These differences in connectivity contribute to varying behavior between adolescents and adults and help to explain why adolescents behave and think the way they do. This includes their preferences for clothing design, music, art, leisure and recreational activities, among other things.

The prefrontal cortex is associated with executive function—regulation and control of cognitive function. This includes reasoning, problem solving, working memory, task flexibility, planning and execution of tasks, controlling impulses and weighing risks vs. rewards. This area of the brain equips individuals with the ability to make rational choices, suppress impulses and foresee future consequences for their behavior (Funahashi & Andreau, 2013; Zelazo, 2004). Once viewed with skepticism, brain science now shows that higher order cognitive processes do not fully develop until adulthood. This means that adolescents likely do not recognize all viable options when making decisions and they are also limited in their ability to recognize the consequences for behaviors they choose. As it relates to popular culture, this partially explains why adolescents choose certain behaviors like posting private information on social media, or getting tattoos or other body art. While these behaviors undoubtedly contribute to their self-image, adolescents often do not fully consider how these decisions affect their future, including their reputation and professional image. In order to understand how these factors contribute to popular culture, it is necessary to consider the significance of adolescent brain development and behavior to both neuroscience and behavioral science. Research findings in neuroscience inform behavioral science and vice-versa. This process provides common ground for the two sciences to achieve greater overall understanding about youth behavior, youth values, and youth mores and contributes to a greater understanding about popular culture among youth, including the choices they make and the way they express themselves.

Policy makers and youth development professionals can benefit from new findings related to brain development by thoughtfully applying the information when making recommendations about adolescent privileges and accountability. Youth in the U.S. generally enjoy privileges with minimal restrictions. But given past statistics on juvenile crime and injury, adolescents likely need *more* guidance and supervision, rather than *less* (Steinberg, 2014). The balance between risk and privilege requires careful assessment of youth privileges with adequate guidance in place to minimize their risk for making decisions that lead to undesirable consequences (NIMH, 2011). Understanding the developmental changes that occur in the adolescent brain enables youth development professionals to provide a suitable environment for adolescents to explore and experiment as they mature. But the myth that adolescence is "just a phase" that individuals must pass through disregards critical research findings that indicate adolescents undergo unique changes in brain development that are necessary in order for them to reach full maturity.

Myth #2—Adolescents Are Immature and Irrational

A second, and equally popular myth suggests that adolescents are immature and irrational. It is common for parents, teachers, law enforcement officers, and youth development professionals to observe an increase in behavior they qualify as deviant around the time of adolescence, and the behavior often leads to stereotyping adolescents as irresponsible with disregard for common rules. Adolescents often choose behaviors that differ from mature adults, but brain science suggests that these differences are at least partially due to variations in brain development (Dobbs, 2011). For example, the reward system in the adolescent brain is more active compared to the adult brain, and areas responsible for logic and reasoning are not yet fully developed (Blakemore, 2012). As a result, adolescents are more likely to choose risk-taking behavior like reckless driving and drug use and are more prone to addictive behaviors like gambling, video gaming, and excessive interaction on social media (Lewis, 2014).

Prior to the 1990s, scientists thought human brain development was complete by around age six years. However, advances in technology over the past few decades have provided information showing brain development in humans continues well beyond this age. Some scholars suggest the brain continues to mature through the age of 25 (Giedd, 1999; Wallis, 2013). These findings suggest that the adolescent stage should be extended through the mid-twenties to reflect this ongoing development. However, the age of majority in the U.S. is 18 years. This is the age when adolescents are considered legally independent, responsible for their actions, and are tried as adults in a court of law. Current policies and laws are structured on the assumption that 18-year-olds are mature enough to understand the consequences for their behavior.

With the use of fMRI, researchers can record brain activity in response to tasks, stimuli and emotional processing. This is particularly significant because adolescents often choose behaviors that provide reward and pleasure. The neurotransmitter dopamine is instrumental in the function of the brain's reward and pleasure centers. Dopamine is produced in the substantia nigra and ventral tegmental area (VTA) of the brain and floods the nucleus accumbens (pleasure center) when an individual experiences situations that evoke feelings of pleasure. As it turns out, areas of the brain that relate to pleasure develop faster than areas in the prefrontal cortex that control decision-making and logical thinking (Blakemore, 2012). Thus, adolescents frequently overlook logically perceived risks and choose behaviors that provide rewards and feelings of pleasure instead. Depending on the choices they make, adolescent behavior can result in consequences that involve serious injury or criminal charges.

Risk Taking Among Adolescents

Adolescents between the ages of 16–19 years are at the highest risk for motor vehicle accidents compared to any other age group (Centers for Disease

Control and Prevention, 2014). While many adolescents are novice drivers and their accidents are likely attributed to inexperience, other accidents result from adolescents taking more risks while driving. The way adolescents perceive risk can cause them to take on riskier driving behaviors (Dobbs, 2011). When individuals make decisions, they typically weigh potential risks vs. rewards to determine the most desirable options. The behaviors adolescents choose more often involve risk taking compared to adults. This includes behaviors like driving over the speed limit and performing dangerous maneuvers in high traffic areas. Consider a situation that involves an adolescent who is late for work. The individual will probably focus more on the benefit of arriving to work on time than the risk of causing an accident. Oftentimes, adolescents in situations like this decide to speed or run yellow lights, especially in the presence of their peers (Chein et al., 2011). A mature adult in the same situation will likely place more focus on the risks associated with causing an accident or being stopped by the police; they might also consider moral issues related to causing physical or emotional harm to others as the result of an accident. With more limited brain development, adolescents are not as well equipped to consider risks compared to adults. This does not mean that adolescents consciously disregard the rights and safety of others, but rather, it is an indication that their decision-making abilities are more limited based on their level of brain development. To the adolescent, the likelihood for an accident seems low.

Another common risk-taking behavior among adolescents is tobacco use. The media greatly contributes to adolescent use of tobacco as TV shows and the media often depict smoking as cool and without consequence. Viewing movies that depict smoking greatly increases the likelihood that adolescents will start smoking (Heatherton & Sargent, 2009). The American Academy of Pediatrics reported that more than $25 billion is spent annually to advertise tobacco, alcohol and prescription drugs (Alden, 2013). But in spite of these influences, smoking among adolescents is currently on the decline (National Institute on Drug Abuse [NIDA], 2014a). This pattern also holds true for recreational drug use, except for marijuana, which has steadily risen over the past few years (NIDA, 2014a). Marijuana is popular among youth because of its low cost, easy access, and its decline in negative stigmas (Motel, 2015). One commonly touted idea is that marijuana is safe because, unlike heroin or cocaine, it is not addictive. While the majority of marijuana users are not addicted, about 9 percent habitually smoke marijuana (Budney, Roffman, Stephens, & Walker, 2007). Because physical addiction to marijuana is not proven—meaning the body does not experience withdrawal symptoms when the substance is no longer present—many individuals do not think there is significant risk in smoking. By definition, addiction indicates a person is not able to control their desire for something in spite of the harm they experience (NIDA, 2014d). Harm from drugs most often results directly from their use, but in the case of marijuana, harm can also occur because individuals ignore critical life responsibilities and experience a decline in social skills, education and career options.

Adolescents, especially at the high school level often abuse Adderall, Ritalin, and other amphetamine drugs that are used to treat disorders like Attention Deficit Hyperactivity Disorder (ADHD) (Barnes & Wadley, 2013). This class of medication generally does not share the same stigmas as alcohol, which is viewed as a "party" drug. While most of today's youth are familiar with the addictive properties of alcohol and tobacco, they are less aware of the addictive properties of amphetamines. These drugs share many of the same addictive qualities as cocaine and methamphetamine. As one teen described:

> I grew up in a household where pop culture was biblical. My mom would buy tabloids every week, speedy music videos were always on TV, and I was never given classic literature, or shown "real music."
>
> I started to do lines of Adderall because I thought heroin/drug chic was glamorous. I did it while looking at myself on my iPhone camera, obviously, because how else would I know it was happening if my reflection on a screen wasn't looking back at me?
>
> I also thought it would make me a better writer. Contrary to belief, it made me numb and distorted. I couldn't write, I could only drool and listen to a million different songs on Spotify as my eyes rolled back.
>
> When I write, I'm usually able to imagine vivid imagery, recall sounds. I can write 15-line poems in under a minute and not know what I've said until I go back and read it. But on Addy—zip. Zero [Kazemi, 2013].

Prescribed medications usually receive approval as necessary drugs, and adolescents who take these medications are often students in good standing at school working to maintain an acceptable grade point average. Individuals with ADHD achieve a greater level of focus with amphetamines. But some adolescents without ADHD use these drugs to induce extra energy that helps them get by without sleep so they can study for exams. Adolescents in this category place themselves at risk for other health problems including decreased sleep and appetite, malnutrition, increased blood pressure, cardiovascular complications and stroke (NIDA, 2014a). Amphetamines trigger the release of dopamine in the brain and activate the reward and pleasure circuitry. When stimulated at normal levels, the release of dopamine results in rewards for natural behavior. But when individuals abuse amphetamines, they over-stimulate this system and achieve a euphoric effect that reinforces the behavior and encourages them to repeat it (NIDA, 2014c).

The majority of drug users are between the ages of 18 and 20 years (NIDA, 2014b). While these individuals are traditionally viewed as adults and are held accountable for their behavior, they have not yet achieved complete brain maturity. Without sufficient supervision and guidance, adolescents often make choices that bring about undesirable consequences. It's not surprising that these individuals are among the most likely to abuse drugs.

Adolescents and Video Games

Another concern for adolescents relates to their involvement in video gaming. Video gaming is a popular activity for this group and addiction to gaming is on the rise. Although arcade games date back to 1971 with *Pong*, video game addiction is a relatively recent concern. Video gaming comprises a large and lucrative industry, and as the industry continues to grow, companies seek ways to expand even further. It is common practice for gaming companies to consult with psychologists for research-based information they can apply to increase the appeal of games for their target audience (Clay, 2012). Gentile (personal communication, 2009) reported that as many as one in ten video game players between the ages of eight and 18 years was addicted to gaming, "although the general public uses the word 'addiction,' clinicians often report it as pathological use. This is the first study to tell us the national prevalence of pathological play among youth gamers, and it is almost 1 in 10" (Iowa State University, 2009, par. 5).

There are also gender-based concerns related to gaming. Brandt (2008) reported findings from a video game study that indicates males naturally resonate more with video games compared to females. Participants in the study gained territory based on their gaming decisions. Results from the study suggest that males are more focused on reward-based stimuli than women. Riess and colleagues conducted another study with 11 male and 11 female Stanford students that measured brain activity while they played a video game that involved gaining or losing territory. Participants clicked on balls to prevent them from hitting a vertical line in the middle of the screen. If they successfully clicked on the balls, then the balls would disappear and not hit the vertical line. This increased their territory in the game. A significant finding from the study was activation of the pleasure circuit in all participants, and the effect was stronger in males (Linden, 2011). These results suggest that males are more at risk for video game addiction compared to females.

While some individuals are addicted to arcade games and invest real money into their addiction, others interact through virtual games using the Internet. A recent trend in video gaming is the inclusion of online activities and communities. The Internet now supports video game consoles that interact with one another so players can participate in virtual gaming. This type of gaming capitalizes on the inherent social qualities of humans. As Aristotle stated long ago, "Man is by nature a social animal" (Aristotle & Davis, 1920). Adolescents who do not make friends in school sometimes find common interests with others while they interact through gaming, similar to the way athletes share common interests around a sport. Parents of adolescents who play video games for long hours each day frequently express concern about their child's limited socialization. But adolescents can form virtual relationships and bond with other individuals through online gaming. A survey conducted by Klinger (1978) showed 89 percent of individuals cited close relationships as a key factor that contributes to their meaning in life. Adolescents who participate in online gaming are not necessarily avoiding social situations, but rather, for some this is a method for developing friendships in a context that is more comfortable for them. Individuals who are introverted by nature sometimes make friends more easily in the online environment (Kowert, Domahidi, & Quandt, 2014). While online social communities provide a comfortable forum for some individuals, these communities should not replace normal social interaction. Digital relationships should be used in conjunction with social interaction, not as a substitution (Taylor, 2013).

World of Warcraft, colloquially known as WoW, is a popular massive multiplayer online role- playing game (MMORPG). This game is especially significant for popular culture because of the way it affects adolescents. Addiction to WoW is common. In fact, the online website *www.wowaholics.com* is available to help members stop playing when they no longer wish to continue. As described by one former Wow addict:

> I just stopped playing a few days ago. I had started in late 2007 and played until early 2009, when I quit because it felt like the game was taking over my life. After I stopped playing I became extremely productive and took that competitive fire that was helping me kill bosses and applied it to real life. What did I do? I enrolled in a computer-programming course, decided that I liked it, took a couple of graduate courses in computer science, and then decided to apply to grad school! Along the way I met a guy that I fell in love with. When things didn't work out I stupidly went back to playing this game because I was "bored" and wanted to forget about him. For anyone that has been addicted to this game, you know how WoW starts out like Solitaire, where you play for an hour or two and shut off the computer and go to bed. As you progress in the game you become more immersed and eventually have to spend all of your free time playing because it required that much work! [Wowaholics, 2012].

Wowaholics Anonymous parodies the well-known support group Alcoholics Anonymous and offers a similar 12-Step Program (Wowaholics, 2012). While other games like *Call of Duty*—an online shooting game—are also associated with addiction, WoW stands out as the poster child for video game addiction.

To address concerns about video game addictions, researchers have performed studies to identify the motivations behind gaming. Hilgard, Engelhardt, and Bartholow (2013) cited escapism, reward through effort, and social interaction as three primary indicators for gaming addiction. With MMORPG games, ongoing interaction is mandatory in order to fully experience the game objectives. Some MMORPG games create a competitive environment by positioning players against each other while others require players to combine efforts to overcome obstacles they would otherwise not be able to overcome. Video games, including MMORPG games, have been described as virtual Skinner Boxes (Yee, 2002). This refers to laboratory boxes used by B.F. Skinner to change the behavior of animals through strategically timed rewards (McLeod, 2007). In his early experiments, Skinner placed hungry rats in boxes that were equipped with levers that dispensed food when pushed. The rats quickly learned how to dispense the food. This process reflects *operant conditioning*. MMORPG games provide a similar reward system through "grinding"—performing repetitive tasks during the game (Thompson, 2008). Grinding is comparable to the lever in Skinner's experiment; the repetitive action provides game players with rewards in the form of character enhancements.

While the addictive properties of video games are apparent, adolescents are especially at risk for addiction because the reward center in their brain is more fully developed compared to the cognitive center. Lewis (2014) reported on a simulated gambling study conducted by Galvan and colleagues. The study used fMRI to scan 19 adults (age 25–30) and 22 teenagers (age 13–17) while they played a gambling game. The participants decided whether to accept a bet with a 50–50 chance of either winning or losing money. The study showed greater risk taking and reward seeking behavior among adolescents compared to adults—the adolescents made more risky bets for greater rewards. Along with these differences, the study also highlighted more activity in the ventral striatum (reward center) of the brain for the adolescents, even when they placed bets for the same amount as the adults. This finding suggests the neural circuitry for the reward system is more mature than the neural circuitry for the cognitive center in the adolescent brain. This relationship carries into decision-making as well; the way the adolescent brain responds to rewards contributes to the choices they make. Video gaming activates the reward center of the brain much the same as gambling (Linden, 2011) and provides ongoing positive reinforcement through frequent rewards. But with most MMORPG games, each achievement or milestone is followed by another goal. This cycle continues and keeps the adolescent engaged in the game, so even though they appreciate a sense of satisfaction and accomplishment, it is immediately followed by another challenge.

Adolescents also achieve a sense of escapism through video gaming. This is a common coping mechanism for adolescents as they experience higher levels of stress compared to adults in similar situations (National Science Foundation, 2010). Hilgard (personal communication, 2013) states, "The biggest risk factor for pathological video game use seems to be playing games to escape from daily life. Individuals who play games to get away from their lives or to pretend to be other people seem to be those most at-risk for becoming part of a vicious cycle" (News Bureau, University of Missouri, 2013).

Social Media

Social media websites such as Facebook and Twitter also serve as forums for adolescents to interact in the online environment. Since its debut in 2004, Facebook has grown to include over 900 million daily users (Facebook, 2015). In the early days of Facebook, adolescents comprised the majority of users, but over the years, individuals in most other age groups have joined as well. Adolescents also use Instagram and Snapchat to interact in the online environment while other age groups are not as active on these forums. As with other activities, adolescents often fall into a pattern of increasing interaction on social media to the point of addiction. This interaction can trigger release of dopamine in the adolescent brain that activates the reward and pleasure areas (Mitchel & Tamir, 2012). Once this occurs, these individuals are drawn even more to interact on social media in order to maintain the feelings of reward and pleasure.

One of the greatest benefits of social media is its structure for sharing instant messages, photos and videos. Individuals who live geographically far apart can instantly share life events. But social media can also be used in more vile ways. In current world affairs, the military terrorist group Islamic State, more commonly known as ISIS, has gained mass attention through their online recruiting practices. In contrast to traditional propagandizing, ISIS disseminates information through high quality videos and information on social media networks to help identify new recruits.

Adolescents and young adults are prime targets for ISIS, especially young women, as ISIS recruits them to be their brides (Mullen, 2015). Twitter is the main platform ISIS currently uses to send messages. It is estimated that they send over 90,000 messages each day (Mullen, 2015). Adolescents typically seek guidance, values and opportunities for activities that help them realize their life meaning, and ISIS appeals to their quest for greater meaning. ISIS relies on many of the same recruiting strategies that cults use including severing ties with family and friends. Once family ties are severed, it is difficult for adolescents to leave ISIS (Furnham, 2014). The combination of all these factors makes adolescents prime targets for recruitment. And many of their age-related characteristics—including stress, anxiety, continuous change, and self-doubt leave them open to new and more radical ideas. Adolescents often seek a sense of self-identity and a desire to belong to larger groups (Milevsky, 2014). If other socially acceptable opportunities are not presented to them, adolescents will grasp at the opportunities within their reach.

Conclusion

Adolescence is a unique life stage characterized by values, norms, morals and behaviors that reflect this age group. The way adolescents express these characteristics defines popular culture. Philosophies about the adolescent life stage continue to change as new technologies, like fMRI, reveal more and more about the development and function of the human brain. Studies over the past few decades clearly show incomplete brain development among adolescents compared to adults. This information is applicable in several arenas—home, school, courts, etc.—and is useful for reframing the way society views the adolescent. Myths about adolescents are common and often result in stereotyping that does not consider developmental differences between adolescents and adults. Information in this essay argues against two popular myths: *Adolescence is just a phase that individuals must get through* and *Adolescents are immature and irrational.* The information presented addresses these myths and provides evidence explaining why they are inaccurate. While the information is not intended to absolve adolescents from responsibility for their actions, or to indicate that there should not be consequences for their behavior, it argues that adolescent norms, values, mores and behavior do not reflect deviant behavior, but rather, these things reflect a unique pattern of brain development that is normal for adolescents. Part of the developmental process between adolescence and adulthood involves learning which actions are permissible and which are not. As the brain develops, it is necessary to reinforce positive behavior and deter negative behavior. This essay provides insight into why adolescents choose the behaviors and values they do. Adolescents analyze situations and weigh risks differently compared to adults. While the choices they make appear logical to them, these choices also reflect brain development that is not yet complete. Adolescent values, mores, behaviors and norms should be considered in this context.

References

Alden, A. (2013). Pop culture portrayal of tobacco: Alcohol and drugs influences teens. Retrieved from http://www.bearingnews.org/2013/04/media-glamorization-tobacco-alcohol-drugs-influences-teens/.

Andianapoulos, G. (2008). *Retrain your brain, Reshape your body: The breakthrough brain-changing weight-loss program.* New York: McGraw-Hill.

Arden, J. (2010). *Rewire your brain: Think your way to a better life.* Hoboken, N.J.: Wiley.

Aristotle, Jowett, B., & Davis, H. W. C. (1920). *Aristotle's Politics.* Oxford: Clarendon Press.

Barnes, S., & Wadley, J. (2013, December 18). Teens more cautious about using synthetic drugs, *University of Michigan.* Retrieved from http://www.ns.umich.edu/new/releases/21880-teens-more-cautious-about-using-synthetic-drugs.

Blakemore, S., & Choudhury, S. (2006). Development of the adolescent brain: implications for executive function and social cognition. *Journal of Child Psychology and Psychiatry, 47* (3–4), pp. 296–312. doi: 10.1111/j.1469-7610.2006.01611.x.

Blakemore, S. (2012). The mysterious workings of the adolescent brain. *TED.* Retrieved from http://www.ted.com/talks/sarah_jayne_blakemore_the_mysterious_work ings_of_the_adolescent_brain?language=en.

Brandt, M. L. (2008). Video games activate reward regions of brain in men more than women. *Stanford study finds. Stanford School of Medicine news release.* Retrieved on August 24, 2015, from https://med.stanford.edu/news/all-news/2008/02/video-games-activate-reward-regions-of-brain-in-men-more-than-women-stanford-study-finds.html.

Budney, A. J., Roffman, R., Stephens, R. S., & Walker, D. (2007). Marijuana dependence and its treatment. *Addiction Science & Clinical Practice, 4*(1), 4–16.

Centers for Disease Control and Prevention. (2014, October 7). Injury prevention & control: Motor vehicle safety. Retrieved from http://www.cdc.gov/vitalsigns/crash-injuries/.

Chein, J., Albert, D., O'Brien, L., Uckert, K., & Steinberg, L. (2011). Peers increase adolescent risk taking by enhancing activity in the brain's reward circuitry. *Developmental Science, 14*(2), F1–F10. doi:10.1111/j.1467-7687.2010.01035.x

Clay, R. (2012). Video game design and development. *APA.* Retrieved from http://www.apa.org/gradpsych/2012/01/hot-careers.aspx.

Dobbs, D., & Conan, N. (2011, September 20). Understanding the mysterious teenage brain. *Talk of the Nation.* Washington, D.C.: Nation Public Radio.

Facebook (2015). *Our History.* Retrieved from http://newsroom.fb.com/company-info/,

Freud, A. (1946). *The ego and the mechanism of defense.* New York: International Universities Press.

Freud, A. (1958). Adolescence. *Psychoanalytic Study of the Child, 15,* 255–278.

Freud, A. (1968). Adolescence. In A. E. Winder & D. Angus (Eds.), *Adolescence: Contemporary studies,* pp. 13–24. New York: American Book.

Freud, A. (1969). Adolescence as a developmental disturbance. In G. Caplan & S. Lebovici (Eds.), *Adolescence: Psychosocial perspectives,* pp. 5–10. New York: Basic Books.

Funahashi, S., & Andreau, J. M. (2013). Prefrontal cortex and neural mechanisms of executive function. *Journal of Physiology-Paris, 107*(6), 471–482.

Furnham, A. (2014, February 24). Why Do People Join Cults? *Psychology Today.* Retrieved from https://www.psychologytoday.com/blog/sideways-view/201402/why-do-people-join-cults.

Giedd, J. N., Blumenthal, J., Jeffries, N. O., Castellanos, F. X., Liu, H., Zijdenbos, A., Paus, T., Evans, A. C., Rapoport, J. L. (1999). Brain development during childhood and adolescence: A longitudinal MRI study. *Nature Neuroscience, 2,* 861–863.

Hall, G. S. (1904). *Adolescence: Its psychology and its relation to physiology, anthropology, sociology, sex, crime, religion, and education* (Vols. I & II). Englewood Cliffs, NJ: Prentice-Hall.

Heatherton, T. F., & Sargent, J. D. (2009). Does watching smoking in movies promote teenage smoking? *Current Directions in Psychological Science, 18*(2), 63–67, doi: 10.1111/j.1467-8721.2009.01610.x.

Hilgard J., Engelhardt C.R., & Bartholow B.D. (2013). Individual differences in motives, preferences, and pathology in video games: the gaming attitudes, motives, and experiences scales (GAMES). *Frontiers in Psychology, 4,* 608. doi: 10.3389/fpsyg.2013.00608.

Huttenlocher, P. R. (1979). Synaptic density in human frontal cortex – developmental changes and effects of aging. *Brain Research, 163,* 195–205.

Huttenlocher, P. R., De Courten, C., Garey, L. J., & Van Der Loos, H. (1983). Synaptic development in human cerebral cortex. *International Journal of Neurology, 16–17,* 144–154.

Iowa State University. (2009). ISU's Gentile authors study finding nearly 1 in 10 youth gamers addicted to video games. Retrieved from http://www2.iastate.edu/~nscentral/news/2009/apr/vgaddiction.shtml.

Johnson, S. B., Blum, R. W., & Giedd, J. N. (2009). Adolescent maturity and the brain: The promise and pitfalls of neuroscience research in adolescent health policy. *Journal of Adolescent Health. 45*(3), 216–221. doi: 10.1016/j.jadohealth.2009.05.016.

Kawashima, R. (2008). *Train your brain more: Better brainpower, better memory, better creativity.* New York: Penguin.

Kazemi, A. (2013). Adderall teen drug confessional: Pop culture didn't trigger me, I triggered myself. *Thought Catalog.* Retrieved from http://thoughtcatalog.com/alex-kazemi/2013/12/260352/.

Klinger, E. (1978). *Meaning and void: Inner experience and the incentives in people's lives.* Minneapolis: University of Minnesota Press.

Kowert, R., Domahidi, E., & Quandt, T. (2014). *Cyberpsychology Behavior, and Social Networking, 17*(7), 447–453. doi:10.1089/cyber.2013.0656.

Lewis, T. (2014, January 13). Teen brains really are wired to seek rewards. *Live Science.* Retrieved from http://www.livescience.com/42532-teens-brains-respond-strongly-to-rewards.html.

Linden, D. J. (2011, October 25). Video games can activate the brain's pleasure circuits. *Psychology Today.* Retrieved from: https://www.psychologytoday.com/blog/the-compass-pleasure/201110/video-games-can-activate-the-brains-pleasure-circuits-0.

Lodish, H., Berk, A., Zipursky S.L., Matsudaira, P., Baltimore, D., Darnell, J. (2000). "Neurotransmitters, Synapses, and Impulse Transmission." *Molecular Cell Biology* (4th ed.) Retrieved from: http://www.ncbi.nlm.nih.gov/books/NBK21521/.

Marsh, R., Gerber, A. J., & Peterson, B. S. (2008). Neuroimaging studies of normal brain development and their relevance for understanding childhood neuropsychiatric disorders. *Journal of American Psychiatry, 47*(11): 1233–1251. doi: 10.1097/CHI.0b013e318185e703.

Mathiak, K., & Weber, R. (2006). Toward brain correlates of natural behavior: fMRI during violent video games. *Human Brain Mapping, 27,* 948–956.

McLeod, S. (2007 – updated 2015). Skinner – operant conditioning. *Simply Psychology.* Retrieved from http://www.simplypsychology.org/operant-conditioning.html.

Mead, M. (1928). *Coming of Age in Samoa.* New York: William Morrow.

Milevsky, A. (2014). Why are teens joining ISIS? *Huffington Post.* Retrieved August 24, 2015 from http://www.huffingtonpost.com/avidan-milevsky/why-are-teens-joining-isi_b_5773668.html.

Mitchell, J. P., & Tamir, D. I. (2012). Disclosing information about the self is intrinsically rewarding. *Proceedings of the National Academy of Sciences of the USA, 109*(21): 8038–8043. Retrieved from http://www.ncbi.nlm.nih.gov/pmc/articles/PMC3361411/. doi: 10.1073/pnas.1202129109.

Moll, J., Eslinger, P. J., Oliveira-Souza, R. (2001). Frontopolar and anterior temporal cortex activation in a moral judgment task: preliminary functional MRI results in normal subjects. *Arq. Neuro-Psiquiatr, 59 (3-B),* 657–664, doi: 10.1590/S0004-282X2001000500001.

Motel, S. (2015, April 14). 6 facts about marijuana. *Pew Research Center*. Retrieved from http://www.pewresearch.org/fact-tank/2015/04/14/6-facts-about-marijuana/.

Mullen, J. (2015, February 25). What is ISIS' appeal for young people? *CNN*. Retrieved from http://www.cnn.com.

National Institute of Mental Health. (2011). The teen brain: Still under construction. Publication No. 11–4929. Retrieved from http://www.nimh.nih.gov/health/publications/the-teen-brain-still-under-construction/index.shtml?utm_source=LifeSiteNews.com+Daily+Newsletter&utm_campaign=2c0fa9560b-LifeSiteNews_com_Intl_Full_Text_12_18_2012.

National Institute on Drug Abuse. (2014a, January). Nationwide Trends. Retrieved on June 14, 2015, from http://www.drugabuse.gov/publications/drugfacts/nationwide-trends.

National Institute on Drug Abuse. (2014b, June). Drug facts: Nationwide trends. Retrieved on August 28, 2015, from http://www.drugabuse.gov/publications/drugfacts/nationwide-trends.

National Institute on Drug Abuse. (2014c, June). Drug facts: Nationwide trends. Retrieved from http://www.drugabuse.gov/publications/drugs-brains-behavior-science-addiction/drugs-brain.

National Institute on Drug Abuse. (2014d, September). The Science of Drug Abuse and Addiction: The Basics. Retrieved on June 14, 2015 from http://www.drugabuse.gov/publications/media-guide/science-drug-abuse-addiction-basics.

National Science Foundation. (2010, September 3). Stressed Out: Teens and Adults Respond Differently. Retrieved from http://www.nsf.gov/discoveries/disc_summ.jsp?cntn_id=117610.

News Bureau, University of Missouri. (2013, September 23). MU Researchers identify risk factors for addictive video-game use among adults. Retrieved from http://munews.missouri.edu/news-releases/2013/0923-mu-researchers-identify-risk-factors-for-addictive-video-game-use-among-adults/.

Redcay, E., Dodell-Feder, D., Pearrow, M. J., Mavros, P. L., Kleiner, M., Gabrieli, J. D., & Saxe, R. (2010). Live face-to-face interaction during fMRI; a new tool for social cognitive neuroscience. *Neuroimage, 50*(4), 1639–1647, doi: 10.1016/j.neuroimage.2010.01.052.

Schreiber, D., Fonzo, G., Simmons, A. N., Dawes, C., Flagan, T., Fowler, J. H., & Paulus, M. P. (2013). Red brain, blue brain: Evaluative processes differ in democrats and republicans. *PLoS ONE, 8*(2): e52970 doi:10.1371/journal.pone.0052970.

Selemon, L. D. (2013). A role for synaptic plasticity in the adolescent development of executive function. *Transl Psychiatry, 3*(3): e238. doi: 10.1038/tp.2013.7.

Skup, M. (2008). Longitudinal fMRI analysis: A review of methods. *Stat Interface, 3*(2), 235–252: doi: 10.4310/SII.2010.v3.n2.a10.

Steinberg, L. (2012). Should the science of adolescent brain development inform public policy? *Issues in Science and Technology, 28*(3), 67–78.

Steinberg, L. (2014). Age of opportunity: Lessons from the new science of adolescence. New York: Houghton, Mifflin, Harcourt.

Taylor, J. (2013, February 27). Are online relationships healthy for young people? *Psychology Today*. Retrieved from https://www.psychologytoday.com/blog/the-power-prime/201302/are-online-relationships-healthy-young-people.

Thompson, C. (2008, July 28). "Back to the grind in WoW — and loving every tedious minute." *Wired: Games Without Frontiers*. Retrieved August 24, 2015, from http://archive.wired.com/gaming/virtualworlds/commentary/games/2008/07/gamesfrontiers_0728?currentPage=all.

Wallis, L. (2013, September 23). Is 25 the new cut-off point for adulthood? *BBC*. Retrieved from http://www.bbc.com/news/magazine-24173194.

Wowaholics (2012, July 12). Quitting WoW feels like you're finally coming up for air. Retrieved August 17, 2015 from http://www.wowaholics.org/top?page=18.

Yakovlev, P. I., Lecours, A-R. (1967). The myelogenetic cycles of regional maturation of the brain. In A. Minkowski (Ed.), *Regional development of the brain in early life*. Oxford: Blackwell Scientific, 3–70.

Yee, N. (2002). Ariadne—Understanding MMORPG addiction. Retrieved from http://www.nickyee.com/hub/addiction/home.html.

Zelazo P. D., Craik , F. I., Booth, L. (2004). Executive function across the life span. *Acta Psychologica, 115,* 167–184.

Public (Youth) Policy and Emerging Culture

How Policy Facilitates an (Unintended) Youth Pop Culture

FAIRY CHAM-VILLAROMAN, CHARLES W. BATES
and FRANCISCO A. VILLARRUEL

Immigration is no doubt a worldwide phenomenon. It has, however, become a contentious issue in the United States over the past decade given that it has become the nation receiving the highest number of immigrants across the globe (Zong & Batalova, 2015), rapidly changing the demographic composition of the United States to a more diverse population. From the United States' founding to the 1920s, Europeans were the dominant immigrants in the United States. Restrictive immigration laws in 1920 coupled with the Great Depression and World War II led to a sharp drop in new arrivals. Immigration reached a record low by 1970, but increased rapidly after that due to the Immigration and Naturalization Act of 1965. From the 1970s to the present, the United States has been attracting an increasing number of immigrants from Third World countries (Pumariega & Rothe, 2010). Presently, there are more than 41.3 million immigrants residing in the United States, wherein 17.4 million are children below eighteen years of age, and live with at least one immigrant parent (Zong & Batalova, 2015). Moreover, an estimated 11.5 million of the immigrant population in the United States are undocumented (Zong & Batalova, 2015), as "an unintended consequence of policies designed to curb undocumented migration and tighten the U.S.-Mexico border" (Gonzales, 2011, par. 2, quoting Nevins, 2010). Many of the reasons for immigration have not changed over the years. Immigrants choose to leave their home country in pursuit of a better life (Delva et al., 2013),

240

better employment (Abrego, 2011; American Psychological Association [APA], 2012) and academic opportunities (Cho & Haslam, 2009), family reunification (Abrego, 2011, APA, 2012; Pumariega & Rothe, 2010), escape from persecution for a variety of reasons or seeking religious or political freedoms (APA, 2012; Roffman, Suarez-Orozco, & Rhoads, 2003), and to escape from war (Abrego, 2006) or environmental catastrophes (APA, 2012).

The percentage of immigrants living in the United States has increased in the last twenty-five years, with immigrants making up about thirteen percent (with nearly 28 percent being younger than 25 years of age) of the current total United States population (Zong & Batalova, 2015). Just as these numbers have increased throughout history so have anti-immigrant attitudes. In a nation that has been built by immigrants, immigration paradoxically has been perceived as a threat; therefore, conversations about immigrants have usually revolved around anti-immigration sentiments and policies that have marginalized them in the social and political constructs of the nation. Although these populations are becoming the numerical majority in the United States, they unfortunately still suffer from inequities in socioeconomic status, educational opportunities, political influence, and access to health and human services.

Media sources often caution that immigrants flood the job market, drain the public resources, and strain the criminal justice system. On the other hand, several findings contradict these anti-immigration sentiments (Ewing, Martinez & Rumbaut, 2015; Rumbaut, 2008). For example, The U.S. Department of Labor (DOL, 2011) found that foreign-born adults in the United States today are more likely to participate in the work force than the typical native-born American. Labor force participation rate of the foreign-born in 2010 was 67.9 percent, compared to the native-born rate of 64.1 percent (par. 7). In another report, the Office of the Texas Comptroller report found that unauthorized immigrants paid a total of $424.7 million more in state revenues in 2005—including sales and school property taxes—than they used in state services, including education and health care (Strayhorn, 2006, p. 20). Similar trends were documented by the Institute of Taxation and Economic Policy (ITEP, 2015), which found that unauthorized immigrants contributed $11.84 billion in state and local taxes collectively in 2012 (par. 4). They are estimated to contribute $2.2 billion annually; increasing 8.7 percent of state and local taxes nationwide (ITEP, par. 5). Further, immigrants, especially undocumented immigrants, have become embedded in the U.S. workforce and have become vital to certain industries that the U.S.-born may be reluctant to enter. Indeed, debates usually focus on economic impacts and the legal status of individuals or groups of immigrants, but with a deficiency on the human and ethical perspective of immigration. Immigrants' skills and education levels in the U.S. environment limit most of their opportunities. Consequently, their incomes are disproportionately low. Most undocumented immigrants are in occupations that are hazardous and low-wage work (Abrego, 2006), increasing their vulnerability to exploitation, yet benefitting the living standards of citizens—low-cost food, better services, and improved leisure time. They pay taxes, yet immigrants—even authorized immigrants—have limited access to entitlements funded by the same taxes (Menjivar, 2006). They live in unsafe neighborhoods, witness violence near their homes and schools, and study in poor educational environments (Abrego, 2006).

Immigration in U.S. has important association in many realms of society and consequently it impacts millions of lives socio-economically and psychologically. Furthermore, although immigration can bring many gains to an immigrant and the host country, it can also bring many challenges that affect the well-being of immigrants during their period of adjustment. Several studies have stated that immigration can be one of the most stressful events in a person's life and can have multiple significant negative impacts on a person. Recent literature of immigrants in general, point out the potential stressors of immigration, characterized by family separations (Roffman et al., 2003), dislocations (Pumariega & Rothe, 2010), loss of cultural values (Pumariega & Rothe, 2010), and multiple traumas, including dangers during the migration journey (Pumariega & Rothe, 2010). Additional stressors often compound these with their experiences of poverty (Zhou, 2015), complex legal proceedings (C. Suzarez-Orozco, Yoshikawa, Teranishi, & M.M. Suárez-Orozco, 2011), threats of arrests or deportations (Delva et al, 2013; Abrego, 2011), and xenophobia (Pumariega & Rothe, 2010; Roffman et al., 2003).

Immigrant Youth

At the forefront, linguistic and cultural challenges generally hamper the immigrant children from tapping their full potential (Cho & Haslam, 2009). They are also more likely to grow up in poverty and suffer long periods of time separated from their parents. Other migration stress factors such as racial discrimination and living conditions may further encumber their growth, and put them at a higher risk of victimization. Having an undocumented status can further exacerbate these challenges, creating "additional layers of stress related to lack of access to resources and fear" (Gonzales, Suárez-Orozco & Dedios-Sanguineti, 2013, p. 1176, citing Willen, 2007).

The implications of immigration are particularly challenging for adolescents living in the "shadows of unauthorized homes" (Suarez-Orosco et al., 2011) in the United States. Raised and educated in American communities, the United States is the only country they call home, yet they live in the shadows of American society. Many of them, including their family members, endure "liminal legality" (Menjivar, 2006, p. 1008), or the ambiguousness of their legal status while their documents remain in a legal limbo. Furthering the problem, many children grow up in "mixed-status families," where some family members are citizens by birth, legal residents, or in the process of obtaining their documentation, while others remain undocumented (Fix & Zimmermann, 2001). The increasing concern on the consequences of immigration and American society's exclusionary reception (Roffman et al., 2004) to immigrants highlight the special need to understand the cognitive, social and emotional development of the vulnerable immigrant youth. Society's imposed social categorization (Kiang, Yip, & Fuligni, 2008) interconnects with their sense of self (Abrego, 2011).

Adolescence is regarded as a vulnerable life phase given the physical and socio-cognitive changes that impact their well-being (Cho & Haslam, 2009; Fisher et al., 2011; Rodriguez, Morrobel & Villarruel, 2003). It is the stage where the young are establishing their identity. Thus, teenagers in the midst of immigration process need special attention, as normative development and immigration challenges also intertwine and pose significant effects on an individual.

Immigrating to a different country can be challenging at any stage of development yet may be even more complicated for those who arrived as children and spent most of their formative years in the United States, because of the confusing transition they make from the relatively protected state of childhood to experiencing the full impact of their undocumented status as young adults (Gonzales, 2011; Gonzales et al., 2013). Those who arrive in the United States as minors are guaranteed their constitutional rights to enroll in the K to 12-school system (as per *Plyler v. Doe*, 1982). They grow up with the same rights and access to education as their citizen peers until they graduate from high school (Abrego, 2006). However, undocumented youth learn the full implications of lacking legal status when they find themselves unable to apply for a driver's permit and unable to work in an after-school or summer job as their peers do (Gonzalez et al., 2013), and learn about the strong barriers they face to higher education and stable, well-compensated employment (Chavez, Soriano, & Oliverez, 2007; Gonzalez et al., 2013; Perez, 2009). Additional difficulties associated with institutional barriers include not being able to vote or have access to primary health care, and complete financial instability (Gonzales & Terriquez, 2013). They also face constant, chronic risk of apprehension and deportation; nationally, 52 percent of undocumented Latinos worry about deportation (Lopez, Morin, & Taylor, 2010), making them not only scared for themselves but also for their family members and loved ones (Ford & Shoichet, 2013; Gonzalez et al., 2013; Suárez-Orozco, Bang, & Kim, 2011). Further, many of the immigrant youth came to the United States with their parents, as minors, too young to have an active voice in the decision making process. In many cases they were forced to immigrate by their parents' aspirations to achieve a piece of the American Dream. Conversely, as they grow older, they take on the adult role of becoming the cultural translator (Chu, 1998) of their parents in a wide range of domains. The child usually learns the new cultural practices (Gonzales, 2011) and language (Chu, 1998) faster than the adult parent because immigrant children are integrated with native-born children in public schools (Gonzales, 2011). Adults, on the other hand, tend to acculturate more slowly and are more likely to retain and pass on to their children the values of the culture of origin (Marsiglia, Kulis, FitzHarris, & Becerra, 2009, p. 3, citing Phinney & Vedder, 2006). As a result, immigrant children and youth become an interpreter (i.e., language broker) to facilitate information and cultural norms that help their families to access resources, and gain knowledge and information in their new society. At the same time, they also play a pivotal role in protecting their families from outsiders intruding into their personal lives (Orellana, Dorner, & Pulido, 2003). This reversal of parent-child roles makes them active participants not only in their own homes, "but also as socializing agents" (Orellana et al, 2003, quoting Tze, 1995) of their communities, crucial to "families' health, survival, and social advancement" (Orellana et al., 2003, p. 521). The immigrant youth therefore transitions to his or her own identity as a young adult while transitioning simultaneously from one culture to another (Chu, 1998). On the other hand, the adolescents' desire and need to integrate social expectations from the host culture with what is expected by their family and culture of origin can result to an "acculturative family distancing" ([AFD], Pumariega & Rothe, 2010, p. 508) or "intergenerational cultural dissonance" ([ICD], Choi, He & Harachi, 2008), and subsequent family conflict. Theoretically, AFD is the distancing in communication and incongruent cultural values between immigrant parents and children (Hwang, 2006), while ICD is the conflict between parents and children over cultural values due to rapid assimilation by adolescents to mainstream society. In addition, youth's developmental need for autonomy can be in conflict with their role as their parents' "cultural brokers" (Weisskirch, 2010). Forms of intergenerational acculturation gaps can negatively affect parenting practices, family relationships, and healthy youth development (Weisskirch, 2006, citing Martinez, 2006), and become an additional stressor to family life because it exacerbates the natural generational gap that exists between adolescents and their parents (Choi et al., 2008). Family, as one of the identified social identities of adolescents (Kiang, Yip & Fulligni, 2008), has been strongly related to youth adjustment outcomes. For instance, a study of Hispanic youth showed that those who learned and engaged in the practices, values, and identification of their Hispanic culture were more resilient than those who completely assimilated and disengaged from Hispanic values, who were found to be prone to symptoms of depression due to the loss of family cohesiveness and increase in family conflict (Lorenzo-Blanco, Unger, Baezconde-Garbanati, Ritt-Olson, & Soto, 2012). Furthering the problem, many of the undocumented youth "transition into illegality" (Gonzales, 2011, p. 605) as they come of age, which requires adopting adult roles that uncover the full meaning of illegality. Because many of them are economically disadvantaged, they have fewer opportunities to attend postsecondary institutions, and are more likely to contribute to the household finances and responsibility to family needs.

The realization of the barriers and implications imposed by their undocumented status however, transforms the youth to a period of disorientation where they "engage in a process of retooling and reorienting themselves for new adult lives" (Gonzales, 2011, p. 606). Gonzales (2011) found that undocumented youth transition to illegality in three stages. First is the "discovery stage" (ages 16–18; p. 608) where they are confronted with the knowledge that they are not able to participate in normative rites-of-passage experienced by their peers (e.g., obtaining a driver's license, applying for college). Vital to identity formation of adolescence is their heightened social comparisons and sensitivity toward peers, and events at home and school, affecting their sense of self (Arnett, 2006). Thus, undocumented youth who have been socialized in the American environment contextualize their undocumented status with stigma and shame (Abrego, 2006). Most of them respond with anger, hopelessness and decreased academic interest with the onset of their exclusionary experiences with different societal institutions (Suarez-Orozco et al, 2011).

The next stage is "learning to be illegal" (ages 18–24; Gonzales, 2011, p. 612) is where they come to realize of their limited life opportunities. Crucial to the experiences of undocumented youth is their context of reception. The depreciatory term "illegal" classifies them as criminals and inferior, affecting their sense of selves and social position in the American society. Undocumented immigrants are barred from legal employment, in-state tuition and financial aid, paid internships, voting, and driving in most states (Abrego, 2006; Gonzales, Terriquez, & Ruxzcyyk, 2014; Perez, 2009). Thus, many of them find themselves employed in the low-wage market, vulnerable to exploitations. Mentally and physically inexperienced, they experience shock and uncertainty for their futures. Outside the protection of the public schools, they become at-risk for arrests and deportation. They create alternative narratives to keep their identity a secret from their social networks, psychologically burdening them with feelings of distrust, isolation and hopelessness (Gonzalez et al., 2013; Suarez-Orozco et al., 2011). Fear of being discovered adds to their ongoing stress and stigmatized status. Moffitt (1993) distinguishes two types of delinquents: the temporary adolescence-limited delinquency behavior, where nothing in the adolescent's childhood puts them at risk; on the other hand, life-course persistent delinquents exhibit behavior in adolescence as a "continuation of problems that began long before adolescence and are likely to continue well into adulthood" (as cited in Arnett, 2006, p. 188). Constant stress and marginalization can lead to risky behavior and precipitate further risk-taking behaviors, aggression, and potential for self-harm in other consequential ways. Undocumented youth may falsify their Social Security cards and drivers' licenses to obtain employment (Gonzales et al., 2013). Some get involved in substance abuse (Gonzales et al., 2013), while others associate with gang membership for the belongingness, solidarity, protection, discipline, and warmth that it conveys (Suarez-Orozco & Suarez-Orozco, 2002). In most cases, the stress manifests in the form of medical issues (APA, 2011; Gonzalez et al., 2013). Yet in some, undocumented adolescents respond to this chronic stress with suicide (Gonzalez et al., 2013).

Those who have strong support systems and stable financial resources are able to postpone the negative consequences of their undocumented status by enrolling in higher educational institutions, only to converge in the job market with other undocumented school drop-outs during the "coping stage" (ages 25–29, Gonzales, 2011, p. 613). It is in this phase where they are forced to accept their untenable position in the formal market regardless of their educational attainment. Many who have adopted the U.S. values of social mobility and equal opportunity are compelled to truncate their aspirations because of the legal barriers they constantly face, recreating the same difficult path that their parents encountered upon arrival (Roffman et al., 2013).

Literature highlights that identity and acculturation are intrinsically tied, and affect the well-being of the undocumented youth. Because they navigate both the normal challenges during the vulnerable adolescent stage and the acculturation process simultaneously, immigration stressors during this life phase complicate their formation of identity and their relationship to people inside and outside the nuclear family (Gonzales et al., 2013). In the long term, the undocumented youth can inevitably internalize the debilitating residence status (Abrego, 2006) and their academic experiences (Abrego, 2006; Perez, 2009) with adverse consequences on their identity, relationships, and mental health (Gonzales et al., 2013), negatively affecting their attitudes at work, in school, and in their communities (Suarez-Orozco et al., 2011). Moreover, the undulated effects of immigration extend beyond the undocumented youth; research indicates that current immigration policies have broken up individuals and families (Abrego, 2006; Abrego & Gleeson, 2013; Chaudry et al., 2010; Delva et al., 2013).

Families and Youth

As previously stated, immigration in the United States is not a new reality; however the dynamics of post 2001 terrorist attacks (Delva et al., 2013; Menjivar, 2006; Suarez-Orozco et al., 2011), media misrepresentations (Gonzales et al., 2013; Rumbaut, 2008), xenophobic rhetoric (Abrego, 2006; Abrego & Glesson, 2013; Rumbaut, 2008; Suarez-Orozco et al., 2011), political divisiveness (Abrego & Gleeson, 2013; Gonzales et al., 2013; Suarez-Orozco et al., 2011), and immigration policies and enforcement (Abrego, 2006, 2011; Abrego & Glesson, 2013; Chavez et al., 2007; Delva et al., 2013; Gonzales et al., 2013; Menjivar, 2006) have led to increasing criminalization and dehumanization (Abrego, 2006; Rumbaut, 2008) of immigrants, bringing significant changes and challenges to their children and families. Paradoxically, the United States, which prides itself in preservation of family values, deportation has steadily been increasing since 2001(Department of Homeland Security [DHS], 2012, Table 38), with an average of 400,000 immigrants deported annually since 2008 (Abrego & Gleeson, 2013).

As debates continue on the broken immigration system, many immigrants continue to live in the shadows or are forced there due to the country's detention and deportation policies. A burgeoning body of research over the past several years has documented the adverse consequences of these immigration enforcements on immigrants' psychological, emotional and social wellbeing (Chaudry et al., 2010; Delva et al., 2013; Satinsky, Hu, Heelleer, & Farhang, 2013). Moreover, experiences from Immigration and Customs Enforcement (ICE) work-site or home raids that have separated families have traumatized detainees and/or deportees, but have an even more profound, long-term consequence on the affected children's development, sense of self, and academic performance. Studies conducted by the Urban Institute (Chaudry et al., 2010) and Human Impact Partner (Satinsky et al., 2013) indicate that separated families experience income loss, housing instability and food insecurity which are all basic essentials to families' well-being. Aggressive immigration enforcement breeds a climate of fear and apprehension. Separated children exhibit symptoms of Post-Traumatic Stress Disorder, including anxiety, frequent crying, changes in eating and sleeping patterns, withdrawal and anger (Chaudry et al., 2010; Satinsky et al., 2013). Mixed status families share the same challenges and hardships, but differ in strains and possibilities because of the different legal statuses of the family members (Abrego & Gleeson, 2013). U.S.-born citizens often fear and worry about their undocumented loved ones, particularly their parents, because of the random enforcement of immigration policies (Abrego & Gleeson, 2013).

When a parent has been deported, the citizen family must face the impossible choice our current immigration system forces upon thousands of families: should they leave the United States and follow the deported family member, or stay behind and attempt to maintain family ties from half a world away? When both parents are deported or a legal parent is unable to take custody, citizen children end up either staying with relatives who have legal status, or entering public foster care or a state of homelessness. Complexities in family reunification in the United States can make it grueling, if not impossible, for deported parents to regain their parental rights.

Acknowledging the power, politics and structure affecting the lives of the immigrants, still immigrants show high resilience related to strengths they bring from their cultures, such as values of family orientation, optimism, and a collectivistic mentality (Camacho & Fuligni, 2014; Lorenzo-Blanco et al., 2012). Studies have also provided a positive set of lens to immigration and acculturation that yield important information about not only the risks but also the protective factors that foster the positive characteristics mentioned, including positive adult influences, meaningful relationships, civic engagement and, advocacy (Chaudry et al., 2010; Gonzales et al., 2013; Lorenzo-Blanco et al., 2012; Perez, 2009; Roffman et al., 2003). Importantly, schools offer a safe refuge in the aftermath of parents' arrests that contribute to students' academic aspirations in the long run (Chaudry et al., 2010) while after-school activities promote "positive behaviors such as pro-social behaviors, academic resilience as well as decreased misconduct at school, delinquency, dropping out and substance use" (Camacho et al., 2013, p. 1252) integral to a sense of school belonging. Moreover, some undocumented youth are able to succeed in schools and higher educational institutions (Chavez et al., 2007; Perez, 2009). Education results in various outcomes to individuals and society. To some, there is an intrinsic or consumptive value from the educational process that individuals are willing to pay, but to most undocumented youth, it as an investment that will generate a higher level of economic integration and social mobility and consequently, improving lives. The risk of perceiving immigration as solely a problem in our society can limit from the shadows and acknowledge the challenges of immigrant families and their children as a precondition for poverty alleviation, discrimination mitigation and sustainable development.

Public Policy and Immigrant Youth

The cry for full legal rights for immigrants has led many pro-immigrant groups and organizations to come out for their inclusion in American society. Undocumented youth, most notably, have been in the forefront of the struggle for dignity and justice for immigrants in recent years. They have challenged the most fundamental notions of what it means to be undocumented, especially when they began in 2010, to come out of the shadows publicly. The failure to pass the Development, Relief, and Education for Alien Minors (DREAM) Act (DREAM Act, 2001) on the federal level has not only denigrated immigrant children's potential as well as the leaping representational measure of education reform and equity but also depicts the immigrant youth's vulnerability in the social and political constructs of the nation. In the absence to pass the DREAM Act legislatively, U.S. president Obama implemented the Deferred Action for Childhood Arrivals (DACA) through executive action on June 15, 2012, suspending deportations with immediate effect and granting temporary Social Security cards and renewable two-year residence permits to the young undocumented population brought up in the United States (Gonzales et al., 2013). The executive action benefits undocumented immigrants under 30 who arrived in the U.S. before the age of 16, who have lived in the U.S. continuously for at least five years, have no criminal record and have graduated from an American high school or served in the U.S. military (U.S. Citizenship and Immigration Services [USCIS], 2014). DACA offers undocumented youth, who President Obama averred are "Americans in their heart, in their minds, in every single way but one: on paper" (White House, Office of the Press Secretary, 2012, par. 2), temporary relief from deportation, and increased opportunities for economic and social incorporation (Gonzales et al., 2013). However, unlike the DREAM Act, DACA is a grant of prosecutorial discretion that does not provide lawful immigration status or pathway for citizenship that will provide access to federal financial aid benefits (Gonzales et al., 2013; Martinez, 2014) or to the Affordable Care Act (Gonzales et al., 2013). On November 20, 2014, Secretary of Homeland Security Johnson issued a memorandum expanding guidelines for DACA in significant ways, including removal of age eligibility; extension of deportation reprieve and work authorization from two years to three years; extension of potential beneficiaries to parents of U.S. citizens and lawful permanent residents through the Deferred Action for Parents of Americans and Lawful Permanent Residents (DAPA), and expansion of provisional waivers for unlawful presence to spouses and children of lawful permanent residents, and sons and daughters of U.S. citizens (USCIS, 2014). As of this writing, however, expansion of DACA and enactment of DAPA has been suspended, and the previously issued three-year Employment Authorization Documents (EAD) to DACA recipients have been recalled.

The resentment and rejection of immigrants is rooted in fear, anger, and grief, as a response to human nature. People initially fear what is different, and they feel anger toward those most readily identifiable because of differences. Fear, anger and grief, however, can be changed if new perspectives and values are fostered. Positive youth development values the young as assets who are able to build and address their own social, moral, emotional, physical and cognitive competencies to actively participate as partners and stakeholders in society. In the absence of political willingness to effectively implement comprehensive immigration reform, undocumented youth are creating public awareness of their shadowed lives. Their civic impact through active participation in advocacy for the DREAM Act, civic organizations, DACA application assistance and social networking cannot be ignored. Given the importance of legal status in an individual's life opportunities, DACA provides a more positive lens in immigrants' socio-economic integration. A survey of DACA's impact on its recipients shows increased economic integration: 61 percent of recipients obtained a new job, 54 percent opened a bank account, 38 percent were awarded their first credit card, and 61 percent obtained a driver's license (Gonzales & Terriquez, 2013). Meanwhile, Kosnac (2014) shows the positive influence of DACA on recipients' sense of belonging and identity. These positive changes on the socio-economic integration of immigrants validate that a "more positive context of reception, through legalization, must be established to increase their life chances in this country" (Abrego, 2006, p. 226). While DACA does not confer legalization, it highlights the importance of sound and unbiased policies that support immigrant youth's optimum healthy development by incorporating a few of the five Cs (Lerner, 2007) through the hope and opportunities that DACA provides.

DACA motivates youth to return or continue their education that fosters and sustains positive connections to their communities, and develops youth's individual competence and character. Character and education are quintessential agents for an active and effective participation of youth in socio-economic and political developments. Higher education and academic resilience in turn cultivate positive pro-social behaviors and human capital, which will increase chances in meaningful employment. Improved wages and employment benefits strengthen confidence and competence. Further, their improved economic incorporation encourages caring characteristics that positive youth development (PYD) aspires. DACA recipients are helping or aspiring to financially support their parents and family members who do not qualify for DACA (Macy, 2013). Aside from the socio-economic integration that DACA offers, it also facilitates for civic associations (Gonzales et al., 2014) and community service. Gonzales and associates (2013) note that "community institutions serve as spaces of information sharing and trust, supporting immigrant integration" (p.1862), a clear reflection of caring, connections and contribution. Moreover, their awareness and participation in the bureaucratic process indicate that they have the potential to develop the knowledge, skills and ethical values needed for them to fulfill their role as equal partners and social agents in their communities, and future contributors to the nation.

Kiang et al. (2008) suggest that multiple social identities such as family, religion and ethnicity interact across multiple dimensions to influence youth outcomes, while Salmond and Schoenberg (2009) included parenting styles and gender differences. Giroux (1999), on the other hand, addressed the educational systems and pop culture. Their studies affirm that relationships between social interactions, youth perceptions of positive and negative influences within their social and physical environments, and ways in which these relationships and perceptions are associated have significant implications on how youth and their families deal with conditions of instability, adversity, limited resources, and social change. Their studies reflect an understanding how youth themselves perceive assets and deficits within their social settings. Most importantly, their studies highlight the need to integrate the youth development research literature with other research on societal development, and to collaborate programs and policies with different institutions and organizations that will build supportive and protective societies for youth and families.

Giroux (1999) challenges the belief that childhood is a natural state of innocence, but is instead a historical construction with outcomes stemming from children's view of themselves through cultural definitions. He calls on reframing cultural politics that will provide parents, educators, and other youth's social contexts better opportunity and understanding of the unique and different experiences of youth that will empower them. Furthermore, he encourages adults to be more self-effacing about "how they wield power over young people, or offering young people supportive environments where they can produce their own cultural experiences, mediate diverse public cultures, and develop diverse social affiliations" (p. 211).

Whereas equal access to higher education is youth's public culture in the DREAM Act; it is in socio-economic integration for DACA. Now that DACA has clearly opened new doors for qualifying undocumented youth, we must also open doors for their families through policies that address the inequities in the labor market and injustices in political and social environments. The expanded DACA period and DAPA are leaping representations of immigrant narratives that also affect the development of immigrant children and youth in other significant ways, since there is no "monolithic undocumented immigrant experience" (Abrego, 2006, p. 340). Recognition of the dynamic and multi-contextual nature of immigrant experiences within their social settings and systems will enable parents and the community to increase their abilities to nurture young people with a goal to provide guidance that ensures that emotional, recreational, academic, mental and physical health and needs of adolescents are explicitly addressed. Awareness and understanding of the context of the immigrant family's challenges, strengths, and reasons for migration—distinct pluralities that give rise to different values and orientation—could help steer the development of our youth toward a life of successful and meaningful contributions.

Conclusion: Policy and Youth Pop Culture

As dawn breaks on what will soon become a typical, picturesque mid-week day, the sun begins its slow, crimson ascent over Lake Victoria. Okullo Nyong'o, a member of the Luo Tribe, hastily dips his fishing net into the tepid water. He is soon joined, somewhat reluctantly, by his sons Ramogi, 15, and Miguna, 13. The youth would much rather continue to sleep in their comfortable beds during the two hours they have agreed to help their father fish, before walking to school. But they know their family must eat—and sell—some fish if they are to continue to meet their daily needs and the boys are to continue attending school.

Okullo plucks 12 very small "Kapenta" out of his net. He and his two sons are using fine-filament nets, which harvest even the very small fish, yet, the nets are not intended to be used as fishing nets. The netting was provided to their family as mosquito nets, its use intended to combat malaria. Governments, religious organizations, foundations, private corporations, charitable organizations, and other entities, world-wide, have funded, manufactured or ensured the manufacture of, and distributed mosquito netting in Africa. This provision—or attempted provision—of mosquito netting to a large sector of Africans is, quite simply, what has become as close to a *world* policy as exists today (McNeil, 2008; World Health Organization, 2003).

Because of the dire need to feed his family, Okullo's use of the mosquito nets for fishing, instead of mosquito protection for family members, does concern him, but it also has the *positive unintended consequence* of providing food and income for his family which otherwise might be out of his reach. It has the *negative unintended consequence* for his immediate community and the people of the nations of Tanzania, Uganda, and Kenya, surrounding Lake Victoria, of depleting future fishing stocks meant to feed their next generation. It also, of course, has the negative unintended consequence of the nets not doing the job they were intended to do—protecting the people of Africa of malaria, and protecting, in particular, the youth who—if they survive—will become their next generation of adults.

It is these complexities in caring for his family that leads Okullo's mind to drift from the duties at hand to a country called the United States of America, or more commonly, America. It is a country he has only imagined, but a place in which he hopes to eventually reunite his sons with their beloved cousins, who moved there five years ago. Okullo and his wife plan to move there in pursuit of a better life and for Okullo in particular, for the hope of better employment, safe from the diminishing fish stocks of Lake Victoria. He wants to move his sons to America for the academic opportunities, and to protect them and his wife from the threat of malaria. Okullo and his wife wish to strive for a life in America that would likely otherwise be out of their reach. He and his wife are, in fact, so desperate to pursue the American Dream that they are willing to immigrate there without the official documents blessing their entry into the country and allowing them to legally work and reside there. Okullo vaguely believes the path for him and his family will be more difficult in America without these documents, but given the roadblocks to obtaining the documents prior to his sons becoming adults—if they live to become adults where they are currently living—Okullo believes their journey is worth the effort in order to reach the better life America has to offer.

Many youth policies—those implemented by local, state, or federal governments, or instituted, de facto, by non-government entities—are intended to promote positive consequences for our youth. Many of those policies will meet their well-intended objectives, partially or fully. Some policies, whether intended for youth development or for broader positive purposes will meet their objectives—or not—but will create unintended negative consequences for our youth or for society as a whole. No matter what the intention of the policy for our youth, policies can, also, trigger a dynamic that results in the creation, modification, or expansion of youth pop culture, which may or may not have anything to do with the policy itself.

Such as it will be for Ramogi and Miguna, when they immigrate to the United States of America. Private developers (e.g., shopping centers) and public entities (e.g., city hall sites) have banned skateboarding and inline skating for fear of damage to property, injury of youth, or disturbance of the comfort level of patrons. This has certainly led to municipal and county development of publicly funded and maintained skate parks (Centralia, WA Northwest Skater, 2015; Olympia, Skatecourt, 2015). Although the skate parks may be attractive, does the activity lose some of its "cool" when it is done in a government-sponsored location intended for skateboarding, abiding by government-imposed rules? So has this driven youth, immigrant and non-immigrant alike, if they wish to continue to use shopping centers and city hall sites for their recreation, under their own (no) rule, to adopt a newer and arguably potentially more injury-prone form of modality—*Parkour*—using only their bodies (Amazing Pakour and Freerunning, 2014)? With parkour, the authorities may no longer have a legitimate concern for damage to property, but still presumably have concern for injury of youth and the disturbance of the comfort level of patrons. It is much more difficult for the youth to get "caught," than with skateboarding or inline skating, given they are moving faster and do not have any equipment with them to be a burden to their mobility. Just as adults have "given up" on fighting skateboarding by trying to regulate and control it through building of skateboard parks and creating safety rules or at least encouraging safety (e.g., use of helmets and elbow/knee pads), are they also beginning to concede on parkour? There are organizations now teaching parkour to our youth, emphasizing the positive physical attributes of the sport, along with its promotion of discipline, with an emphasis on safety (Parkour Visions, 2015). Public policy has resulted in unintended consequents by youth asserting themselves through their activism. Most schools have some form of dress code—increasingly more have implemented uniforms for daily school wear. Has activism, again driven by youth, immigrant and non-immigrant alike, led them to express their individuality—and their unity with other youth—in the only way they can: the smaller, subtle ways of dress beyond the basic uniform? Those may be with shoes, shoelaces (e.g., colored, often different for each shoe), belts (e.g., rope, web), or hats (e.g., pork-pie, fedoras). Public policy has again resulted in unintended consequents by youth asserting themselves through their activism.

Immigrant youth—documented or not—are influenced by and in turn influence the evolution of a pop culture that emerges from the intended and unintended consequences of public policy development and implementation that is aimed at all youth. This is true whether the policy pertains to what most adults would consider the fairly innocuous activity of youthful skate-boarding or to the innocent rebellion of youthful individuality expressed in modes of dress beyond school uniforms. Likewise, the more serious topic of public policy on immigration that has evolved in the past 20 years presumably would push immigrant youth underground. It has instead resulted in the emergence of those underground youth from the shadows, encouraging them to lead the creation of a phenomenon where undocumented, documented, and native youth have joined forces, publicly uniting in the creation of a pop culture of youthful civic activism. This civic engagement and advocacy (Caudry et al., 2010; Gonzales et al., 2013; Lorenzo-Blanco et al., 2012; Perez, 2009; Roffman et al., 2003) that sparked this growing pop culture of civic activism among our youth and young adult immigrants will go a long way toward ensuring their attainment of the 5 Cs and ultimately their success. Responses to DACA and the Dream Act have contributed to an emerging voice of immigrant youth (Wong, Shadduch-Hernandez, Inzunza, Monroe, Narro & Valenzuela, 2012; Wong, Shadduch-Hernandez, & Rivera-Salgado, 2008), and the recognition that they are shaping not only youth culture, but culture in the U.S.

References

Abrego, L. J. (2006). "I can't go to college because I don't have papers": Incorporation patterns of Latino undocumented youth. *Latino Studies, 4*(3), 212–231.

Abrego, L.J. (2011). Legal consciousness of undocumented Latinos: Fear and stigma as barriers to claims-making for first- and 1.5-generation immigrants. *Law & Society Review, 45,* 337–369.

Abrego, L. J., & Gleeson, S. (2013). Immigration policies hurt immigrant families more than they help. James A. Baker Institute for Public Policy Rice University.

Retrieved from http://bakerinstitute.org/media/files/Research/ed981bd8/LAI-pub-AbregoGleesonImmigrantFamilies-04813.pdf.
Amazing Pakour and Freerunning. (2014). Retrieved from https://www.youtube.com/watch?v=1UINrjP2onM.
American Psychological Association. (2011). Stress: The different kinds of stress. Retrieved from http://www.apa.org/helpcenter/stress-kinds.aspx.
American Psychological Association. (2012). Crossroads: The psychology of immigration in the new century. Retrieved from http://www.apa.org/topics/immigration/report.aspx.
Arnett, J. J. (2006). G. Stanley Hall's adolescence: Brilliance and nonsense. *History of Psychology, 9*(3), 186–197. doi: http://dx.doi.org/10.1037/1093-4510.9.3.186.
Berry, J. W., Phinney, J. S., Sam, D. L., & Vedder, P. (2006). Immigrant youth: Acculturation, identity, and adaptation. *Applied Psychology, 55*, 303–332.
Camacho, D.E., & Fuligni, A.J. (2014). Extracurricular participation among adolescents from immigrant families. *Journal of Youth and Development 44*, 1251–1262.
Centralia, W.A. (2015). Northwestskater. Retrieved from http://www.northwestskater.com/centralia.html.
Chaudry, A., Capps, R., Pedroza, J., Castaneda, R.M., Santos, R., Scott, M.M.. (2010). Facing our future: Children in the aftermath of immigration enforcement. The Urban Institute. Retrieved from: http://www.urban.org/sites/default/files/alfresco/publication-pdfs/412020-Facing-Our-Future.PDF.
Chavez, M.L., Soriano, M., & Oliverez, P. (2007). Undocumented students' access to college: The American dream denied. *Latino Studies Journal, 5*, 254–263.
Cho, Y.B., & Haslam, N. (2009) Suicidal ideation and distress among immigrant adolescents: The role of acculturation, life stress, and social support. *Journal of Youth and Adolescence 39*, 370–379.
Choi, Y., He, M., & Harachi, T. W. (2008). Intergenerational cultural dissonance, parent-child conflict and bonding, and youth problem behaviors among Vietnamese and Cambodian immigrant families. *Journal of Youth and Adolescence, 37*, 85–96.
Chu, C.M. (1999) Immigrant children mediators (ICM): Bridging the literacy gap in immigrant communities. *New Review of Children's Literature and Librarianship, 5*, 85–94.
Delva, J., Horner, P., Martinez, R., Sanders, L., Lopez, W. D., & Doering-White, J. (2013). Mental health problems of children of undocumented parents in the United States: A hidden crisis. *Journal of Community Positive Practices, 13*, 25–35.
Department of Homeland Security. (2012). Yearbook of immigration statistics: 2010. Retrieved from: http://www.dhs.gov/yearbook-immigration-statistics-2010.
DREAM Act (2001). Development, Relief, and Education for Alien Minors Act. S.1291, 107th Congress (2001–2002). Introduced in the U.S. Senate on August 1, 2001, by Senators Dick Durbin and Orrin Hatch, and since reintroduced several times.
Ewing, W.A., Martinez, D.E., & Rumbaut, R.G. (2015). The criminalization of immigration in the United States. Immigration Policy Center. Retrieved from http://immigrationpolicy.org/special-reports/criminalization-immigration-united-states.
Fisher, J., Cabral de Mello, M., Izutsu, T., Vijayakumar, L., Belfer, M., & Omigbodun, O. (2011). Adolescence: Developmental stage and mental health morbidity. *International Journal of Social Psychiatry, 57*(1), 13–19.
Fix, M., & Zimmermann, W. (2001). All under one roof: Mixed-status families in an era of reform. *The International Migration Review, 35*, 397–419.

256   The Young Are Making Their World

Ford, D., & Shoichet, C. E. (2013). Immigrants' days filled with fear, uncertainty, separation. *CNN*. Retrieved from http://www.cnn.com/2013/01/29/us/immigrants-change/.

Giroux, H. (1999). Public intellectuals and the challenge of children's culture: Youth and the politics of innocence. *Review of Education, Pedagogy, and Cultural Studies, 21*, 193–224.

Gonzales, R. G. (2011). Learning to be illegal: Undocumented youth and shifting legal contexts in the transition to adulthood. *American Sociological Review, 76*(4), 602–619.

Gonzales, R.G., Suárez-Orozco, C., & Dedios-Sanguineti, M.C. (2013). No place to belong: Contextualizing concepts of mental health among undocumented immigrant youth in the United States. *American Behavioral Scientist, 57*, 1174–1199.

Gonzales, R.G., & Terriquez, V. (2013). How DACA is impacting the lives of those now DACAmented: Preliminary findings from the National UnDACAmented Research Project. Washington, D.C.: Migration Policy Institute and the Center for the Study of Immigrant Integration. Retrieved from: http://dornsife.usc.edu/csii/daca/.

Gonzales, R. G., Terriquez, V., & Ruszczyk, S. P. (2014). Becoming DACAmented: Assessing the short-term benefits of Deferred Action for Childhood Arrivals (DACA). *The American Behavioral Scientist, 57*(14), 1852.

Gardner, M., Johnson, S., & Wiehe, M. (2015). Undocumented immigrants' state & local tax contributions. Institute on Taxation and Economic Policy. Retrieved from http://itep.org/itep_reports/2015/04/undocumented-immigrants-state-local-tax-contributions.php#.VaS9amC4mMI.

Hwang, W. (2006). Acculturative family distancing: Theory, research, and clinical practice. *Psychotherapy: Theory, Research, Practice, Training, 43*, 397–409.

Kiang, L., Yip, T., & Fuligni, A. J. (2008). Multiple social identities and adjustment in young adults from ethnically diverse backgrounds. *Journal of Research on Adolescence, 18*, 643–670.

Kosnac, H. S. (2014). *One step in and one step out: The lived experience of the deferred action for childhood arrivals program.* Available from ProQuest Dissertations & Theses A&I; ProQuest Dissertations & Theses Global. (Order No. 1568170).

Lerner, R.M. (2007). *The good teen: Rescuing adolescence from the myths of the storm and stress years.* New York: Three Rivers Press/Crown.

Lopez, M.H., Morin, R., & Taylor, P. (2010). Illegal immigration backlash worries, divides Latinos. *Pew Research Center.* Retrieved from http://www.pewhispanic.org/2010/10/28/illegal-immigration-backlash-worries-divides-latinos/.

Lorenzo-Blanco, E., Unger, J. B., Baezconde-Garbanati, L., Ritt-Olson, A., & Soto, D. (2012). Acculturation, enculturation, and symptoms of depression in Hispanic youth: The roles of gender, Hispanic cultural values, and family functioning. *Journal of Youth and Adolescence, 41*, 1350–65.

Macy, B. (2013). Deferred action for childhood arrivals is not a dream, but it works for now. *McClatchy - Tribune Business News.* Retrieved from http://ezproxy.msu.edu/login?url=http://search.proquest.com/docview/1433912420?accountid=12598.

Marsiglia, F.F., Kulis, S.K., FitzHarris, B., & Becerra, D. (2009). Acculturation Gaps and Problem Behaviors among U.S. Southwestern Mexican Youth. *U.S. National Library of Medicines National Institute of Health.* Retrieved from http://www.ncbi.nlm.nih.gov/pubmed/23888125.

Martinez, L. M. (2014). Dreams deferred: The impact of legal reforms on undocumented Latino youth. *American Behavioral Scientist, 58*(14), 1873–1890.

McNeil, D.G. (2008). *A $10 mosquito net is making charity cool. New York Times,* June 2. Retrieved from http://www.nytimes.com/2008/06/02/us/02malaria.html?_r=0&pagewanted=print.

Menjívar, C. (2006). Liminal legality: Salvadoran and Guatemalan immigrants' lives in the United States. *American Journal of Sociology, 111*(4), 999–1037.

Olympia Skatecourt (2015). Olympia Skate Court, Olympia, WA. Retrieved from http://olympiawa.gov/city-services/parks/parks-and-trails/olympia-skate-court.

Orellana, M.F., Dorner, L., & Pulido, L. (2003). Accessing assets: Immigrant youth's work as family translators or "para-phrasers." *Social Problems, 50,* 505–524.

Parkour Visions (2015). Parkour Visions RSS. YouTube. Retrieved from http://parkourvisions.org/.

Pérez, W. (2009). *We are Americans: Undocumented students pursuing the American dream.* Sterling, VA: Stylus.

Plyler, James, Superintendent, Tyler Independent School District, et al. v. John Doe, et al., 457 U.S. 202 (U.S. Supreme Court, 1982). Opinion issued in 1982 by the United States Supreme Court, published in No. 80–1538, 102 S. Ct. 2382.

Pumariega, A. J., & Rothe, E. (2010). Leaving no children or families outside: The challenges of immigration. *American Journal of Orthopsychiatry, 80*(4), 505–515.

Rodriguez, M.C., Morrobel, D., & Villaruel, F.A. (2003). Research realities and a vision of success for Latino youth development. In F.A. Villarruel, D.F. Perkins, L.M. Borden, & J.G. Keith, J.G. (Eds), *Community youth development: Programs, policies and practices* (pp. 47–78). Thousand Oaks: Sage.

Roffman, J.G., Suarez-Orozco, C. & Rhodes, J.E. (2003). Facilitating positive development in immigrant youth: The role of mentors and community organizations. In F.A. Villarruel, D.F. Perkins, L.M. Borden, & J.G. Keith, J.G. (Eds), *Community youth development: Programs, policies and practices* (pp. 90–117). Thousand Oaks: Sage.

Rumbaut, R. (August 2008). Undocumented immigration and rates of crime and imprisonment: Popular myths and empirical realities. *Immigration Enforcement and Civil Liberties: The Role of Local Police.* Invited address at the National Conference, Police Foundation, Washington, D.C. Retrieved from http://ssrn.com/abstract=1877365.

Salmond, K., & Schoenberg, J., (2009). Good intentions: The beliefs and values of teens and tweens today. New York: Girl Scouts of the USA.

Satinsky, S., Hu, A., Heelleer, J., & Farhang, L. (2013). Family unity, family health: How family-focused immigration reform will mean better health for children and families. *Human Impact Partners.* Retrieved from http://www.familyunityfamilyhealth.org/uploads/images/FamilyUnityFamilyHealth.pdf.

Strayhorn, C. K. (2006) Undocumented Immigrants in Texas: A financial analysis of the impact to the state budget and economy. Special Report (December). Retrieved from http://www.window.state. tx.us/specialrpt/undocumented/.

Suárez-Orozco, C., Bang, H. J., & Kim, H. Y. (2011). "I felt like my heart was staying behind": Psychological implications of immigrant family separations & reunification. *Journal of Adolescent Research, 26,* 222–257.

Suarez-Orozco, C., & Suarez-Orozco, M.M. (2002). *Children of Immigration.* Cambridge: Harvard University Press.

Suárez-Orozco, C., Yoshikawa, H., Teranishi, R. T., & Suárez-Orozco, M.M. (2011). Growing up in the shadows: The developmental implications of unauthorized status. *Harvard Educational Review, 81,* 438–472,619–620.

United States Citizenship and Immigration. (2014). Consideration of Deferred Action for Childhood Arrivals (DACA). Washington, D.C. Retrieved from http://www. uscis.gov/humanitarian/consideration-deferred-action-childhood-arrivals-daca.

United States Department of Labor. (2011) Labor force characteristics of foreign-born workers: Summary. *Bureau of Labor Statistics*. Washington. Retrieved from:http:// www.bls.gov/news.release/archives/forbrn_05272011.pdf.

Weisskirch, R.S. (2010). Child language brokers in immigrant families: An overview of family dynamics. *mediAzioni, 10*. Retrieved from http://mediazioni.sitlec. unibo.it, ISSN 1974–4382.

White House, Office of the Press Secretary. (2012). Remarks by the President on immigration. Retrieved from https://www.whitehouse.gov/the-press-office/2012/06/ 15/remarks-president-immigration

Wong, K., Shadduch-Hernandez, J., Inzunza, F., Monroe, J., Narro, V., & Valenzuela, A. (2012). Undocumented and unafraid: Tam Tran, Cinthy Felix and the Immigrant Youth Movement. Los Angeles: UCLA Labor Center.

Wong, K., Shadduch-Hernandez, J., & Rivera-Salgado, G. (2008). Underground undergraduates: UCLA students speak out. Los Angeles: UCLA Labor Center.

World Health Organization (2003). *Insecticide-treated mosquito net interventions: A manual for national control programme managers*. Edited by Roll Back Malaria. Geneva. ISBN: 92 4 159045 9.

Zhou, M. (1997). Growing up American: The challenge confronting immigrant children and children of immigrants. *Annual Review of Sociology, 23*, 63–95.

Zong, J., & Batalova, J. (2015). Frequently requested statistics on immigrants and immigration in the United States. *The Online Journal of the Migration Policy Institute*. Retrieved from http://www.migrationpolicy.org/article/frequently-requested-statistics-immigrants-and-immigration-united-states

About the Contributors

Willie S. **Anderson** is an educator, writer, speaker and community advocate. For 22 years, she has been a volunteer at Austin Community Radio, KAZI 88.7 FM. She has produced and hosted "Educating Our Children," "The KAZI Review," and "In the CLEar" (Community Learning Exchange Advocacy Radio).

Charles W. **Bates** has worked for more than 40 years in the private and public sectors and has been a volunteer in various capacities for numerous youth development organizations. He is the education and employment coordinator for Cocoon House in Everett, Washington, Snohomish County's only resource exclusively providing a continuum of care serving homeless and at-risk youth and young adults.

Vicki **Burns** is a visiting assistant professor in women's and gender studies at Florida International University. Her research and advocacy interests focus on violence against women, gender role socialization and the objectification of women and girls. She is also the co-founder of *Girl Talk,* a psycho-educational program for young girls that covers self-esteem, relationships, friendships and sexism.

Fairy **Cham-Villaroman** is a program assistant at the Middle School Teen Center at Joint Base San Antonio. She was a consultant and entrepreneur for ten years in the Philippines before immigrating to the United States. She has served as a volunteer for various Fil-Am organizations, the American Red Cross, the Family Readiness Group and various programs of the Army Community Services (ACS).

Alison **Chrisler** is a doctoral candidate at Michigan State University in human development and family studies. She worked as a research analyst in early childhood development at Child Trends in Washington, D.C. Her program of research focuses on promoting the wellbeing and resiliency of families and youth who identify as lesbian, gay, bisexual, transgender and queer (LGBTQ).

Noah S.L. **Crimmins** is an undergrad at Michigan State University, planning to pursue a career in supply chain management with a minor in psychology. He completed studies in brain development under the mentorship of Lori Hoisington in preparation for continued studies in psychology.

Bryan **Currie** is the lead pastor at Holy Trinity Community Church in Nashville, Tennessee. During his 15-plus years of professional youth experience, he has worked with teenagers in both religious and community settings. He has also managed

259

youth programs for a non-profit organization that serves LGBT (lesbian, gay, bisexual, and transgender) youth in New York City schools.

Asia A. **Eaton** is an assistant professor of psychology and women's and gender studies at Florida International University. Her research explores the relationship between social power and gender in the United States. She has been published in *Archives of Sexual Behavior, The Journal of Sex Research, American Psychologist* and other peer-reviewed psychology journals.

Daniel **Gould** is the director of the Institute for the Study of Youth Sports and a professor in the Department of Kinesiology at the Michigan State University. He has published widely on topics such as mental preparation, the psychology of excellence, coaching psychology, motivation, children in sport, stress and the development of life skills in young athletes.

Lori **Hoisington** is an assistant professor in human development and family studies at Michigan State University. She teaches online courses on brain development, evolution and behavior and interpersonal relationships. She is also a core faculty member of the Great Plains IDEA Youth Development program.

Mariko **Izumi** is an associate professor of communication at Columbus State University. Her research focuses on the intersection of ethics and politics, especially how human suffering is communicated across temporal, spatial and cultural boundaries and shapes humanitarian agendas in cultural politics.

Darla J. **Johnson** is a choreographer, teacher and writer. She is the author of *The Art of Listening: Intuition and Improvisation in Choreography* (2012). She was a contributor to *Experiments in a Jazz Aesthetic: Art, Activism, Academia, and the Austin Project* (2010).

Naomi **Kagawa** is an associate professor of education at Shimane University in Japan, where she works to integrate communication aspects and globalization into teacher education curriculum. She also studies theoretical models of interpersonal, family and intercultural communication mainly using quantitative methods.

Yuya **Kiuchi** is an assistant professor in the Department of Human Development and Family Studies at Michigan State University. His research interests include African American studies and history, popular culture studies and youth development. He serves on the editorial advisory board for the *Journal of Popular Culture*.

Jenifer K. **McGuire** is an associate professor of family social science and an extension specialist at the University of Minnesota. Her research areas have focused predominantly on adolescent sexual identity and health, with a secondary focus on community service and civic identity. She has a growing research and outreach area focused specifically on the well-being of transgender young people.

Martha **Montero-Sieburth** is a guest researcher in migration and ethnic studies in the Department of Sociology and Anthropology at the University of Amsterdam and a lecturer in social sciences and humanities at Amsterdam University College. She has published a wide variety of topics related to education around the world.

John A. **Oliver** is an assistant professor of educational and community leadership at Texas State University. His research interests include the intersection of youth and adult partnerships for community change. His teaching specialties include understanding the self as an educational leader, the role of school leaders in facilitating school improvement and the leadership praxis of principal preparation.

Nicole **Polen-Petit** is an assistant professor of psychology at National University where she teaches a variety of courses to a diverse student body. Her research interests center on identity and orientation, sexual fluidity in women and sexual coercion experienced by women in sororities.

Joshua **Quinn** is a recent graduate in student affairs in higher education at Texas State University. His research interests include diversity, LGBTQIA students, students of color, masculinity development, first-generation students and intersectional identities and cultures.

Elizabeth **Sharp** is an associate professor of human development and family studies and an affiliate faculty member of women's studies at Texas Tech University. She has published broadly in the fields of human development and family studies, sociology, psychology and family therapy.

Jesse **Silva** currently is an assistant director of the Office of Student Diversity and Inclusion at Texas State University. His areas of interest and practice include intersectionality, social justice, diversity, inclusion, race, hip hop, first-generation students, male students, college recruitment of K-12 students, LGBTQIA students, student veterans and undocumented students.

Stella **Silva** is an associate director of the Office of Student Diversity and Inclusion at Texas State University. Her areas of interest and research include diversity, inclusion, first-generation college students, Latinas and their experience in higher education and the recruitment and retention of Mexican American and Latino/a students.

Francisco A. **Villarruel** is a university outreach and engagement senior fellow, the associate chair for education and outreach and a professor of human development and family studies at Michigan State University. He is also one of the founding faculty members of the Great Plans IDEA Youth Development Program.

Nicole **Wesley** is an assistant professor of dance at Texas State University, performer and choreographer. Her research interests include community building through authentic performance (The JUSTICE Project) and Laban Movement Analysis (LMA) as a methodology in the realm of technical training and performance process.

Scott **Westfall** has been a teacher, coach, and athletic director at the middle school level and has completed a Ph.D. at Michigan State University. He conducts research at the Institute for the Study of Youth Sports (ISYS) and works with the Michigan High School Athletic Association (MHSAA) on student-athlete leadership programs.

Index